THE TECHNICAL INTELLIGENTSIA AND
THE SOVIET STATE

Studies in Soviet History and Society
General Editor: Professor R. W. Davies

The series consists of works by members or associates of the interdisciplinary Centre for Russian and East European Studies of the University of Birmingham, England. Special interests of the Centre include Soviet economic and social history, contemporary Soviet economics and planning, science and technology, sociology and education.

Nicholas Lampert
The Technical Intelligentsia and the Soviet State:
A Study of Soviet Managers and Technicians 1928–1935

Robert Lewis
Science and Industrialisation in the USSR:
Industrial Research and Development 1917–1940

Further titles in preparation

THE TECHNICAL INTELLIGENTSIA AND THE SOVIET STATE

NICHOLAS LAMPERT

HOLMES & MEIER PUBLISHERS, INC.

New York

First published in the United States of America 1979 by
HOLMES & MEIER PUBLISHERS, INC.
30 Irving Place, New York, N.Y. 10003
Copyright© 1979 Nicholas Lampert

Library of Congress Cataloging in Publication Data

Lampert, Nicholas.
  The technical intelligentsia and the Soviet State.

  Bibliography: p.
  Includes index.
  1. Intellectuals—Russia. 2. Professions—Russia.
3. Russia—Economic policy—1917–1928. 4. Russia—
Economic policy—1928–1932. 5. Technologists—Russia.
I. Title.
HT690.R9L35 1979   301.44'5   79–15419
ISBN 0–8419–0534–7

ISBN 0–8419–0534–7

Printed in Great Britain

Contents

List of Tables

Acknowledgements

Many people have helped me to finish this study. My first thanks must go to Professor R. W. Davies, who supervised the thesis which provided the starting point for this work, and expended much effort in criticising, always carefully and constructively, the material he finally managed to cajole out of me. I am very grateful for his assistance.

Others who have helped are too numerous to mention individually. But I would like to thank especially Professor M. Lewin, whose stimulating comments in many conversations gave me a lot to think about; Dr V. Andrle, who pertinently criticised papers that formed part of the study; and members of the Soviet social history seminar at the Centre for Russian and East European Studies, University of Birmingham—especially Peter Kneen, Steve Wheatcroft and the late Geoff Barker—who gave me ideas in responding to research papers. Their comments will have improved the product, but its failings are not their responsibility.

Finally, I would like to record my thanks to the SSRC, under whose auspices the study was extended into its present form as part of the project on Soviet social and economic history on which I worked as a research associate.

Glossary

brak	defective goods
Gosplan	State Planning Commission
GPU	Security Police
ITR	Engineering and technical personnel
ITS	Engineers' and Technicians' Sections under the All-Union Central Council of Trade Unions
khozraschet	cost accounting
kolkhoz	collective farm
komsostav	leading executive personnel
kraikom	regional party committee (administering an area equivalent to that administered by an obkom)
nepmen	those engaged in private enterprise during the NEP period
NKTP	People's Commissariat of Heavy Industry
obkom	regional party committee
okrug	district
partiinost	party-mindedness
promfinplan	industrial-financial plan
Promparty	Industrial Party (alleged to have been formed by specialists working in Soviet industrial and planning agencies for the purpose of subverting the Soviet order)
rabfak	workers' faculty
raikom	district party committee
Rabkrin or RKI	Workers' and Peasants' Inspection
RKK	Assessment and Conflict Commission
serednyak	middle peasant
spets	specialist
SSSR	Union of Soviet Socialist Republics
troika	triangle (referring to management, party and trade union in enterprises)

TsU or	
TsUNKhU	Central Statistical Administration
uravnilovka	wage-levelling (with a pejorative connotation)
VAI	All-Union Association of Engineers
VARNITSO	All-Union Association of Scientists and Technicians for Assistance to Socialism
VMBIT	Central organ of the ITS
VSI	All-Russian Union of Engineers
VSNKh	Supreme Council of National Economy (in charge of industry)
VTsIK	Central Executive Committee of the Congress of Soviets of the RSFSR
VTsSPS	All-Union Central Council of Trade Unions
vtuzy	institutions of higher technical education

1 Introduction

The chief aim of this book is to examine the relationship between the technical intelligentsia and the Soviet state in the late 1920s and the early 1930s. It is offered as a contribution to an analysis of the USSR in a period of major social upheavals which brought certain critical shifts in the character of the Soviet state. The object is to try to throw light on some elements in that process through an investigation of its impact on the technical intelligentsia. The account rests upon, and at the same time attempts to explore, a number of general assumptions about the role of the Soviet state in this period. The first part of Chapter 1 sets out briefly what those assumptions are. The second part outlines the particular issues to be investigated and the way they relate to the general questions underlying the study.

1A INDUSTRIAL EXPANSION, COLLECTIVISATION AND THE SOVIET STATE

Any analysis of the social transformations in the USSR in the 1930s will contain some premises, explicit or implicit, about the relation between these changes and the Russian revolution. Here it will be accepted as a background assumption that the peculiarity of the Russian revolution arose from its dual character. It was the conjunction and interpenetration of worker and peasant struggles in 1917 that provided the conditions for the successful October uprising, and enabled the Bolsheviks to carry out the historic 'bourgeois democratic' tasks, especially the redistribution of the land.[1] But the same dualism of the revolution was a source of major dilemmas in the post-revolutionary situation, dilemmas that became more acute when the European-wide revolution that the Bolsheviks were fully expecting in 1917–18 did not materialise. Instead they faced a period of civil war and foreign intervention in which they were fighting for survival under conditions of growing material devastation.

The civil war years brought a general 'statisation' of the social order.[2] Under war communism—the conventional term for the form of political rule that emerged during the civil war—the agencies of the state, in order to concentrate diminishing resources on the requirements of the military struggle, tried to establish a direct control over production. In the case of industry, this led to a wholesale nationalisation of the means of production. In the countryside, the Soviet power proved unable to offer the peasantry an acceptable rate of exchange for agricultural produce. Political agencies therefore resorted to a forcible extraction of grain and other products in the attempt to bypass the market.[3]

Two features of the form of state that became established under war communism can be singled out. First, the Bolshevik party consolidated its position as the dominant political agency within the state. Second, the conditions of life or death struggle gave the coercive apparatuses—the political police as well as the military—a key role in the conflict. In the civil war conditions, according to the view of one leading Bolshevik, the dictatorship of the proletariat was to become the 'most ruthless form of the state, which embraces the life of the citizens authoritatively in every direction'.[4]

By the spring of 1921, the civil war had been won but the ruling party found itself fighting for its life in the face of internal unrest. The New Economic Policy (NEP) was an attempt to salvage some measure of stability from the wreckage of war communism, and especially from the battered relationship between the Soviet power and the peasantry. By re-establishing market relations between the state and the independent producers on the land, by setting in motion a revival of industrial production, and by dismantling to some extent the repressive state apparatuses, the party leadership was able to reach a compromise between the state power and a variety of private interests whose activities now appeared vital to its survival. During the NEP the state no longer embraced the life of the citizens 'in every direction'. There was a partial retreat from the forms of political domination of the civil war, as a means of preserving the post-revolutionary state itself. But the NEP generated its own contradictions, which were confronted by means of a thoroughgoing reassertion of state power.

The ending of the NEP, set in motion by the 'left turn' in 1928, was the outcome of a new political conjuncture. The decisive development leading to it was the growing strain in the relations between the state and the peasantry, which took on a critical significance because of the decision to step up the rate of industrial investment. After a two-year period of recurrent and increasing conflict in the countryside, the decision was made in late 1929 to dismantle private production on the land by means of a wholesale collectivisation of agriculture. By intention the party would then overcome opposition to state procurement policies and establish a direct access to grain and other agricultural products, avoiding the uncertainties of the market.[5]

The key elements, then, in the left turn at the end of the 1920s were first, the proposed rapid industrial expansion, to be effected through a 'command' form of planning, and second, closely linked with it, the transformation of the relations of production in the countryside. These processes formed the basic elements of what in Soviet accounts is termed the 'reconstruction' of the post-revolutionary social order.

In the established Soviet view, the period of reconstruction was also the period in which socialism was built, when the party vanquished the enemy classes—the rural and urban petty bourgeoisie, established an overwhelming predominance of state and cooperative property and thus consolidated the proletarian dictatorship. The process involved a prolonged class struggle, because the USSR was surrounded by hostile capitalist powers, and because the capitalist and restorationist forces within the country had not abandoned their resistance; the struggle was in fact intensifying as a result of the attack on private production and trade. The socialist forces had to contend not simply with the private sector as such; the struggle was also a result of the influence of class enemies within the collective farms, among industrial workers and the intelligentsia, and within the political apparatus itself. In these circumstances, the role of the state could not diminish. On the contrary, the agencies of the state became increasingly important as an instrument of repression and education in the battle against forces resisting the victorious march of socialist construction.

This picture is recognisably Stalinist in origin.[6] It was by reference to the class struggle that Stalin sought to legitimate in Marxist terms the growing role of the state apparatuses in the early 1930s, while retaining in theory the formula of the withering away of the state. Following Stalin's lead, the political discourse of these years relied heavily on an imagery of combat. This imagery is less in evidence in recent Soviet historical accounts of the period. The edges of the conflict have been smoothed down, and it now sometimes looks like a battle without enemies. But the broad lines of thought to be found in Stalin's pronouncements have not been questioned in the orthodox Soviet literature.

The orthodox perspective will appear in this book as an object of analysis but not as a framework of inquiry. The assumption will be that the Stalinist conception was not so much a form of trickery as the ideological reflection of a real struggle. It was a struggle by political officialdom to carry through a crash programme of industrial expansion by imposing particular forms of political control over production. In the countryside this brought a massive show of force against the peasantry in the effort to establish a direct link between the state and agricultural production, and involved a prolonged confrontation between political officials and peasants, whether inside or outside the collective farms. Collectivisation meant not only a rapid extension in the scope of state intervention; it meant too a more active role for the coercive agencies in the grain collection campaigns, and in the administration of the labour camps which were rapidly expanded at this time with deportees from the countryside. Alongside the battle for grain, political officialdom was also engaged in a 'war' to secure a firmer hold over industrial production and to ensure the implementation of centrally established plans and priorities by managers, technicians and workers. This again had direct consequences for the role of different political agencies in relation to industry and the groups working within it.

It is suggested then, that Soviet reconstruction brought certain critical shifts in the pattern of state activity. From one perspective, these shifts can be seen as effects of a drastic social dislocation. In a persuasive analysis, it has been argued that the political transformations of the 1930s were the result of a general 'unhinging' of the social structure. The agencies of the state were engaged in a continuous effort to contain the consequences of a rapid social flux generated by industrial expansion and collectivisation. The transformation of individual producers into collective farmers, the sudden influx of peasants into the cities, the rapid turnover in the factories—to mention only some of the processes involved—created a series of social tensions which were confronted by means of a further enlargement of state activity, especially through the law and order agencies. A particular form of 'state building' thus appears as both cause and consequence of a radical social dislocation. The mutual influence of these processes provides a key part of the explanation for the emergence of the 'Stalinist' form of the state.[7]

This involved important changes in the character of the political apparatus itself, and in the relative role of different sections of it: for example, the party leader, the party apparatus, the political police and the judiciary. But these changes were effects of a transformation in the pattern of state activity *within* society, or a change in the position of the state as part of the totality of social relations.

From a somewhat different vantage point, one could say that Soviet reconstruction brought a generalised struggle by the defenders of the 'public' interest against the pursuit of a variety of 'private' interests that were seen to be sabotaging state objectives. In a sense this formulation is not so different from some official formulations of the period. But it does not carry the implication that this was a class struggle, nor that it was a process of socialist construction. To adopt these formulae is to accept an equation between the interests of 'state' and 'class', or between building socialism and constructing the state itself. Such equations formed the basis of a powerful political imagery and were important in the ideological defence of state property and public interests in general against erosion by the pursuit of private goals that were defined as anti-state. But it is more fruitful to try to understand how and why these equations were used as political weapons than to accept the assumptions underlying them.

In referring to the state in a global way, it is not being implied that this concept represents a homogeneous entity. The clash between public and private—if one adopts a broad understanding of the term private—was manifested not just in the tension between political officials and non-officials, but also in the friction between different levels and sections of political officialdom itself. There was no preordained unity between the decisions of the centre and the manner in which these were implemented by local political authorities, nor between, for example, the activities of the party, the police and the managers of industrial and agricultural production. A constant energy was needed in order to control agencies and citizens who were not 'in control', and to confront networks of local political interests which threatened to undermine the public interest as interpreted by the central party authorities. The dominant position of the party is to be seen not so much as a guarantee of unity between the different sections of political officialdom, or between political officials and those involved in the management of production, but as a necessary condition for its coordinating efforts in the face of the constant tendency for the practices of political officials and managers of production, as well as of rank and file workers and farmers, to conflict with the currently defined general interest.[8]

If this perspective is accepted, then the emergence of the Stalinist state cannot be seen as the product of an omnipotent officialdom— nor of an omnipotent leader. To be sure, the process was set in motion by a 'voluntarist' solution to the contradictions of the NEP: politics was in command. But the particular forms of state domination that developed were an effect of the continuous effort to respond to activities that were out of 'control', and to confront the unintended consequences of previous political decisions. Thus the concept of state domination, or the concept of 'politics in command'—which we accept—is *not* the same as the concept of an all-powerful officialdom, which could do anything it wanted with 'society'. The type of social formation called Stalinist was the product of particular forms of state activity within society, and linked to this, a set of relations between different sections and levels of officialdom. But to suppose that the political ruler or rulers were omnipotent requires the assumption of a full 'Weberian' bureau-cratic rationality in which the activities of subordinates could be controlled (and predicted) through the application of clearly established general rules to particular cases. This assumption, as will emerge, is radically at odds with any plausible interpretation of the role of political agencies under Stalinism. It also makes it impossible to explain the dynamic elements of the social formation, except in terms of some notion of pure political will.

The concept of the totalitarian state has sometimes been used to denote a radical extension of the scope of state activity, or a 'politicisation' of social relations, without at the same time adopting the notion of an all-powerful political officialdom. But more usually, especially in the postwar period, the concept of the totalitarian state has had a rather different usage, in which the whole pattern of social relations—especially under Stalinism—has been seen as an effect of the total control exercised by the political centre through a monolithic single party organisation, ubiquitous police penetration, and a number of other features.[9] But the idea of a radical extension of state activity is not the same as the idea of unlimited political control; the latter simply erases all questions about the possible contradictions which might characterise a state-dominated society, and which might account for its internal transformations. Since it is those sorts of questions that are central to the study, there is little point in making an issue of 'totalitarianism' in its typical postwar usage. The matter will be set aside, on the assumption that the concept is inadequate for an analysis of the Stalinist state. At the same time, state domination will be a central idea, and the object will be to throw light on how it worked by observing its consequences in certain specific social contexts.

IB THE TECHNICAL INTELLIGENTSIA AND THE STATE: THE ISSUES

Having set out some of the general assumptions underlying the study, a brief account will now be given of the particular issues to be investigated. The intention is to explore some of the consequences of the emerging Stalinist form of state domination by examining its impact on the technical intelligentsia. But before outlining the matters involved, an explanation of some key terms will be necessary. A distinction is drawn at the outset between the intelligentsia—or those engaged in 'intellectual' work—and the functionaries of the state or the political apparatus, that is, the central and local organs of party and government. This separation is admittedly difficult to make in a clearcut way, because political functionaries are 'intellectuals' in the broadest sense, and because the decision as to who is and is not a functionary of the state may to some extent be arbitrary. But this does not invalidate the distinction in principle.

The term intelligentsia is still left with a very broad reference. Its members perform a wide variety of cultural, scientific, technical and managerial functions. The term *technical intelligentsia*, as used in the study, means intellectual workers closely concerned with production. Unless otherwise stated, the scope of reference is restricted to the technical intelligentsia in industrial enterprises. The category subsumes (a) *managerial (or 'line') personnel*, including directors, technical directors and chief engineers, managers of shops, foremen, (b) *technical (or 'staff') personnel*, including engineers and technicians without managerial functions. A third category of 'mental labour' in industrial enterprises, which in the Soviet definition customarily includes accountants, bookkeepers and the clerical staff of the enterprise, will not be discussed.

The technical intelligentsia is thus synonymous in this study with the Soviet category 'engineering and technical workers' (henceforth ITR), which incorporates both 'line' and 'staff' personnel whose work is more or less closely linked to production. The term 'line' conventionally refers to the hierarchy that is most directly involved with the production process itself, while 'staff' refers to activities that are less immediately connected to production, within which technical experts perform advisory functions, and lack the authority over subordinates associated with the line. But the boundary between line and staff is not always easy to draw in practice. Some staff, for example maintenance, quality control or work study engineers, may have intimate links to the process of production, and some staff functions may involve authority over subordinates similar to that conventionally associated with the line.[10]

Finally, the term 'specialists' is sometimes used in Soviet sources synonymously with ITR, and it is in this restricted sense that the term is used here. We have therefore a trio of coextensive terms: technical intelligentsia, ITR and specialists. 'Managers' refer to line personnel, 'technical staff' to ITR not on the line. The scope of reference is confined to *industry* (excluding transport and construction), with the bulk of evidence, though not all of it, taken from the heavy industry sector.

In the period (1928–35) providing the main focus of attention, the social position of the technical intelligentsia in the USSR was affected in important ways by the changing mode of state domination that has been briefly discussed. To explore this question, the analysis takes the following course.

First, in order to give some historical depth to the account, and to make sense of the emphasis on the transformations involved, some attention must be given to the period preceding the rapid industrial expansion of the late 1920s and early 1930s. Chapter 2 is therefore devoted to a discussion of the technical intelligentsia during the decade following the October revolution. For the most part the account is concerned with the position of the so-called bourgeois specialists, that is the managers and technical staff who were 'inherited' by the post-revolutionary state. It looks briefly at their response to the revolutionary events and examines their relationship to the party, to the Bolshevik industrial managers and to the trade unions and workers in the period 1917–27.

Chapter 3 examines some of the effects on the technical intelligentsia of the 'left turn', the beginning of which can be dated from early 1928, and which can be seen as the start of the breakup of the NEP. One of the striking features of the left turn was a political offensive against the old generation (bourgeois) specialists who were singled out as enemies of the state, which had now embarked on a new phase of socialist development by stepping up the rate of industrial investment, establishing a new form of planning, and trying to put its relationship with the peasantry on a new footing. The campaign against the old generation technical intelligentsia was presented in the prevailing political imagery as one element of a class struggle in which party and state were engaged against all enemies of socialist construction. Part of what was meant by the class struggle in this context was an attack on the intellectuals' claim to authority based on specialised or professional knowledge. It was an attempt by the party, through drastic means, to impose its own definition of the situation in the face of the tension between political demands and corporate or professional commitments within the intelligentsia. The aim is to find out what was involved in this effort to redefine—and 'politicise'—intelligentsia roles.

Together with an offensive against the old generation technical intelligentsia, the period of reconstruction, since it involved a rapid industrial expansion, also meant a rapid growth in the size of the technical intelligentsia. The sudden increase in the rate of recruitment to managerial and technical positions was determined by the technical requirements of industrialisation. But the process of recruitment was also seen by the party leadership as a vital element in the attempt to form a new relationship between the technical intelligentsia and the state in which a closer harmony would be established between political demands and professional self-images. This question is explored in Chapter 4. By examining some of the patterns of recruitment to ITR positions and considering the effects on the 'new' specialists of the campaign against the old generation, some further suggestions are made about the consequences of the effort to 'politicise' the relationship between the technical intelligentsia and the state.

The character of this relation (and the effects of politicisation) cannot, however, be adequately understood without a study of the work roles of the ITR. The focus of discussion therefore shifts in Chapter 5 to examine the work situation of managers and technical staff during Soviet reconstruction. We shall look at the consequences for the ITR of adopting a particular form of political control over production—'command' planning—and explore the impact on the technical intelligentsia of different political agencies which were asked to overcome obstacles hindering the implementation of plans. Special attention is given in this context to the role of the coercive agencies in the arena of industrial production, in order to highlight the question of the degree of job security for the ITR. The discussion here is crucial in considering the extent and limits of 'control' over the technical intelligentsia by agencies of the state. It is also possible to consider in a concrete way whether the notion of a 'Weberian' bureaucratic rationality is relevant to an understanding of this relationship.

While faced with a variety of pressures from above, the ITR—especially line managers—at the same time stood in authority over the industrial workers. The technical intelligentsia was asked to play a key part in imposing 'culture' and 'discipline' on the workforce in order to extract the necessary effort to meet pressing production targets. This issue is explored in Chapter 6. The organisational environment was conducive to a tough style of direction and reduced to a minimum the possibilities of any organised response by workers or mass organisations of the enterprise to management demands. But the question is also asked in what ways managerial authority may have been limited from below, and whether the image of an unconditional authority over the workforce is accurate.

Finally, in Chapter 7, a further dimension is added by looking briefly at certain material privileges that benefited the ITR in the period under review, and the possible significance of this for a statement about the relationship between the technical intelligentsia and the state.

By examining these different dimensions it is hoped to give a convincing characterisation of the social position of the enterprise technical intelligentsia during Soviet reconstruction. It should be stressed that the features to be identified are not connected in a merely contingent way, but will be seen as different manifestations or effects of a change in the mode of state domination which affected the whole pattern of social relationships in the USSR in this period.

Further, the assumption is that the features in question were historically specific to the USSR in the period under review. It could quite plausibly be argued that certain elements in the situation were 'formative' and that one would find some important continuities in the position of the technical intelligentsia in the early 1930s and in the present day. But it is not part of the exercise to demonstrate this. It is not intended, then, that any conclusions be drawn from the study about the contemporary Soviet Union.

Also, we shall take the view that the role of the technical

intelligentsia in this period was specific when set against the position of the technical intelligentsia in past or present capitalist formations. Certain parallels can be drawn. For example, it can be said that in both cases the technical intelligentsia played a mediating role, being subject to domination from above and also acting as agents of domination over industrial workers. This is important, since it may point to common elements in the social division of labour in industrial production. But similarities in the social division of labour will not be taken as an indication of the presence of capitalist relations of production. In Marx's analysis, the position of the technical intelligentsia in capitalist production—the labour of the 'foreman, engineer, manager, etc.'—is defined by a certain relationship to *capital* and *wage labour*. This position is complex, since managers and technicians are wage workers, but wage workers of a special type because of their 'superintendent' role on behalf of capital. But this ambiguity is defined in the context of a capitalist mode of production.[11] If capitalist relations of production were not present in the USSR, then the meaning of 'mediation' is not the same.

Some parts of the story that the book is concerned with have been discussed elsewhere. The studies by Carr and Davies, Granick and Azrael[12] are especially important and the debt to these will be apparent. But the analysis here is informed by a specific set of questions and does not substantially rely on these studies. The argument is based mainly on a reading of Soviet publications of the time. The most important of these are: contemporary newspapers and journals, official directives of party and government, stenographic reports of various conferences, memoirs by participant observers, and statistical handbooks.

2 The Technical Intelligentsia 1917–27

The purpose of this chapter is to try to give a historical depth to the later discussions of the technical intelligentsia during Soviet reconstruction, and to make some sense of the emphasis on the dynamic elements in the situation after 1927. It has not been possible to give the same amount of attention to the post-revolutionary decade as to the later years. But the present discussion is nonetheless intended to be more than a backdrop. It forms a necessary part of the whole argument. The first section looks at the role of the technical intelligentsia during the revolutionary period and the civil war, and examines some of the disputes within the party which arose in this connection. The second section identifies some of the key changes affecting the technical intelligentsia during the NEP, focusing on party policy towards the bourgeois specialists and their response to it, on the relations between Bolshevik enterprise directors and non-party specialists, and on the role of the managers in relation to the workers and trade unions.

2A REVOLUTION AND CIVIL WAR

The first few months after the October revolution, between October 1917 and the spring of 1918, witnessed what Lenin described as a civil war between the Soviet government on the one side, and on the other, representatives of capital and sections of the intelligentsia.[1] A number of groups, including officials and employees of government departments and banks, teachers and doctors, refused to cooperate with the Bolsheviks, doing what they could to subvert the new political order.[2]

In the case of the technical intelligentsia, or that section of the technical intelligentsia which was employed in production, the 'war' with the Soviet government during the revolutionary period took the form of a struggle for control over industry. Controls over capitalist production, from above by the state and from below by workers' organisations, were already established before the Bolshevik takeover of power.[3] But in the immediate post-revolutionary period, these controls were extended and given a new content as a result of the political upheaval. Industrial managers and technical staff were in the thick of the ensuing struggle.

In the early phases of the struggle, the Bolshevik leaders did not propose any drastic changes in the form of control over capitalist production—at least in the sense that no sweeping measures of nationalisation were proposed. The immediate aim was to seize certain key economic positions, and to keep industry in operation, preventing a possible 'strike of capital' designed to bring down the government. Within the proposed framework, the existing managerial and technical personnel were to keep their jobs. But production and distribution would be subordinated to the 'accounting and control' (*uchet i kontrol*) of the proletarian dictatorship, exercised from above by the Councils of National Economy (VSNKh and its subordinate *Sovnarkhozy*) and at the point of production by the factory committees. Workers' control in this conception belonged to a phase of partial socialisation of the means of production, a phase which Lenin later liked to call 'state capitalist'. The working class would be in command not by virtue of an overnight abolition of the capitalist basis of production, but by virtue of the political power of workers' organisations and the workers' state which decisively transformed the conditions under which capitalist production could go on.[4]

The state capitalist–workers' control pattern was fundamentally unstable. The decree on workers' control of November 1917,[5] which gave the factory committees access to all company records, and the right to supervise the production of goods, the purchase of materials, and finance, in effect legitimated a continuing war between management and factory committees. There were some cases of cooperation—or at least mutual toleration—between the enterprise administration and workers' organisations.[6] But most managements resisted the implementation of workers' control and often closed down their plants or attempted to do so. Where the administration was held to have sabotaged production, individual enterprises were either nationalised by a decision from above or else taken over by the factory committees. In the process, managers and technical staff often chose to leave their jobs or were forced to.[7]

It was the role of the technical intelligentsia in the struggle for control over industry in the revolutionary period which earned them the Bolshevik epithet 'bourgeois specialists'. If understood as a reference to the social origins of the Russian technical intelligentsia in 1917 the label would be misleading.[8] Even if one considers only the more prestigious section, the engineers, their family background was more often petty-bourgeois than bourgeois in the conventional sense.[9] However, the label referred to ideological conditioning and structural position within capitalist production rather than to social origin, and it is in those contexts that the appropriateness of the label has to be judged.

A proper analysis of how the technical intelligentsia responded to the revolutionary events and the reasons for this response would need more investigation than has been possible within the confines of this study. But a few suggestions will be made, based on the comments of different speakers at a single conference of the All-Russian Union of Engineers (VSI) in January 1918.[10]

First, one gets a strong sense of injured professional self-esteem. According to one speaker, the technical personnel had been deprived of their 'autonomous and responsible role', and industry was in the hands of a ruling party which 'does not have even the simplest understanding of the concrete economic conditions of the moment'. It was essential that 'the most competent technical and economic forces in the country be given leading and responsible positions'. Workers' representatives were incompetent to manage industry, but the Bolsheviks were encouraging them through workers' control and were generally unleashing mob rule.[11] In the view of one delegate, the Bolsheviks were leading industry to destruction because their chief aim was to 'pander to the crowd and its crude instincts and destructive impulses . . . with narrow class slogans and with an attempt to preserve authority in the eyes of the masses. An epoch of demagogy, conceit and ignorance has begun'.[12]

A second feature that emerges, implicit in the first, is a commitment to maintaining a capitalist form of production; this was what the 'concrete economic conditions' demanded. One speaker referred to the 'extremely difficult and ambiguous position of capital, deprived of profits and legal perspectives', and said that the government should 'define its attitude towards capital'. A certain measure of state control was essential, but the limits should be clearly set.[13]

Finally, the discussion revealed a third important element: a

strong nationalist commitment. Fears were expressed that Russia
would be turned into a German, English or American colony when
the war ended.[14] The Bolsheviks were expected to fail the *nation*
because of the policy they had adopted in relation to industry. The
choice facing the country was. either a decisive attempt to re-
establish 'industrial discipline' by ending workers' control, or a
temporary industrial death, after which the workers and everyone
else would be doomed to a full subordination to foreign capital.[15]

On the basis of this view of the situation, the conference passed
the following 'tactical resolution':

> The VSI, as a professional organisation defending the pro-
> fessional interests of its members, must struggle with expressions
> of social anarchy which are destroying the economic life of the
> country and putting its members in a position where they cannot
> freely, in accordance with their conscience, fulfil their pro-
> fessional duties of managing and developing Russian
> industry . . . The VSI therefore forbids its members to join any
> organisation whose politics contributed to the collapse of in-
> dustry, and to support it with its knowledge and experience.
> Members of the union cannot take on the function of commissars
> in industrial enterprises, participate in workers' management
> boards, or in control commissions with managerial functions, and
> in general must struggle against the interference of irresponsible
> forces . . .

In cases where workers' representatives or appointed commissars
took over managerial posts that had been occupied by engineers,
those positions were to be boycotted by members of the union.[16]

To what extent the members of the VSI fell in line with this
resolution is not known. Nor is it known how far the responses
identified were typical of the Russian technical intelligentsia. But
the assumption that they were is consistent with other evidence and
may help to explain the basis on which an accommodation between
the technical intelligentsia and the Soviet power was later made.

By the spring of 1918, if we can judge by Lenin's comments, the
tension—or at least overt conflict—between the Soviet power and
the technical intelligentsia (together with other groups of intellectuals) was less than in the first few months after the October
revolution. In December 1917 Lenin was demanding 'military
measures' against uncooperative capitalists and their lackeys,

'messrs. bourgeois intellectuals'.[17] But in April 1918 he was saying that sabotage by the intelligentsia had in the main been 'broken' and even that there had been an 'enormous change of mood and political behaviour among former saboteurs'.[18]

During the civil war from the summer of 1918 to late 1920, the specialists who remained in Soviet territory were incorporated as administrators, managers and technical advisers within a now wholly nationalised industry. They were working in central and local economic agencies, and, in so far as the factories and mines were kept going, in production itself. One Soviet writer later described the relationship between the Soviet power and the technical intelligentsia during the civil war as a 'forced marriage'.[19] The Bolsheviks had no choice but rely on the available technical skills, while the specialists were obliged to earn a living. Neither of these points need be disputed, but there was more to it than that.

First, although representatives of the technical intelligentsia strongly opposed the rapid extension of nationalisation in summer 1918,[20] the form of organisation of industry that was established during the civil war was less injurious to professional self-esteem than in the revolutionary period. Externally, enterprises were administered within a highly centralised framework in which they were heavily dependent on the various departments of the All-Russian Council of National Economy (VSNKh) at the centre, or its local branches (the *Sovnarkhozy*). Within enterprises the work of specialists was supervised either by collegial boards or by 'commissar' directors appointed by the *Sovnarkhoz* with the participation of the trade unions. In this scheme of things the factory committees continued to play an important role through participation on collegial boards. But they were less influential than in the revolutionary period, and by the end of the civil war there was a trend away from collegial administration towards one-man management at the enterprise level.[21] According to one prominent specialist, the position of the old managers and technical staff to some extent improved in 1918 because of the introduction of 'strict organisation'.[22] The strengthening of a system of administration from above, because it meant the atrophy of workers' control from below, did give back to the specialists some of the authority that they had lost during the first post-revolutionary months, and thereby conceded some of their claims to a special professional competence.

A second point concerns the possible importance of patriotic considerations during the civil war, which may have modified the specialists' basic antipathy to the new political order. The Bolsheviks, it could be argued, were defending national interests in their own way. Some evidence on this point has been found,[23] but further documentation would certainly be necessary to establish it.

Finally, it should be noted that a certain attempt was made not only to give jobs to the technical intelligentsia, but also to look after their material interests. In April 1918, Lenin proposed paying high wages to specialists as an alternative to 'military' incentives to work. He described this as a 'departure from the principles of the Paris Commune and of every proletarian power'. Only bourgeois methods would enable the Soviet power to put the skills of the bourgeois specialists to work, and the benefits would far outweigh the expense involved.[24] But one should not perhaps make too much of this concession to material incentives. The absolute decline in living standards was precipitous during the civil war, and the relative privileges of the rank-and-file managers and technical staff were probably minimal. According to one source, the engineer in a factory usually did not earn much more than a skilled worker.[25] In the case of 'top specialists', to judge from figures cited by Lenin in March 1919, the ratio of average workers' wages to top salaries was 1 to 5, as compared with a ratio of 1 to 20 before the revolution.[26] The civil war trends can thus be seen as only a minor concession to a bourgeois mode of distribution, though it was acknowledged that there was 'widespread dissatisfaction' with the relatively high earnings of specialists.[27]

2A (i) SPECIALISTS AND FORMS OF MANAGEMENT: SOME POLITICAL ARGUMENTS

The question of what relationship the Soviet power was to establish with the 'old' managerial and technical cadres was the subject of much dispute within the party during the civil war, closely connected to a debate about the appropriate forms of organisation of industrial production. The basic position that was being urged from the centre, backed up by frequent cajoling from Lenin, was summed up in his slogan 'combat the counter-revolution, utilise the bourgeois-cultural apparatus'.[28] The implications of this slogan were spelt out in the party programme of March 1919:

The task of developing the productive forces demands the immediate, widespread and all-sided (*vsestoronny*) utilisation of the specialists of science and technique left to us by the capitalist inheritance, despite the fact that they are in most cases steeped in a bourgeois outlook and bourgeois habits. The party considers that the period of sharp struggle with this stratum, caused by the sabotage organised by them, has ended, since this sabotage has on the whole been broken. The party, in close cooperation with the trade unions must carry out its former line: on the one hand, not give the slightest political concession to this bourgeois stratum and ruthlessly suppress any counter-revolutionary impulses, on the other hand, equally ruthlessly struggle with the pseudo-radical but in fact ignorant opinion that the workers are in a position to overcome capitalism and the bourgeois order, not learning from the bourgeois specialists, not utilising them, not going through a long period of education with them.[29]

Underlying this injunction were certain general assumptions about the role of the intelligentsia in a socialist revolution. The forms of cultural domination within capitalist society made it impossible for the working class to produce its 'own' intellectuals in the sense that this had been possible for the third estate before the bourgeois revolutions. Some intellectuals would join the workers' movement, and in Russia the conditions for this may have been peculiarly favourable. But generally the intelligentsia—perhaps especially the technical intelligentsia because of its structural position in capitalist production—would have no sympathy with socialism. Yet the existing technical knowledge was concentrated in the heads of the intellectuals, and they must in one way or another be accommodated within the new political order, especially under the Russian conditions of 'Asiatic' cultural poverty. In such a context, the idea of developing a proletarian technical or scientific culture was farfetched. Gaining a modicum of honest bourgeois culture was the best that could be hoped for.[30]

There does not seem to have been much contention within the party about these general propositions, though there was within anarchist and anarchosyndicalist circles.[31] But argument arose over what *forms of organisation* should be adopted in industrial production. This was logically separate from the question about what role the inherited managers and technical staff would play. But since the forms of organisation would determine how much authority was to be given to the '*spets*'—a current colloquialism for the old generation specialists—the two issues were closely related in practice. Lenin's position, eventually adopted as official party policy, was that one-man authority was 'called for' by modern large-scale industry itself.

> . . . it must be said that large-scale machine industry—which is precisely the material source, the productive source, the foundation of socialism—calls for absolute and strict *unity of will*, which directs the joint labours of hundreds, thousands and tens of thousands of people. The technical, economic and historical necessity of this is obvious, and all those who have thought about socialism have always regarded it as one of the conditions of socialism. But how can strict unity of will be ensured? By thousands subordinating their will to the will of one.
>
> Given ideal class-consciousness and discipline on the part of those participating in the common work, this subordination would be something like the mild leadership of a conductor of an orchestra. It may assume the sharp forms of a dictatorship if the ideal discipline and class consciousness are lacking. But be that as it may, *unquestioning subordination* to a single will is absolutely necessary for the success of processes organised on the pattern of large-scale machine industry.[32]

This statement was made in 1918, but the matter of one-man management became a topic of major political argument only in 1920 when collegial forms of management were being abandoned in practice in industrial enterprises. Lenin then resurrected his earlier arguments, saying that the problem of forms of organisation was a technical matter that did not affect the 'rights of class'. According to a resolution of the 9th Party Congress in April 1920 (drafted by Lenin):

> One-man management in no way destroys or limits the rights of the class, nor the 'rights' of trade unions, since the class can rule in any form, and this form depends on technical expediency; in all cases the ruling class 'appoints' the directing and administering personnel. One-man management, even where a '*spets*' directs, is in the last resort an expression of the proletarian dictatorship . . .[33]

A more spelt-out version of a similar position can be found in Bukharin's *The Economics of the Transition Period*. Bukharin distinguishes two elements of the social relations of production: 'class relations' and 'technical relations'. The seizure of power by the working class led to the reordering of class relations, but 'the logic of the productive process itself demands a quite definite type of relationship' between the 'human technical' elements of production, namely the labour power of the director, engineer, foreman, worker, etc. Collegial management was to be seen as a temporary phenomenon of the revolutionary upheaval—the technical intelligentsia, by refusing to cooperate, had left the factories 'without a master'. But rule by the factory committee, and *election* of managerial personnel, was technically an imperfect system, which had meant a rapid decline in productivity. A collegial system could be dispensed with, and the principle of *selection* established, once the revolutionary crisis was overcome and the workers' state was firmly established. In the new scheme of things, the old technical intelligentsia would retain its 'middle place' in the hierarchy, since 'the engineer or technician must give orders to the workers, and must therefore stand *over* them . . . ' But the technical intelligentsia would no longer serve as the agent for the extraction of surplus value. Political and economic power would be concentrated in the hands of the proletariat, and 'no engineer can carry out any function except that which the proletariat demands of him'.[34]

Against this or similar positions, a number of oppositional factions, the Left Communists (1918), the Democratic Centralists (1920–21) and the Workers' Opposition (1920–22), argued in favour of a collegial and an elective form of enterprise management, on the grounds that this was the best 'school of administration' and that the 'technical' role of managers and engineers as established under capitalist conditions was incompatible with any attempt to establish socialist forms of labour organisation.[35] A strong version of the argument can be found in a Workers' Opposition document written by Kollontai, where she suggests that one-man and collegial management are 'historically irreconcilable', one-man management being a 'product of the individualist conception of the bourgeois class'. Further, it was a 'fallacy to suppose that "practical" men, technicians, specialists and managers of capitalist production can suddenly release themselves from the bonds of their traditional ways of handling labour . . . and acquire the ability to create new forms of production, of labour organisation and of incentives to work'.[36]

These arguments, which unfortunately cannot be adequately

explored here, need to be taken seriously. The way that one-man management was defended, depended on a rather mechanical distinction between technical and class relations, according to which it was possible to take on the 'good' parts of the capitalist organisation of labour and reject the 'bad'. But this bypassed the question of the link between economic relations and the forms of the labour process under capitalism.[37] Lenin may well have been right that workers' control in the 1917 sense could not solve the problem that technical knowhow was indeed concentrated in the heads of the specialists. There was a fundamental inherited division of labour which could not be transcended simply by means of an electoral system of industrial management. The 'organising' role of the technical intelligentsia was a consequence of its specialist knowledge: specialists would necessarily be telling workers what to do. But the question remained, what were the conditions for transcending that division of labour, and whether any *particular* forms of organisation were 'called for' by 'large-scale industry'.

The debates in the party can be taken as an indication of the uncertain political conditions in which the bourgeois specialists worked during the civil war. Lenin generally defended the specialists, though his own position was ambivalent; after all, these were ex-saboteurs. But when he was defending them, it was in a context of conflicting views within political officialdom about the appropriate form of relationship to establish with the technical intelligentsia. Trotsky's remarks on this in 1919 give some idea of the underlying tensions:

> Only a sorry Soviet bureaucrat, jealous of his new post, valuing this post for its personal privileges, not in the interests of the proletarian revolution, can have an attitude of groundless mistrust towards everyone who has mastered his profession, towards an outstanding organiser, technician, scientist . . . deciding in advance that 'we shall manage by ourselves one way or another'.[38]

In similar vein, Lenin later attacked 'communist boasting' (*komchvantstvo*) and the 'bureaucratic inattention to practical experience'[39] and began to compare communist planners and administrators unfavourably with the down-to-earth experts who at least knew their business.[40]

These injunctions do not suggest that the specialists were easily accommodated within the post-revolutionary order under the civil war conditions. Rather, they testify to a struggle that was being carried out by some political officials to offer more concessions to the intelligentsia than other officials were prepared to allow.

2B   THE NEP

The introduction of the NEP in 1921 brought important changes for the technical intelligentsia, both in the political climate and in the organisational environment of industrial production. But before discussing these, something must be said about patterns of recruitment to ITR positions in the years 1921–27.

In 1921–22, many 'commissars' who had acted as directors during the civil war were replaced by '*spetsy*'. But from 1923 onwards 'red' managers were again replacing the *spetsy* in top positions in industrial enterprises. This was one result of the effort by the party apparatus, especially after the 12th Party Congress in 1923, to extend its influence over the appointment of managers at all levels. According to one of the resolutions of the Congress, 'the party is now in no case able to limit itself only to general propaganda and agitation . . . [the party] cannot forget for a moment that it has the chief responsibility for the economic organs . . . still closer to the economy, still more attention to the economic organs—this should be the slogan of the party in the next period'. Accordingly the party and trade union organisations were instructed to 'pay the most serious attention to increasing the cadres of worker-managers, especially communists, in the organs of industrial administration at all levels of the economic hierarchy, making their primary task to provide factories and plants with cadres of red directors'.[41]

Some of the ensuing changes can be seen in the information on directors in Table 1.

There seems to have been very little published information on other managerial and technical positions during the NEP. But some observations can be made on patterns of recruitment relying on a sample survey of August 1929. The survey covered 8995 managerial and technical personnel in Soviet industry (the total number of ITR at that time was about 100,000), and included a selection of the largest enterprises in the USSR.[42] Of the sample 67 per cent were in industrial enterprises, 3.5 per cent in construction, 5.4 per cent in

TABLE 1: *Enterprise directors 1923–28*

	Party members (per cent)	Former workers (per cent)	No higher or secondary education (per cent)
1923[a]	29	–	52
1924[b]	48	36	–
1926[c]	78	58	66
1928[c]	89	63	72

Sources: [a]*Nash promyshlenny komsostav* (1923), p. 11 (sample of 1300 directors); [b]*Komsostav promyshlennosti* (1924), p. 37, (sample of 639 directors); [c]*Bolshevik*, 1928, no. 8, p. 64 (samples of 770 and 766 directors for 1926 and 1928 respectively).

trust offices, 5.9 per cent in design organisations, and 18.2 per cent in scientific and technical research establishments.

The categories covered at the enterprise level were defined as follows (the figures in brackets give the relative weight of each category as a proportion of all enterprise ITR covered): 1. directors and their assistants (1 per cent); 2. heads of shops, departments, workshops and their assistants (24 per cent); 3. chief engineers and engineers (12 per cent); 4. foremen (29 per cent); 5. technicians (15 per cent); 6. designers (9 per cent); 7. other managerial–technical personnel (10 per cent). A little recalculation yields the figures in Table 2 concerning the length of work experience of the ITR at the end of 1927. The 'ITR' in the table includes all the above categories, and 'higher administrative and technical personnel' lumps together categories 1, 2 and 3.

TABLE 2: *ITR in the NEP period*

Began work as specialists	ITR (total)		ITR (enterprise level)		Higher administrative and technical personnel	
	No.	per cent	No.	per cent	No.	per cent
Before 1905	756	12.0	458	11.2	391	13.9
1906–17	2002	31.8	1277	31.4	1037	36.8
1918–25	2881	45.8	1921	47.1	1151	40.8
1926–7	654	10.4	419	10.3	242	8.5

Source: A. Beilin (1935), pp. 134, 144–7.

Thus at the end of 1927 the 'old generation' specialists who started working in industry before 1918, formed about 43 per cent of ITR as a whole, and about half of 'higher administrative and technical personnel'. According to one source, most of the *trained* specialists who started working in industry between 1918 and 1925 were pre-1918 graduates, since very few people graduated from Soviet technical institutes in this period.[43] If the 'old generation' is understood more broadly—as it often was by Soviet observers—to include those with a largely prerevolutionary training, the proportion of old specialists would look considerably higher.

There is not enough information to get a picture of sources of recruitment to the different ITR positions during the NEP. Our impression is that the older specialists typically occupied posts as chief engineers or technical directors, as managers in production shops and departments, and as higher-level technical staff. New generation specialists, either *praktiki* (people without formal technical qualifications) who had been promoted to ITR positions since the revolution, or else trained specialists who had graduated from technical institutes in the post-revolutionary period, were still, at the end of the NEP, in lower supervisory or staff positions. But this division was not clearcut, since it is known that a certain proportion of foremen were of the prerevolutionary formation, and many of the shop heads were *praktiki* who had been promoted since 1917.[44]

Finally, it should be noted that there was a clear contrast between the red directors and the incumbents of other ITR positions in relation to party membership and social background. The August 1929 survey indicates that at the end of 1927, about seventeen per cent of all ITR were party members, and about twenty per cent had once been workers on the shop floor.[45] These figures were mostly accounted for by the relatively high party membership among foremen, and by the fact that most foremen had been promoted from manual jobs.[46] Among engineers, on the other hand, party saturation was about two per cent and the proportion of former workers about five per cent.[47] The NEP enterprise thus typically incorporated 'non-expert communists' with 'good' biographies, and 'non-party experts' whose claim to authority was based solely on training and experience. This social division had a definite resonance for contemporaries, which will be explored later.

2B (i) THE PARTY AND THE BOURGEOIS SPECIALISTS

During the NEP, by contrast with the war communist period, a more emphatic effort was made by the central party authorities to enlist the technical intelligentsia as full citizens of the post-revolutionary order. With the inheritance of a war-shattered industry and the shift of attention from military objectives to the restoration of production, the party leaders became more conscious of the scarcity of technical knowhow and sought to establish conditions in which the *spetsy* would be able to get on with their work without political harassment. This shift in political stance, together with the key NEP concessions to rural and urban private production and trade, provided the basis for a further political accommodation between the specialists and the Soviet power, although it did not remove all the tensions between political demands and professional self-images.

To get some idea of the impact of the NEP on the technical intelligentsia, we shall again rely on statements made in a trade union context, starting with a few words of explanation on the organisational setting. The previously mentioned All-Russian Union of Engineers (VSI), set up in March 1917, was dissolved at the end of 1918. After internal struggles within the VSI, it was agreed that trade union issues should become the province of new 'sections' of engineers under the All-Russian Central Council of Trade Unions (VTsSPS), while a separate organisation, the All-Russian Association of Engineers (VAI, eventually dissolved in 1929) would continue to exist as a scientific and technical body.[47] In the event it proved very difficult during the civil war period to establish a working relationship between the sections and the trade union leadership. There was at first, according to Tomsky, a 'horror on both sides' about the prospect of working together,[48] and the organisational forms and tasks of the sections tended to be defined by the trade unions without the participation of the specialists themselves.[49] Most sections atrophied during the civil war, and were re-established only after a coordinating 'Engineering Centre' had been established under VTsSPS in December 1921. After 1921 'engineers' sections' and from 1924 onwards 'sections of engineers and technicians' (ITS), were established for all major industries, and by 1927 covered the great majority of ITR.[50] The idea of a separate trade union for the technical intelligentsia was still 'very popular' at the time of the 1st Congress of Engineers in December

1922,[51] but this did not happen. Thus the position was that the ITR remained formally integrated within the trade unions, but were separately represented through the sections, whose day-to-day affairs were run independently of the central trade union leadership.

In January 1922, a resolution of a conference of engineers (VAI) described the NEP as a 'very big step forward'. It was said that 'we do not adhere to the ideology or tactics of any political party', that 'we wish to be accused neither of counterrevolution nor of excessive leftism', and that the task of the engineers was to 'struggle for the development of the productive forces of Russia . . . and for their restoration independently of any transient (*prekhodyashchikh*) political situations'. At the same time, it was said, 'under no circumstances can one allow the engineer to be regarded as an observer from the sidelines or as a hired *spets* (*naemnika-spetsa*). According to our view, the engineer is a citizen of the highest qualifications, boldly and honestly fulfilling his duties as a technician and a citizen'.[52] Similar remarks could be heard at another conference of engineers in December 1922. One delegate described the 'present tactic' (that is, the NEP tactic) as 'more acceptable' to the engineers and said that it was now possible to find 'points of contact'. He had this appeal to make to the political leadership: 'Since the engineers said that they did not share the ideology and tactics of communism, we were regarded with suspicion and our good motives were not believed . . . now the engineers can say to the communists: 'take us as we are, not as communists, but don't suspect us of counterrevolutionary intentions, since we do not have any'.[53]

The extent to which the party leadership wanted to smooth things over can be judged from an address by Bukharin to the second All-Union Conference of Engineers' and Technicians' Sections in December 1924. The task for the political leaders ('*kadrovy sostav politikov*' was the expression) and the technical intelligentsia was to 'learn from one another', and it was 'essential for us [the political leaders] to listen in the most attentive way to the voice of the specialists . . . '. Bukharin stressed that the 'radicalisation' of the economic structure during the civil war was 'not the product of a change in our views' but was 'forced on us by objective circumstances'. Yet this radicalisation had saved not only the proletarian power but also the *nation*, 'irrespective of the class nature of its socio-economic order'. Without the civil war 'radicalisation', Russia would now be in the subjugated position of China or Persia, or at best Germany. Even without the world war, he assured the audience, Tsarism would have fallen, because of the basic contradiction between the development of industry and a declining market capacity. The government's chief aim now was to ensure that 'we do not tear ourselves away from our peasant base', and its policy in general was founded on a 'cold, calm analysis of . . . sociopolitical and economic relationships'. 'In essence', he said, 'we decide all problems as technical problems.'[54]

In these remarks Bukharin was clearly bending over backwards to made concessions to the professional self-esteem, the nationalism and the self-image of non-political 'objectivity' of the specialists. He did, however, appeal for a 'higher level of political consciousness' among the technical intelligentsia. This was essential if a proper understanding was to be reached between the political and specialist cadres: 'if we achieve this link (*smychka*) between the engineers and the leading party cadres . . . then we can say that your social group will play a colossal role . . . not simply in the technical construction of the country but in the sense that you will become a kind of lever for the transformation of the whole people'.[55]

In the same spirit, a resolution of the conference offered the following assurance:

> the broad masses of engineers and technicians . . . regard themselves as an inseparable part of the working class and reject any ideology which does not come into contact with the ideology of the Soviet power . . . The main task for the mass of engineers and technicians is not to defend a caste separateness, not to demand the special privileges of the bourgeois engineer, but to seek the mutual trust of engineers and technicians with the working class as a whole . . .[56]

One can infer from all this that Bukharin's envisaged *smychka* was something to be worked for rather than actually achieved, and that the self-image of 'caste separateness' among the ITR was also something that had not yet been transcended. The legacy of tension from the revolution and the civil war was unlikely to be quickly erased, and political criteria, as suggested by the information presented earlier, remained important in assessing the suitability of ITR for particular posts. The guidelines used by a party commission in 1923 to consider the question of party control over industrial personnel are revealing in this respect. The following categories, based on the reports of local party and GPU organisations, were identified: (a) '*spets*-communist', said to be a mere handful; (2) 'Soviet *spets*', described as loyal, 'all right with the trade unions, do not forget themselves', 'understand that their careers are bound up with the Soviet power'; (3) 'wait and see *spets*': these were allegedly the majority, who were not dishonest, but 'do not believe in the strength of the Soviet power'; (4) *spetsy* who were only concerned with personal gain; (5) '*spets* white guardists' who were 'carrying out destructive work on the sly'.[57]

These indications—admittedly they are only fragments—suggest that political suspicion remained, and had concrete effects. But the NEP conditions did make it possible to establish a less fraught relationship between the non-party specialists and political official-dom. This was reflected in some remarks of Dzherzhinsky, then chairman of VSNKh, in 1925: 'if we have achieved a level of industrial recovery and development that we did not anticipate, it is only because our party has been able to draw the non-party technical personnel into our creative economic work'.[58] In similar vein a Rabkrin (Workers' and Peasants' Inspection) official said in 1926 that 'the specialist has ceased to worry us as a bearer of alien political traditions; he interests us now, above all, as the bearer of business-like qualities in his narrow speciality'.[59]

It seems, then, that the NEP conditions made it possible to reach an accommodation based on this, that political officials were more ready to concede the specialists' claims to authority based on professional competence or experience, on condition that 'alien political traditions' did not get translated into concrete 'destructive' actions. It could be argued that this accommodation was easier to reach with the *technical* than the cultural intelligentsia, because the technical groups had fewer political pretensions. In this connection Lunacharsky observed that 'we were closer to the philistine intelligentsia [he was talking about the engineers] than to the Mensheviks and SRs . . . because the former had no programme . . . This kind of person is the more valuable in the present circumstances, the fewer ideas he has . . . if a specialist has a lot of ideas, this is worse because it prevents us fully using his services . . . '.[60] This did not mean, however, that in the case of the technical intelligentsia the tension between political demands and professional self-images disappeared. Later, in the transformed political environment of the post-NEP period, this tension would again become a major political issue, and the historical antagonisms would reappear in another form.

2B (ii) RED DIRECTORS AND SPECIALISTS

We now turn to a brief discussion of some elements in the work situation of the ITR during the NEP. This section takes a look at the position of the enterprise specialists in relation to their superiors in the industrial hierarchy, and the next section considers the relations between the ITR and the workers.

During the NEP the work of the factories and mines was defined within the framework of a gradually emerging centralised structure in which the director, in overall charge of production, was subordinated to the trusts and through them to VSNKh. In 1921–22 there was a period of relatively free market relations—the concessions to private enterprise were at this time at their peak—but after 1923, when the trusts were established, factory management came increasingly under the control of the higher economic agencies. In a law of 1923, the factory failed to acquire independent legal status, and responsibility for all the actions of the factory remained with the trust. The factory, according to Carr and Davies, 'was generally recognised in industry as an underprivileged unit whose functions should be properly delimited'.[61] In the new statute on trusts of June 1927 the legal status of the factory—now officially designated 'enterprise'—was improved; the director was given a certain financial autonomy, and the right to hire and fire administrative technical personnel. It seems, however, that in practice very few trusts put the regulations into effect.[62]

Enterprise management thus had very limited room for 'market manoeuvre' during the NEP. One director complained that 'the role of technical executant of the directives of the trust in the enterprises entrusted to him, granting him the right of personal initiative only in seeking methods for the replacement of raw materials, and making small-scale orders, will never satisfy the red director',[63] and this sort of protest recurred.[64] The trend towards centralisation was criticised in the latter years of the NEP, but the emphasis on a centralised control over investment decisions, together with the extension of operational planning, proved inimical to decentralisation.[65] However, it should be emphasised that it was the individual factories and not the trusts that were deprived of autonomy, and that the form of central planning during the NEP was not the command form of planning that was to be established later. According to the account of Carr and Davies, in 1923–24 the plans were 'an aggregation of the expectations and desires of the trusts, trimmed to the available finance, rather than an instrument for moulding the behaviour of individual industries and factories to the will of the central administrators in VSNKh'.[66] After 1925, there was a closer control from the centre, especially of capital investment, and the beginnings of physical planning. But up until 1927, at any rate, the 'command economy' in the full sense had not yet been established.

Given the limits to enterprise autonomy, it can be judged that the scope for initiative of subordinate managers and technical staff was correspondingly restricted. The latter positions, however, were often occupied by *spetsy* distinguished by their relatively long experience and near-monopoly of engineering skills. On this basis they were able to retain a certain *esprit de corps*—'caste separateness' was the term referred to earlier—and a degree of influence in the enterprise.

As far as is known, the relationship between the red directors and the non-party specialists was fairly harmonious during the NEP. The directors acted as general overlords and did the necessary negotiating with officials outside the enterprise, but usually left the day-to-day control over production with the chief engineer or technical director and the production managers under him. In 1925 Krzhizhanovsky said that 'one does not have to be a particularly acute observer to notice the elements of close cohesion between the technical personnel and the proletarian staff . . . a merger in friendly work is occurring between the old technical personnel and selected executives from the political leadership'.[67] A similar picture could be inferred from the criticisms to which the directors were subjected in 1928—then in a changed political conjuncture—when it was said in a party resolution that the red directors had established a 'blind faith' in the specialists' work, 'rubber stamping' their proposals and spending too much time giving speeches and dealing with other officials to get acquainted with production matters.[68]

A potential for conflict did exist in this relationship if either side was thought to be overstepping the limits of their legitimate authority. For example, a chief engineer who worked under the celebrated Likhachev in the mid-1920s recalled that disagreements arose because the director—in this respect Likhachev was probably quite unusual—tried to make all the decisions himself and tried to 'do without a chief engineer'.[69] On the other hand, when in connection with the 'rationalisation' campaign in 1926 the VSNKh authorities tried to strengthen the formal position of the technical director and shop management, this was evidently unpopular with the red directors. New VSNKh regulations were published in that year which established, among other things, that the technical director was 'fully in control of the whole technical productive part of the enterprise on the basis of established programmes' and that his powers included the 'hire, fire and transfer of leading technical personnel, subject to the approval of the head of the enterprise'.[70] In this connection an editorial in the VSNKh paper said that 'in the interests of the best allocation of work, the director should restrict himself to overall leadership . . . giving the technical personnel freedom of action within the boundaries of the director's powers'.[71] This looked very much like an attempt to formalise an already existing state of affairs. But one director said that a 'silent attempt is being made to counterpose the qualified specialist to the non-qualified director, to diminish [the director's] present importance and even to challenge his role as the chief director-organiser of the enterprise'.[72] But in the event, no such challenge seems to have been made. It seems, then, that in practice the relations between the 'commissar' and his subordinate ITR remained quite amicable under the NEP conditions.

2B (iii) SPECIALISTS AND WORKERS

During the NEP years managerial authority in relation to the trade unions and workers seems generally to have been strengthened. But it was not beyond challenge, since industrial disputes occurred and were not always resolved in favour of management. Also, since a large proportion of the ITR at shop level were old generation *spetsy*, they were for this reason more likely to be criticised by the trade union and party organisations, and workers' protests over demands for higher productivity could perhaps be expressed with greater impunity.

To take first the relationship between management and trade unions. To begin with, the institutional principle of one-man authority became securely established at the enterprise level, and the role of the trade unions correspondingly reduced. There had already been an important shift in this respect during the civil war, when collegial administration in the factory had been partially replaced by a one-man management structure. But the process was carried further during the NEP. A resolution of the 11th Party

Congress in 1922, following earlier party decisions, set the tone by saying that 'the restoration of large-scale industry demands, in the present situation, the unconditional concentration of full power in the hands of the enterprise administration'. This meant that the trade unions, though they were to 'participate in the socialist organisation of industry', should not 'directly interfere in the administration of enterprises'.[73]

An earlier party decision had established that the trade unions under the dictatorship of the proletariat were 'transformed from organs of struggle on the part of sellers of labour power against the class of capitalists, into an apparatus of the ruling working class'. Their tasks were now to be fulfilled 'not as a self-contained, organisationally isolated force, but as one of the basic apparatuses of the Soviet government led by the Communist Party'.[74] This position was basically retained in the case of state enterprises. At the same time, the NEP, because it had reintroduced certain commercial principles into industrial management, had set up 'some opposition of interests, in matters of labour conditions . . . between the worker masses and the managers', so that the trade unions had the duty to defend the interests of the workers against the 'excesses' of the enterprise management and against possible violation of the labour laws.[75]

There was thus a basic tension in the role that was formally assigned to the trade unions. On the one hand, they were organs of the state in the proposed coordinated effort by management and unions to restore production by raising labour productivity. On the other hand, they were to be defenders of workers against over-zealous managers who ignored the workers' interests.

In the face of these conflicting pressures, the trade unions were generally to be found siding with management, as can be judged from some apprehension in the party about the extent to which trade union officials had lost their separate identity. In October 1925, a Central Committee decision noted that the trade unions were 'overburdened with a variety of economic, political and social activity . . . and sometimes have pushed into the background their most important task—the defence of the economic interests of the mass of trade union members . . . '. A harmful confusion of functions had developed, with an 'indiscriminate defence of all the measures and proposals of management before the workers'.[76]

Again, the trade unions were unable to make much impact in another role which in formal terms was important: to organise, through the 'production conference', mass worker participation in the discussion of production problems. One director noted in 1924 that the trade union committee almost always followed the initiative of the administration in matters concerning production policy, that 'nothing new' had emerged from production conferences and worker meetings, and added: 'I am not against drawing in the masses to a discussion of production-technical and administrative matters . . . but for the workers as a mass, as for the workers' organisations in the enterprise, it is difficult to understand technical questions. Hence we cannot expect . . . any real assistance in this respect'.[77] Another director admitted that 'up till now all our impressive resolutions about drawing the proletarian masses into participation in production matters have remained on paper and have not moved forward one millimetre'.[78] A third said that 'discussion of technical questions with the workers simply creates uncertainty among the administrative and technical personnel, and is really a waste of working time'.[79]

After 1925, production conferences seem to have become less of a formality than in the early NEP years. Also, the enterprise party organisations became more influential, with a tendency for the party to usurp what were regarded as trade union functions. But the more active role of the party and trade union officials seems to have been a result of enlisting them in a campaign for higher productivity in 1926–27. In this connection one director said that the trade union and party cell had become important because of the 'painful transition' to new norms and wage rates in 1926, changes which must be carried out with the help of the party and trade union organisations.[80]

The undoubted pressures on the trade unions to go along with demands for greater productivity did not mean that managerial authority went unchallenged. The trade unions were entitled to, and sometimes did, contest managerial decisions in relation to working conditions and wages, and the hire, fire and transfer of workers. They could do this through the Assessment and Conflict Commission (RKK), which was an arbitration board comprising trade union and management representatives; or if this failed, then appeal could be made to the courts. Disputes were not always decided in favour of management.[81] One thus finds managers complaining that disciplinary measures taken by directors, shop heads and foremen were being reversed by the RKK, that the RKK was an 'anonymous' organisation which did not answer for the course of production, yet limited management authority in a crucial area.[82] According to one director, the RKK was particularly irritating to the old engineers, technicians and foremen who 'look back to the good old days when there was one boss, when everyone did what they were told and didn't discuss'.[83]

The authority of the ITR—especially those in managerial positions—may also have been affected by the high proportion of old generation specialists in the enterprise: they were still not trusted by the enterprise organisations, and the workers could take advantage of this. It is not being suggested that this was a crucial element in determining the pattern of relations between the ITR and the workers. The extent of conflict depended basically on the demands that workers were facing in terms of labour productivity, the amount of pressure on work norms and wages, and the rigour with which these demands were being implemented. But the residue of political mistrust could perhaps affect the extent to which the workers' antagonism to the ITR was seen as legitimate.

The *spets* was unpopular with the workers and with the enterprise trade union and party organisations, and party resolutions against '*spets*-baiting' (*spetseedstvo*) were a recurrent theme of the period. At the 11th Party Congress in April 1922 Tomsky explained that despite previous party directives defending the specialists, the question of the *spets* remained 'very painful'. He summed up the workers' attitude as follows: 'The *spets* lives better, gets paid better, he gives the orders, makes demands; the *spets* is an alien person, the *spets* did not make the October revolution'. Furthermore, if communists spoke against ITR at party and general worker meetings, then this was because, given widespread resentment against the specialists, they were following the line of least resistance.[84] Later, at a conference of engineers, Tomsky noted that the introduction of the NEP had created special difficulties because it was 'still not clearly understood by the workers'; it had created 'much roughness' and had 'increased dissatisfaction with the technical personnel'.[85] According to a VSNKh official in 1924, the problem was this:

On the one hand, the production process demands unconditional one-man authority . . . On the other hand, the vast mass of engineer-specialists, even those who are undoubtedly devoted to the Soviet power, cannot draw close to the worker masses and win their trust. Since the pressure (*davlenie*) on the workers come from the *spets*, then for the backward strata he becomes the personification of all the evil forces. All the dissatisfaction and indignation come out against him, even though he is no more than an executant of the workers' state.[86]

In December 1924 Bukharin claimed that 'the relationship between the workers and the technical intelligentsia, which is one of the most important elements of social and economic progress, has entered a new [i.e. improved] phase of its development'.[87] Yet enterprise organisations and workers were still being told, in connection with efforts to tighten up work discipline, to establish more 'comradely' relations with specialists. Directors complained that the organisation of production was still weak because 'lively and normal relations' had not been established between workers and ITR, and appealed to trade union officials to 'cease adopting a supercilious attitude to the specialists'.[88] In September 1925 the party published a directive, 'On the work of the specialists', which said among other things that 'there must be a decisive struggle against indiscriminate criticism of the specialists in party, trade union and other press organs and in wall newspapers, while not refraining from a business-like criticism of specialists and giving concrete indications of genuine inadequacies in their work . . .'[89] It was explained by a VSNKh official that this directive was designed to bring to an end a situation where specialists, especially shop heads and technical directors, had to spend time 'politicking [engaging in *politikantstvo*] with the enterprise organisations' in order to check the acceptability of their orders.[90] Later, again, in connection with the rationalisation campaign and the attempt to raise the authority of the ITR, a VSNKh directive criticised 'superfluous interventions' which were a result of 'all sorts of commissions, conferences, collegial meetings, instead of one-man management'.[91]

2C CONCLUSIONS

An attempt has been made in this chapter to give some idea of the social position of the enterprise technical intelligentsia in the decade following the October revolution, focusing especially on the 'bourgeois specialists' inherited by the Soviet state, since they continued to occupy a majority of the higher level (though not the highest) managerial and technical positions in Soviet industry.

It was suggested that the response of the technical intelligentsia to the revolutionary events was shaped by the conditions of struggle for control over industry in the first post-revolutionary months. Workers' control was an affront to professional self-esteem since it deprived the technical intelligentsia of what was described as their 'autonomous and responsible role' as organisers of production. Later, during the civil war, the forms of organisation that were established—a trend away from collegial and elected management to one-man authority and appointed management—were less injurious to professional self-esteem. These forms involved a heavily centralised industrial administration, but because they meant the atrophy of workers' control they brought concessions to the claims of the specialists to professional competence. But these developments in industrial organisation did not occur without some major political arguments about the proper extent and limits of the authority that was to be given to the old generation *spetsy*, and during the civil war the political conditions in which the specialists worked remained precarious.

The NEP brought important changes for the technical intelligentsia, both in the political climate and in the organisational environment of industrial production. The combined effect of these changes, it can be said, was a more systematic attempt to bolster up the authority of the specialists in order to restore Soviet industry after its decimation during the pre- and post-revolutionary period. Concretely, this meant that party and other political agencies were instructed to refrain from political harassment of specialists, even if they had a bad record in the past struggle against the counter-revolutionary forces. At the same time, professional authority was supported by the usually amicable relations between the 'commissar' director and the *spets*, by the trend towards a strengthening of managerial authority in relation to trade unions and workers, and by the inability of the latter to make effective the formal right of participation in the discussion of production problems.

But the position was more complex than this. On the one hand, the tension between political demands and intelligentsia self-images persisted. The specialists still incurred political mistrust, as is evident from patterns of recruitment to the top managerial positions, and from the efforts of the party centre to restrain local political officials from excessive criticism of the ITR. On the other hand, the authority of the technical intelligentsia was limited from below by the possibility of successfully contesting some kinds of managerial decision, and because of a certain tolerance of '*spets-baiting*' at the local level.

3 The Bourgeois Specialists and the Class Struggle

During the NEP the party leadership adopted a conciliatory line towards the old specialists. With the 'left turn' in early 1928 there was a radical switch in policy. Over the next three years the old specialists bore the brunt of a political campaign directed at the intelligentsia, a section of whom were depicted, alongside the rural and urban petty bourgeoisie, as class enemies and counter-revolutionaries. The image was dramatised and made concrete through a charge of *wrecking*, and large numbers of suspect specialists were arrested, imprisoned and otherwise harassed by the judicial and security organs.

The conditions for this switch in policy were set by a critical shift in the political situation. The decisive development leading to it was the growing tension in the countryside, which in turn was linked to the drive to accelerate the rate of investment in industry. But the left turn, as suggested earlier, was to have major consequences for the whole pattern of social and political relations, including a change in the relationship between the state and the technical intelligentsia. In this chapter we can explore some of the effects of that change by looking at certain features of the campaign against the old generation specialists. The full ramifications of the campaign were complex and will emerge only in the course of discussion in several parts of the book. Here attention is focused on one aspect: a drastic assertion of the primacy of *political* definitions of the situation against the intellectuals' claim to authority on the basis of *specialised knowledge*. This was part of an attempt, directed at the intelligentsia as a whole, to undermine existing professional commitments and thereby to establish a closer harmony between the activities of intellectuals and the currently interpreted interests of the state.

Before going into this question, however, it will be necessary to provide a brief account of the campaign. In what follows it should be borne in mind that the political attack was focused mainly on the self-proclaimed professionals within the old generation technical intelligentsia—the engineers—whether in line or staff positions. But technicians and foremen were also involved, and political attention was often focused in a more general way on the ITR as a whole. The meaning of 'old generation' will have to remain somewhat imprecise, since Soviet contemporary observers themselves used the term loosely. But broadly speaking, it refers to those who had started working, or who had completed most or all of their training, before the revolution.

3A THE OFFENSIVE AGAINST THE BOURGEOIS SPECIALISTS 1928–31

The beginning of the offensive against the technical intelligentsia can be dated from March 1928, when the Soviet press announced the arrest by the GPU of some 60 engineers and technicians working in the coal mines of the Shakhty district in the Donbass. They were charged, among other things, with arson, deliberate flooding of mines, concealing the existence of coal seams, conscious misuse of equipment, and ordering imports of the wrong machinery from abroad. They had been provocative towards the workers: they had cheated the miners of their wages, left housing unrepaired, and had carried out dangerous work ignoring the most elementary safety rules. Over a number of years they had systematically fooled directors and trade union and party officials.[1] Later it was revealed that the sabotage was part of an organised plot. A Moscow 'centre' was involved, connected with organisations in other branches of industry, and these were linked to counter-revolutionary organisations in France, Poland and England.[2] The trial of the Shakhty specialists, amidst maximum press publicity, took place between May and July 1928; 53 people appeared as defendants, of whom four were acquitted, four given suspended sentences, and 34 given prison terms of one to ten years; eleven were condemned to be shot, of whom five were in fact executed.[3]

Soon after the arrests, the resolutions of the April 1928 plenum of the Central Committee drew a number of political conclusions from the Shakhty affair. Among them was the demand for a 'merciless struggle against wrecking', in particular through a closer check on the work of specialists by economic, trade union and party officials. Furthermore it was now vital to train more 'red specialists' to replace the 'alien bourgeois specialists', and to improve the system of promotion to managerial and technical posts.[4]

When the arrests were announced, and in the following months, there were at the same time voices of caution from political officials against making hasty inferences from the case of the Shakhty engineers. In March Kuibyshev, chairman of VSNKh, warned that 'not one innocent engineer must suffer as a result of the Shakhty affair',[5] and Zatonsky, a leading official of the Central Control Commission, said that 'if, because of tens of specialists, hundreds are taken into suspicion, then this too might cost us hundreds of millions of rubles'.[6] In July, Stalin offered the reassurance that 'we do not throw aside those specialists who do not think in a Soviet way or who are not communists . . . we by no means demand that they should renounce their social and political opinions all at once . . . '[7]. Molotov was even more emphatic: 'every good old specialist—even if by conviction he is the most counter-revolutionary of counter-revolutionaries, the whitest of whites—must be used by us, as long as he has not committed a crime . . . as long as he does the tiniest bit of work in his speciality for the proletarian state'.[8]

But more ominous tones could also be heard. Krylenko, the prosecutor at the Shakhty trial, warned that the affair was 'not an exception . . . if it could happen in the coal industry, then why not in the oil industry . . . in the railways . . . in construction?' Furthermore, the trial demonstrated that 'the Soviet state must now give a new meaning to the notion of Soviet loyalty'.[9] In the event, the political pressure on the technical intelligentsia gathered momentum after the Shakhty affair. In February 1929 Molotov spoke of the case as the beginning of a new period of counter-revolutionary activity by the bourgeois intelligentsia. With the intensifying class struggle in the countryside, 'the whole question of the old technical forces and of the intelligentsia in general has acquired a new sharpness', and the question 'for or against' socialist construction stood with unprecedented urgency before every member of the intelligentsia.[10] At the 16th Party Conference in April 1929, the bourgeois intelligentsia appeared, together with the *kulaks* and *nepmen*, and assisted by world capital, as part of a trio of class enemies 'furiously resisting socialist construction'.[11]

Wrecking was now exposed as a ubiquitous phenomenon, so that by April 1929 Stalin was able to say that ' "Shakhtyists" are at present entrenched in every branch of industry'.[12] During 1929 and early 1930 there were specific reports of GPU arrests in at least the following sectors: metallurgy, engineering, chemical, fuel, ship-building, military production, gold and platinum, transport and communications.[13] In February 1930 Kuibyshev assured an audience of ITR that 'there is not one branch of industry where wrecking organisations have not been created with quite definite directives from abroad',[14] and at the 16th Party Congress four months later Stalin made the same assertion.[15] An image was created in which the struggle in the countryside found its precise counterpart in the class struggle on the industrial front. In the words of a resolution of the Moscow party committee in July 1929: 'The sharpening class struggle in the countryside and the wavering of petty-bourgeois elements connected with it lead in exactly the same way to wavering among the *serednyak* part of the engineers . . . '[16] In accordance with this conception the aim of the party was to defeat the alien procapitalist elements, to give full support to the progressive ITR, and thereby to gain the loyalty of the mass of *serednyaks* to socialist construction. Neutrality was tantamount to surrender to the forces of national or international capitalism. The technical intelligentsia was faced with the drastic choice: either with the Soviet power and the general line, or against it and with the counter-revolution.

There are indications that the new stance was opposed by some sections of the party. 'Some comrades,' wrote one party official, 'seriously doubted whether the Shakhty affair warranted so much fuss.'[17] At the time of the arrests, according to Ordzhonikidze, Rykov 'came to the Politburo with a whole pile of Lenin quotations and began to prove . . . that Ilich had shown that without the bourgeois specialists we cannot build socialism'.[18] At the April plenum in 1928, Rykov was reported to have said that the 'cadres question can be decided in one way or another, not involving classes. This is not a question about our relationship to the countryside or about class differentiation.'[19] In the mounting attack in 1929 on the 'right deviation', one of the accusations was that the right had failed to see the political importance of the cadres question.[20] By criticising the demand that specialists should say unequivocally if they were for or against government policies, the right deviationists had shown that they were incapable of understanding the 'class essence' of the problem.[21]

After the showdown with the right opposition at the 16th Party

Conference in April 1929, the political attack on the technical intelligentsia was stepped up. In late 1929 and early 1930, now running parallel to the all-out drive for collectivisation, the campaign became more virulent and was extended to include the old specialists in the central planning and industrial agencies. Some of the former right oppositionists—no doubt as part of an effort to regain credibility—joined in. In an address to a gathering of ITR, Bukharin said that wrecking had turned out to be 'far bigger in scale than any of us would have thought possible, more ramified in form and more insidious in method'. The proletarian dictatorship could not be complacent: in conditions of intensifying class warfare, it must act with the sword. The ITR *'must not dare* to lag behind . . . stay on the sidelines, look for some comfortable philistine "golden mean"'. Just as collectivisation was impossible without crushing the kulak, so economic advance could not be achieved without overcoming the class enemy on the industrial front.[22] In February 1930 Rykov attacked political neutrality among the ITR and said: 'if the old technical intelligentsia . . . does not wish to be crushed by the wheels of history . . . it must reorganise itself'.[23]

While in 1928 and 1929 public attention was concentrated on engineers in enterprises and in the intermediate agencies of industrial administration, in 1930 it was focused more on the planners. In 1929 the old specialists in Gosplan and VSNKh were already under heavy pressure,[24] but in 1930 the final reckoning came when economists and engineers working in the central economic agencies were charged not only with wrecking production but with sabotage of the planning process itself. The Promparty trial in November 1930[25] and the Menshevik trial in March 1931[26] served as the high point of an offensive which at the outset, in the Shakhty case, had singled out people who were mostly in modest positions.

The effect of the whole campaign was to create the image of a conspiracy within the technical intelligentsia against the Soviet power, to which the state responded by an openly punitive policy, with the political police playing the principal role. How plausible was this image? An adequate answer to that question must await a later discussion of the shifting definitions of political crime in this period. But it is safe to say at this point that the GPU scenario of organised counter-revolutionary plots linked to western intelligence agencies was a fabrication. As there is no access to the archives of the economic department of the GPU, in that sense it cannot be documented from the horse's mouth. But evidence is not lacking. The contradictions in the material of the show trials themselves, discussed in some detail by Medvedev, could be taken as an indirect indication.[27] But there is also more direct testimony. Medvedev cites, for example, the statement of an old Chekist that wrecking as a 'conscious policy', as opposed to 'criminal mismanagement', never existed.[28] Another revealing account may be found in a book by Ciliga, a Yugoslav communist imprisoned in 1930 as a left oppositionist, who came into contact with engineers arrested on wrecking charges at the time of the Promparty affair. Though no friend of the engineers, he remarked that 'the only truth in the affair was the discontent of the specialists and their secret desire to see the communists come to grief in a failure of the Five Year plan . . . All the rest of the accusations were lies and moonshine on the part of the GPU'. Later, Ciliga also met specialists who had been involved in the Menshevik trial, and was able to establish that the confessions were forced.[29]

How far the charges were accepted by contemporaries is not easy to say. It is possible that within some sections of party officialdom and within the party rank and file, and perhaps often among the general public, they were taken at face value. Kravchenko, who was at the time a factory party organiser, has this comment on the Promparty affair:

> Though the picture was full of absurdities, I believed it, as the majority of the country did. At that time party men of the new generation accepted uncritically the assumption that many of the engineers and technicians educated before the revolution would as a matter of course be partisans of the old order—potentially if not actually enemies of the industrialisation effort.[30]

But among economic officials, as within the technical intelligentsia itself, it is clear that there was a lot of scepticism. At the 16th Party Conference there was an argument between Rabkrin officials and some other delegates on this score,[31] and at the 16th Party Congress in June 1930, Ordzhonikidze (then chairman of Rabkrin) said: 'an enormous number of our [economic] officials did not believe in this—they thought that the GPU was overdoing it and it was with the greatest difficulty that they could be persuaded that wrecking really existed'.[32] In the same connection, Krylenko noted that 'there is a tendency among workers (*rabochie*), and among the technical intelligentsia especially, to distrust in a philistine way the statements of the Soviet power'.[33]

If the charges of organised conspiracy are discounted, one still has to answer the question why the charges were brought and why there was a campaign against the technical intelligentsia at all. Three elements will be singled out for analytical purposes. One level of explanation relates to the attempt to pinpoint responsibility—or to find a scapegoat—for breakdowns in production and for the failure of industrial enterprises to meet production targets. This aspect of the matter will be discussed in detail in Chapter 5.

Secondly, the attack on the bourgeois specialists was used by the dominant party faction to help establish a political climate in which it would be easier to silence critics of the left turn within political officialdom itself. This aspect cannot be fully considered, but some remarks on it will not be amiss. The kind of publicity given to the Shakhty affair suggested that it was directed as much against different sections of the political apparatus as against the technical intelligentsia itself. It was tied in with the campaign of 'self-criticism' in 1928, which in turn was the prelude to purges within the party and government apparatus. In the words of a Central Committee directive in June 1928, self-criticism was to be a 'mass struggle against all enemies, starting with the *kulak* and wrecker and ending with corrupt elements in our own ranks'. Without a purge of party elements 'united' with the enemy, there was no guarantee against a repetition of Shakhty-type affairs.[34] It was in this way that the campaign against the specialists became linked with the attack on the 'right deviation'. Stalin later stated the matter plainly at the April 1929 Central Committee plenum, when settling accounts with 'Bukharin's group'. Referring to a number of slogans that had been raised in 1928—self-criticism, the struggle against bureaucratism in the Soviet apparatus, the offensive against the *kulaks*, the purge of the party, etc.—Stalin said:

> The whole thing began when, as a result of the Shakhty affair, we raised in a new way the question of new economic cadres, of training red specialists from the ranks of the working class to take the place of the old specialists.
>
> What did the Shakhty affair reveal? It revealed that the bourgeoisie was still far from being crushed; that it was organising and would continue to organise wrecking activities to hamper our work of economic construction; that our economic, trade union

and, to a certain extent, our party organisations had failed to notice the subversive operations of our class enemies, and that it was necessary to exert all efforts and employ all resources to reinforce and improve our organisations, to develop and heighten their class vigilance. [It would be] ridiculous to think that it is possible to strengthen our Soviet-economic, trade union and cooperative organisations . . . without giving a sharp edge to the party itself [since the party was the] guiding force of all these organisations.[35]

The attack on the technical intelligentsia could thus serve as one instrument in the intraparty struggle. After the defeat of the right opposition in 1929, disquiet within the party failed to evaporate, in the face of mass collectivisation, the developing crisis in Soviet industry in 1930, the disruption in the food supply and the sharp reduction in living standards. The exposure of wreckers again helped to show that critics in the party were 'objectively' assisting the class enemy. Thus, the oppositional activities of the so called 'right- "left" *bloc* in late 1930 had 'objectively turned them into a branch of the Promparty'.[36] Again, at the December 1930 Central Committee plenum, Kuibyshev attacked Rykov and Bukharin on the grounds that they had not fully capitulated, and as a way of driving home his argument, referred to the 'now historical fact . . . that forces hostile to us took their ideological weapons from the platform of the right opportunists . . . the wreckers of the Promparty all hoped for a victory of the right opportunists'.[37] Wrecking, then, was 'proof' of the intensifying class struggle, and any opposition to the current political line could only give comfort to the enemy. Also, if necessary, the confessions of the wreckers could be produced to show that the latter relied for the success of their plans on a victory of the right wing within the party.

Finally, in a third dimension, the attack on the specialists involved an attempt to browbeat the technical intelligentsia into political compliance and to redefine the relationship between political and professional roles. This element in the situation will provide the focus of attention in the rest of the chapter.

3B   POLITICAL DEMANDS AND PROFESSIONAL SELF-IMAGES

The 'class struggle' against and within the technical intelligentsia was part of an attempt to establish the primacy of a political definition of intelligentsia roles over against claims to authority based on special or professional knowledge. The tension between the 'political' and the 'professional' was not new, and had not disappeared in the post-civil war years. But under the NEP this was not a major issue in the way that it had been in the revolutionary period. During the NEP political officials were asking that non-party specialists should do a good professional job, without making further political demands. Now, under the rapidly changing conditions brought by the left turn, pressure was brought to politicise the relationship between the technical intelligentsia and the state. In what follows we shall try to spell out what this pressure involved.

At one level, there was a generalised declaration by representatives of the state that 'anti-Soviet' ways of thinking and talking would no longer be tolerated. Furthermore, to adopt a standpoint of political neutrality was in effect to condone anti-Soviet positions and was tantamount to subversion. The aim of the party and government was to isolate the anti-Soviet elements, to give full support to the progressive ITR, and thereby win over the mass of specialists in the 'middle' to a complete identification with the Soviet power and the current political line.

To use this idiom as a framework for trying to understand the range of political views within the technical intelligentsia would not be helpful. Some remarks by Lunacharsky in 1930 may give a better idea of what the range of views was, although this was still an account from the standpoint of the state itself:

Here we have as it were a whole cluster, a whole series of social types: some have not differentiated out at all (*sovsem ne differentsirovalis*) and remain on the level of a political philistinism, others are simply honest employees for a Soviet wage, a third group sympathise with us to a certain extent, but do not believe very much in our strength, a fourth go along with us and work with us, but there are many things they don't like, including, incidentally, the insufficient rights given to the intelligentsia itself; a fifth fully accept the general line of the party and, though they waver sometimes on individual questions, are still our real allies; a sixth may be genuine Communists without a membership card in their pockets.[38]

Lunacharsky is here implicitly rejecting the formula 'anti-Soviet'/'pro-Soviet'/'neutral': it does not tell you *which* things an engineer or technician may have liked or disliked about the Soviet power, and may have been forcing people into a mould that they would not recognise. To take one obvious example: there may well have been specialists who would have been happy to see an end to Bolshevik rule, but were fervent patriots who welcomed industrialisation as a way of building up the national strength. How would they fit into the trichotomous image?

However, the formula was not intended as a piece of social analysis. Rather, it was the result of generalising the imagery of the class struggle—in a class struggle neutrality is a myth—and thereby legitimating the injunction 'if you are not for us you are against us'. The use of this idiom was not a trick. It was an ideological reflection of the real battle between public and private interests which Soviet reconstruction involved. In this struggle, political neutrality or indifference could look almost as bad, from the standpoint of party or police officials, as direct opposition or 'counter-revolutionary whispering'.[39]

But the pressure to politicise the intelligentsia was not simply a question of demanding that specialists should identify themselves as pro-Soviet. More than this was involved, since what was at issue was the political content of the professional role itself. The organisation of the technical side of the production process might appear to be an activity without political implications, but this was not the case. As one writer put it: 'The work of the engineer and technician is not at all purely technical . . . The mastery of technical processes always presupposes the particular social character of this master'. Just as the work of the manager and engineer in capitalist enterprises was embedded within a particular social and ideological context, so too the engineer in Soviet conditions was (or ought to be) a 'representative of the Soviet state in the production-technical process itself'.[40] Thus, against the professional ideology according to which the functions of the expert in production were purely technical and had no political content, was set the view that these functions had a social meaning which should be openly acknowledged.

What was meant by asking the technical intelligentsia to be 'representatives of the Soviet state in the production-technical process itself'? Two main images emerge from a reading of the Soviet press. One image counterposed 'Bolshevik' willpower and enthusiasm to professional scepticism, apoliticism and 'philistinism' (*obyvatelshchina*). The second image set 'public-spiritedness' (*obshchestvennost*) against a corporate or 'guild' spirit (*kastovost*).

3B (i) BOLSHEVIK WILLPOWER AND PROFESSIONAL SCEPTICISM

The pejorative epithets 'apoliticism' and 'philistinism', which seem to have been used almost synonymously, were constantly cropping up in critical discussions of the technical intelligentsia, and in contrast to these imputed characteristics, the image of a conscious identification with the interests of party and state. During the NEP the view of one engineer—said to be typical—that 'I know what a ball bearing is but what the struggle of the proletariat is . . . doesn't interest me',[41] was quite tolerable. But in a period of rapid party initiated industrial expansion and a life-or-death struggle for the plan,[42] it began to look almost subversive. In order to carry through the transformation of Soviet industry, more was required than technical knowledge. In the words of a leading ITS official, 'people who do not sympathise with the construction of socialism in our country and do not work hand in hand with the state power . . . cannot be regarded as useful technical cadres'.[43]

After the left turn, not only red directors, but also the chief engineers and junior managerial and technical staff were expected to act according to the ideal of the warrior on the industrial front who by means of 'subjective' enthusiasm would overcome the massive 'objective' constraints in the way of industrial expansion. These fighting appeals belonged to a period of increasingly extravagant production targets which, it was said, Bolshevik willpower could achieve, but which were met with widespread scepticism among the technical intelligentsia. There were numerous critical comments on this matter in the press. At the time of the 16th Party Conference in April 1929 (when the 'optimum' version of the Five Year plan was adopted), engineers were saying at factory meetings that the plan targets were impossible, and some were trying to 'persuade' foremen and workers of the absurdity of the plans assigned to them.[44] The 4th Congress of the ITS in April 1929 passed a resolution on the plan which welcomed it and noted that 'the country's natural resources and the existing achievements in practical work in the spheres of industry, agriculture and transport, provide every basis for stating that in the main the Five Year plan is realistic and can be fulfilled'.[45] But the element of restraint in the formulation is clear and it was accordingly attacked as 'almost sceptical' because it spoke only of 'natural resources' and 'practical work' and said nothing about the engineers' 'will to victory'.[46]

In January 1930 some delegates at an ITS conference attacked the 'intolerable attitude of the ITR towards the plan'.[47] Later it was said that there was constant talk among specialists about the critical economic situation, and 'malicious comments on the plan'.[48] 'There is no pessimism amongst us', ITR were quoted as saying, 'but we don't believe in the Five Year plan'.[49] In late 1930, *Pravda* complained that party members among the ITR had been quite unable to overcome the 'feelings of fright' in the face of rapid tempos.[50] In 1931 a chief engineer in the metal industry said to Ordzhonikidze that 'the existing psychological situation is not conducive to success . . . Plans are given to factories not on the basis of an assessment of real conditions, but on the basis of what those conditions ought to be . . . '. The constant commotion (*sumatokha*) in the pursuit of unreal targets led to 'enormous losses of iron and steel'.[51]

The specialists did not always take well to the appeal to enthusiasm as a means of overcoming objective constraints. As one engineer remarked in 1929, 'for us technicians, with our peculiar psychology . . . "enthusiasm" is irrelevant; what is essential is that the success of all our undertakings should be adequately ensured with the necessary materials and means'.[52] In similar vein, an old specialist wrote in a letter to the Menshevik journal in 1931: 'the technical intelligentsia is sentenced to work with "enthusiasm", but this is . . . the highest punishment. We are all, at whatever level we work, obliged to burn with enthusiasm and by this means to surmount the insurmountable'.[53] 'Everything we propose to the centre,' said a chief engineer in 1931, 'is criticised. It is studied not from an engineering but from a "political" standpoint.'[54]

The tensions reflected in these remarks did not involve the *spetsy* alone. It was not only the self-proclaimed experts who would have liked to see more modest plans, but—as will be discussed at a later stage—the enterprise administration as a whole. But the changes in the style of Soviet planning seem to have brought a particular form of antipathy from the technical specialists who wanted (but were unable) to defend 'rational' principles against the perceived irrationality of a politically determined plan.

3B (ii) PUBLIC SPIRITEDNESS AND GUILD LOYALTY

The tension between political demands and professional self-images can be examined further by looking at a second type of polarity, between 'public spiritedness' (*obshchestvennost*) on the one hand and 'guild spirit' (*kastovost*) on the other. Part of the purpose behind the offensive was evidently in some sense to divide and rule by breaking down professional solidarity within the technical intelligentsia. At the April 1928 Central Committee plenum the trade unions were instructed to 'eliminate the caste isolation and narrow corporate spirit among the specialists . . . ',[55] and some time later *Pravda* was demanding a struggle against the 'aristocratic attitudes of the specialists, their guild spirit'.[56] In February 1930 Rykov had the following comment: 'A caste separateness, disgusting prejudices of intellectual philistinism . . . a resentment at having been offended by the proletarian rebel—these are the things that still unite a large part of the engineering-technical cadres'.[57] In similar style, Kalinin reproached those specialists who 'are in love with themselves, regard themselves as the salt of the earth, and are offended because they have found themselves out of place (*ne u mesta*)'.[58]

Specialists were asked to exercise 'self-criticism'—that is, to criticise one another—as a way of breaking down these corporate attachments. Some specialists, as will be seen, took advantage of such appeals in the attempt to advance their own fortunes or in an act of self-preservation. But there was also some resistance to the attacks on professional solidarity. At the 4th VTsSPS plenum in June 1928 one ITS official warned that the policy of encouraging differentiation could become dangerous and that 'we must avoid counterposing one part of the technical intelligentsia to another'.[59] One engineer was cited as saying that ' "self-criticism" contradicts a basic premise of the professional ethic'. It was 'not ethical', 'not comradely'.[60] 'We do not criticise our superiors,' said another specialist, 'we consider this unethical.'[61] The notion that 'we should keep our quarrels to ourselves' was said to be common and was something to be overcome.[62]

In contrast to this corporate separatism was the image of 'public spiritedness' (*obshchestvennost*). The Russian word is difficult to translate; it seems to have had the following connotation. First, it was an attribute of someone who was active in the party or trade union organisations, or else took an active part at factory meetings (especially production conferences) in which party or trade union officials played a leading role. But also, since the party and the trade union at enterprise level served in some sense as a link with the mass of workers, an *obshchestvennik* was someone who was not cut off from the workers, but who knew how to talk to them in such a way as to gain their cooperation.

In both these respects, the specialists—by contrast with the non-expert red managers—were said to be distant from the desired image. The engineers and technicians were 'standing aside' from the social organisations and from public discussions of production problems.[63] They did not bother to attend production conferences or else took only a passive part in them.[64] They were lukewarm towards 'socialist competition', the much heralded attempt to increase labour productivity which began in 1929.[65] According to a report in one factory newspaper, this cool response to the new forms of labour was due to 'technological arrogance',[66] and elsewhere it was said that many specialists disapproved of socialist competition on the grounds that it would actually retard the pace of industrial development.[67] In general, it was said, the ITR were 'not drawn into the social (*obshchestvennaya*) life of the enterprise'.[68]

Secondly, the specialists did not know how to talk to the workers in such a way as to gain their cooperation. 'The Soviet engineer,' wrote one party official, 'must be able to utilise, apart from dead capital, also that social energy which the masses can give with the correct leadership. We have few engineers of this quality.'[69] 'With very few exceptions,' in the view of a mining engineer in 1928, the social gulf between specialist and the worker was such that 'the *spets* as *obshchestvennik* does not exist.'[70] But the 'mutual coldness' between workers and specialists could be overcome, suggested one government leader, if the engineers approached their work not just as specialists but as 'citizens of the Soviet Union'.[71]

3B (iii) THE ITS

The efforts at politicisation of the technical intelligentsia can be explored further by looking at the attack on the engineers' and technicians' sections of the trade unions and attempts at political education among the ITR.

At the time of the Shakhty affair, the ITS came under heavy criticism. According to the resolutions of the April 1928 Central Committee plenum, 'the trade union organisations of engineers and technicians are imbued with caste spirit and narrow guild-like attitudes. Often they are infected with elements hostile to the proletariat who set themselves against the proletarian state and the trade unions and in practice work without direction from the latter'.[72] At the 4th plenum of the Central Trade Union Council in June 1928, trade union officials were also critical, although they themselves were being partly held to blame for the state of affairs. Ever since the sections had been set up, it was said, the ITS had been quite apolitical; the whole tone of their work had been that of 'consumer Leninism', in which the sole aim had been to defend group economic interests with Lenin citations. They had made no impact on the enterprise administration in terms of assistance in the discussion of production issues, and the party organisations were scarcely aware of their existence.[73] According to Tomsky, the leading officials of the ITS were still 'blindly reflecting the opinions of the philistine engineer'. Tomsky said:

> We built the sections understanding the peculiar psychological condition of the ITR. But our aim in this was to bring the trade unions closer to the sections . . . Yet in recent years the gulf has in no way diminished . . . We shall continue the struggle against *spets*-baiting in the future, but we shall demand that there be a genuine engineers' *obshchestvennost* . . . in order to eliminate the gulf between specialists and workers which was a result of the old conditions.[74]

In line with this, the resolutions of the plenum demanded that in the future the ITS should be headed by people who were 'genuinely dedicated to socialist construction'.[75]

The strongest pressure for an overhaul of the ITS came, however, not from the trade union apparatus but from VSNKh, which through its daily paper recurrently attacked 'right wing views, apathy and bureaucratic leadership' in the sections.[76] Since this meant a continued implicit criticism of the central trade union apparatus as well, the trade union paper eventually started defending the sections against VSNKh, and in late 1930 a polemic developed between the two over whether or not a wholesale expulsion of top ITS officials should be carried out.

There were changes in the leadership of the ITS in 1928 and 1929,[77] but it was apparently not until the end of 1930 that a big overhaul took place. It is not known how many old specialists were pushed out but the tenor of the discussion suggested that they were still occupying responsible positions in the ITS at the end of 1930. At that time, the VSNKh daily was still speaking of the ITS as 'stillborn, bureaucratic and apolitical organisations', which had become 'objective supports for wrecking activity'. It was reported that left elements in the ITS were demanding 'surgical measures' to enable the new specialists to take over, so that they could struggle against right-wing views and the defence of minimal plans among the ITR.[78] The trade union daily argued that Lenin's directives on the bourgeois specialists were still relevant and that the old generation should still be asked to occupy leading positions in the sections.[79]

After re-elections to the ITS bureaux in late 1930, it was reported that their membership had been renewed by an average of 70 per cent.[80] But suggestions that the ITS should be abolished were not adopted. In 1929 and 1930 there was pressure from some local trade union officials and rank and file ITS members to do away with the sections altogether, on the grounds that they simply helped to maintain a corporate interest incompatible with the common interest of all groups within the working class.[81] In fact in some enterprises and areas the ITS were liquidated 'spontaneously',[82] but in June 1930 *Pravda* published an article by a VMBIT official which demanded that 'all talk of abolishing the ITS should cease'.[83] This injunction was apparently heeded. Thus the technical intelligentsia retained a separate formal representation within the trade union: the attack on corporate loyalty did not go so far as to remove all institutional supports for a corporate existence.

3B (iv) POLITICAL EDUCATION

It was intended that political education should be an important instrument in the struggle for political support among the engineers and technicians. Two main organisations were in theory involved in this work at the enterprise level, the party and the ITS. But not much seems to have happened in practice.

During the late 1920s and early 1930s the party propaganda machine in industry was almost entirely directed towards the workers, and propaganda efforts aimed at the technical intelligentsia were by comparison negligible. A Moscow party resolution spoke of the 'great weakness, and sometimes total absence of social-political work by the local party organisations among the mass of engineers'.[84] Over the next two or three years the same complaint recurred, although certain plants were singled out as exceptions to the rule.[85] In mid-1932 it was still being said that 'party committees do not consider that re-educating the old specialists and extending political education for the new specialists is their business'.[86]

The position with the ITS was similar. According to a party resolution of November 1929, ITS educational activities were 'extremely weak'.[87] By 1930, ITS political circles had been set up in some enterprises, but the section organizers said they got little help from the party with speakers and literature. The circles were poorly attended, and often those who did come saw it as a matter of 'sitting out the political hour (*politchas*)'.[88] According to one enterprise newspaper report, ITS meetings on political matters were sometimes cancelled because nobody turned up.[89] The situation was different in some of the newer plants where there tended to be a higher concentration of young specialists and where the party was more interested in giving assistance.[90] But in 1931 the ITS journal was still demanding that the 'political illiteracy of the specialists must end once and for all', because every politically illiterate ITR was an 'objective fellow-traveller of the wrecker and counter-revolutionary'.[91]

The feeble outcome of political propaganda in the narrow sense is not surprising if one remembers the prevailing political atmosphere in which the technical intelligentsia found itself in this period. The main form of 'education' was frankly coercive, and this meshed badly with the other professed aim of ideological guidance. Early in 1930 a party official tried to assure his readers that 'our struggle against wrecking does not at all mean that we want to act on the *serednyak* stratum of specialists by frightening them'.[92] But a few months later Radek could describe the situation like this: 'The broad mass of specialists are stunned by the shootings and arrests, are dashing about in various directions and are frightened by the hostile atmosphere with which events have surrounded them, do not know to whom to submit, and meanwhile try to hide their heads under their wings, in expectation of better times'.[93]

In the light of this it is not surprising to find one commentator saying that the atmosphere was such that most specialists wanted to 'get away from politics'.[94] Kuibyshev conceded as much when he said that 'many engineers say: I am not a communist . . . not a wrecker, I work honestly, carry out what is demanded of me . . . leave me alone, and give me a chance to work . . . '[95]

Given this evidence, it is legitimate to ask whether the policies adopted had any of the intended effects on professional 'apoliticism' and 'corporate spirit'. In some sense, it seems, the consequence of the campaign was to reinforce those traits against which it was directed. But in certain ways it did have the effect of undermining professional solidarity, setting up tensions between the older generation specialists and more especially, as will be seen in Chapter 4, between the younger and the older generation. According to a VMBIT official the 'abnormal situation' created for the ITR by the Shakhty affair had encouraged a wave of 'careerism' and 'violations of comradely ethics'.[96] But such violations were sometimes commended, as when a party official praised engineers 'who have in a Bolshevik way named the names of others who were refusing to take on responsibility for production, or were undermining the five year plan . . . or were putting their own personal interests above those of the collective'.[97] When old specialists wrote letters to the press with such titles as 'I don't want to be a fellow-traveller', or 'Away with political neutrality',[98] or when an alleged wrecker published his 'confessions', dissociating himself from all those specialists who 'have not understood the revolution',[99] this too reflected a breakdown in solidarity, even if the statements looked patently concocted.

Another effect of the campaign was to encourage recruitment into the party, especially in 1930 when, according to the party journal, there were 'numerous individual and collective applications'.[100] The information available does not usually indicate the age and career background of ITR who were recruited, so it is not possible to say what was the proportion of old specialists. All that can be said is that some did join. The main reason may well have been an attempt to provide some insurance against political harassment. For example, the case was cited of an old engineer who had been charged with wrecking and who applied to join the party 'direct from prison'. Another specialist sent in his application 'immediately after his flat was searched by the GPU'.[101] But even if such motives prevailed in the case of the older generation specialists, joining the party was still a move of some importance which helped to modify the historically inherited social division between 'non-expert communist' and 'non-party expert'.

3C   A CHANGE IN THE PARTY LINE

In 1931 the line which the party leadership had been following for three years was officially abandoned in favour of a policy of conciliation. The change was hinted at by Molotov in April, in a speech to the First All-Union Conference on the Planning of Scientific Research. Since the Soviet power had 'in the main solved the important tasks of the revolution' which it had faced in the past two or three years, 'the wavering of the intelligentsia is coming to an end'. Molotov therefore rejected the 'leftist' position according to which the intelligentsia could only be 'either friends or enemies'.[102] The new line was spelt out by Stalin in June 1931, in a statement that formed one part of a much-publicised speech to industrial managers:

> The fact that . . . even certain former wreckers . . . have begun to work at a number of plants and factories together with the working class—this fact shows without doubt that the turnabout among the old technical intelligentsia has already begun.
>
> If in the period of . . . wrecking our relationship to the old technical intelligentsia was expressed chiefly in a policy of repression (*razgrom*), now, in the period of its turn towards the Soviet power, our relationship to it must be expressed chiefly in a policy of attraction (*privlechenie*) and solicitude (*zabota*).
>
> It would be stupid and irrational to regard almost every specialist and engineer of the old school as an uncaught criminal and wrecker. . . .[103]

At a conference of ITR in July 1931, the Commissar of Justice insisted that the government had decided to give the ITR 'equal rights as builders of socialism'. The government had settled the matter in such a way that 'the old specialists should feel that they are not objects to be utilised, but subjects of socialist construction, active companions of the working class'.[104] The specialist journals were now full of quotations from Lenin against 'communist boasting (*komchvanstvo*)', against communists who were unable to 'unite and modestly direct the work of the specialists', and perhaps most significantly, Lenin's remark that 'to compel a whole social stratum to work under the lash (*iz pod palki*) is impossible'.[105] One could now read the admission that 'honest specialists' who had nothing to do with wrecking had suffered in the past two or three years,[106] and many engineers formerly convicted on wrecking charges were now released.[107]

Later there were recurrent official reminders that despite the rapidly decreasing relative numerical significance of the old generation specialists, their skills and experience were still greatly valued. In 1932 a leading official said that it would be 'extremely stupid' for the government to rely solely on the young generation of technical forces and that the youth were 'excessively self-confident'.[108] Molotov explained that despite the small numbers of old specialists, 'we cannot do without them in any branch of industry'.[109] In July 1933, a Pravda editorial explained that 'one of the peculiar features of socialist construction lies in the fact that the growth in the proportion of young ITR not only does not mean that the old cadres of specialists get pushed out, but on the contrary increases their role'.[110] Again, in May 1934 the industrial paper reminded readers that the old specialists were still 'highly valued'.[111]

According to the official image, the chief reason for the change in policy in 1931 was that 'profound changes have occurred among the old engineers', that the counter-revolutionary intelligentsia was now broken, and the mass of specialists, impressed by the successes of industrialisation and collectivisation, had rallied round the general line.[112] It will be assumed that this was a necessary way of legitimating the new line, but that as an explanation it does not carry much conviction. Some of the conditions for the change seem to have been the following.

First, it must be related to a shift in the general political conjuncture. The first massive confrontation with the peasantry was now over. The battle for a viable collective and state farm sector went on, but the initial stages of collectivisation had been accomplished in one way or another, and there may have been a sense that serious internal challenges within the political apparatus were at this point unlikely. In his June 1931 speech Stalin explained the position as follows: Wrecking was a result of the 'intensification of the class struggle in the USSR, the Soviet government's policy of offensive against the capitalist elements . . . the complexity of the international situation and the difficulties with collective farm and state farm development'. But the situation had now changed since 'we have overcome the grain difficulties' and 'we have routed and are successfully overcoming the capitalist elements in town and country'.[113] In a period, then, of relative calm in the class struggle, the GPU would be less active in discovering wreckers and saboteurs among the technical intelligentsia.

A second set of conditions relates to the disruptive effect of the whole campaign on the work motivation of managers, engineers and technicians. In the context of a severe shortage of technical and managerial cadres, this brought pressure from the industrial establishment for a reduction in the role of law and order agencies in the arena of production, and a less punitive policy in relation to the specialists. This point will be explored in detail in Chapter 5.

What were the effects of the change in policy in 1931 on the relationship between the old specialists and the Soviet state? After 1931 the old technical intelligentsia was not again specially singled out for political attack. An attempt was made to put the relationship on a new footing by making certain renewed concessions to professional self-esteem and by retreating from some of the coercive forms of political pressure on the specialists. The emphasis in official statements was now on social harmony within the technical intelligentsia and between the technical intelligentsia and the state. We read, for example, in various injunctions by political leaders, that 'the old specialists are now with us', that 'young and old specialists must work hand in hand', that 'we can now say that the old engineers are with us'.[114]

In this respect there were analogies between the changes affecting the position of the old generation specialists and those affecting the cultural intelligentsia. In a decree of April 1932 the Central Committee criticised the existing 'proletarian' literary organisations, which were now 'torn away . . . from important groups of writers and artists who are sympathetic to socialist construction'.[115] It was explained by Vyshinsky that the decree had a far wider significance than for literature and art, in fact, an 'exceptional significance for the whole front of cultural and economic construction', since it was designed to overcome the 'exclusiveness (*kruzhkovoi zamknutosti*)' of 'proletarian' intellectuals in general.[116] In other words, the ruling political officialdom did not wish to antagonise the 'non-proletarian' intelligentsia by giving all its support to those groups of intellectuals who were most demonstrative in their support for the Soviet power.

A similar stance can be found in a speech by Molotov at the 5th Congress of Engineers' and Technicians' Sections in November 1932, where he said: 'In these circles [that is among the ITR] there is, of course, no unanimity in evaluating the results of the October revolution. We cannot expect such a unanimity if only because the social roots of the separate strata within the ITR are very heterogeneous'.[117] But this was not to prevent the establishment of a fundamentally harmonious relationship between the Soviet state and the technical intelligentsia. A hundred per cent Soviet-mindedness was no longer, then, a necessary criterion of political dependability.

But these changes and concessions did not mean that there was a return to the NEP form of the relationship between the technical intelligentsia and the Soviet state. First, mere professional competence was no longer a sufficient criterion of loyalty. Engineers and technicians, said Molotov, should be 'drawn into politics'. The 'mask of political neutrality' was 'in the best of cases a sign of profound social backwardness . . . even if the citizen in question be a person with a diploma and a "name" . . . '. Thus 'the attitude of the Soviet power to the technical intelligentsia will depend on the attitude of the technical intelligentsia to the Soviet power'.[118]

Secondly—to make a point that will be taken up in detail below—the technical intelligentsia continued to some extent to come up against the agencies of law and order, which retained a function in relation to industry. GPU activities in this sphere became less conspicuous, although in the early 1930s many specialists on political charges were still working in or out of prison under some form of GPU supervision. But specialists working in production remained vulnerable to criminal charges arising out of their work. Also, the boundary between ordinary and political crimes was vague and changing, and there was always the possibility that the label of class enemy or wrecker would make a reappearance. Stalin was careful to explain in 1931 that the change in government policy 'does not mean that there are no longer any wreckers in the country . . . Wreckers exist and will continue to exist as long as we have classes and as long as capitalist encirclement exists'.[119] The new-found security of the technical intelligentsia was thus unstable. It depended on the general political situation, on how active the law and order agencies were in conditions of disrupted production, and on the ability of industrial officials and managers to withstand the resulting pressures. But a demonstration of these points will be reserved for a later discussion.

4 Patterns of Recruitment

The changes examined in Chapter 3 took place in the context of a rapid industrial expansion, one of the effects of which was a rapid growth in managerial and technical positions. The question of recruitment to these positions was a major source of party and government concern. First, the training and promotion of new cadres involved a massive organisational task, which to a large extent had to be improvised. But the whole process was also seen to be of the first political importance in the 'class struggle' in industry, or, to revert again to an earlier formulation, in establishing 'representatives of the state in the process of production itself'. The object was to produce a 'Soviet' intelligentsia which by virtue of background and commitment would identify more closely with currently defined political interests. Thus the forms of recruitment were seen as a vital element in establishing the conditions for a change in the relationship between the intelligentsia and the state.

The political importance attached to the forms of recruitment to the rapidly expanding managerial and technical positions can be readily seen by looking at some party resolutions on the matter. The training of new 'red specialists' was put on the historical agenda at the April and July 1928 plenums of the Central Committee,[1] and at the time of the latter, Stalin had this to say: 'The essence of the Shakhty affair is that we proved to be practically unarmed and . . . scandalously backward in the matter of providing our industry with a certain minimum of specialists devoted to the cause of the working class'.[2] By November 1929, the problem of cadres was being described as the 'key problem of socialist construction'. A Central Committee resolution referred to the 'enormous widening of the scissors between the demand for specialists and their present rate of growth', and elaborated on this as follows:

> The present period poses acutely, in connection with new demands, the question not only of the quantity but also the quality of specialists. The development of industry and agricul-

ture on the basis of the latest achievements of world science, the radical reconstruction of the whole productive apparatus, the complexity of socioeconomic processes in conditions of struggle between socialist and capitalist elements, demand a new type of technical director and organiser of the construction of a socialist economy . . . These cadres must have a sufficiently deep mastery of special-technical and economic knowledge, a broad socio-political outlook and qualities essential for the organisers of the productive activity of the broad masses of working people.[3]

From this the conclusion was drawn that the Soviet government should 'strengthen in every way the training of new proletarian specialists on whom the Soviet power can fully rely in its grandiose work in the construction of socialism, which would satisfy our growing needs and which would replace the elements hostile to us among the specialists and radically improve the whole cadres staff (*kadrovy sostav*) of industry . . . '.[4] The theme came up again in a major statement by Stalin in 1931:

> . . . we do not need *any* kind of executive (*komandnye*) and engineering-technical forces. We need the *kind* of executive and engineering-technical forces who are able to understand the policy of the working class of our country, able to master this policy and prepared to carry it out conscientiously . . . This means that our country has entered a phase of development when the working class must create its own productive-technical (*proizvodstvenno-tekhnicheskaya*) intelligentsia, capable of upholding its interests in production as the interests of the ruling class . . . not one ruling class has managed without its own intelligentsia. There is no reason to think that the Soviet working class can manage without its own industrial-technical intelligentsia. . . .[5]

The formulation here transposes into a post-capitalist context the idea of an instrumental link between a social class and 'its' intellectuals. In this sense it could be compared to Gramsci's concept of organic intellectuals, which he explained as follows:

> Every social class, coming into existence on the original basis of an essential function in the world of economic production, creates with itself, organically, one or more groups of intellectuals who give it homogeneity and consciousness of its function not only in

the economic field but in the social and political field as well: the capitalist entrepreneur creates with himself the industrial technician, the political economist, the organiser of a new culture, of a new law, etc.[6]

Since Gramsci was concerned with the role of the intelligentsia in feudal and capitalist social formations, and not with post-capitalist ones, the question arises whether it is legitimate to transfer a concept of organic intellectuals—or some analogous concept of an instrumental link between social classes and intellectuals—to the Soviet context. Also, of course, Stalin's statement is question-begging because it posits an unexamined identity between the Soviet power and the working class. But setting aside these problems for the moment, it is worth asking what were the effects of the attempt to establish 'our own' technical intelligentsia, and whether it is possible in any sense to describe the changes involved as a process of creating an organic technical intelligentsia in production.

The aim of the following discussion is to provide a basis for examining this question first by getting a selective picture of the patterns of recruitment to ITR positions between 1928 and 1935, based on some Soviet statistical information, and secondly by offering a few suggestions about the significance of the processes involved for a statement about the relationship between the technical intelligentsia and the state.

The rapid expansion in the number of ITR in the seven-year period under review is shown in Table 3, which also gives a comparison with the rate of increase in the number of workers and of white-collar personnel not directly involved in production (*sluzhashchie*).

Thus while the number of workers increased 2.3 times and the *sluzhashchie* 2.5 times, the expansion of the ITR was almost fivefold. This expansion took place through three main channels: first, by assigning party, trade union or government officials to managerial posts, with a greater or lesser amount of preparatory training; second, by promoting people without formal technical qualifications (*praktiki*) from the enterprise ranks to managerial and technical positions; third, by recruiting those with a 'regular' training (that is, those who had no work experience before getting trained) to line or staff positions. In what follows we shall try to illustrate the variety of career paths by looking first at some information on selected positions within line management: direc-

TABLE 3: *Personnel in large-scale industry 1928–35 (thousands)*

	All personnel	Workers	ITR	Sluzhashchie
1928	2924.9	2531.9	92.1	173.8
1929	3207.6	2788.7	97.3	189.4
1930	3605.9	3116.2	112.6	230.2
1931	4962.0	4256.4	193.1	327.9
1932	6326.2	5271.3	290.9	485.6
1933	6395.8	5139.7	376.6	543.1
1934	6386.1	5215.0	391.7	434.7
1935	6859.5	5658.3	446.0	438.2

Source: *Trud v SSSR* (1936) p. 91.
Note: (1) All figures are for 1 January; (2) Figures cover industrial enterprises, not industrial agencies at central and intermediate level.

tors, chief engineers and shop heads. We shall then look at sources of recruitment of engineers (those who went through higher technical education) employed in both line and staff positions. The picture is, therefore, strictly selective, but it covers the key positions within the stratum that Soviet sources usually dub the 'commanding staff' (*komandny sostav*) of the industrial enterprise.

4A MANAGERS

A very rough picture of the rate of growth of managerial positions, based partly on informed guesswork, is given in Table 4.

TABLE 4: *Managers in industrial enterprises*

	October 1929	May 1930	November 1933	October 1934
Directors and deputies (including chief engineers)	–	11800[b]	19600[b]	–
Heads of shops and production departments and deputies	13800[a]	17400[b]	53500[b]	70000[c]
Foremen	21800[a]	28900[b]	97400[b]	127600[c]

Sources: [a]*Inzhenerno-tekhnicheskie Kadry* (1930) pp. 46–7. The figures are revised upwards, since the sample covered 83 per cent of ITR; [b]A. Beilin (1935), p. 216. The figures are revised upwards, since the 1930 sample covered 72 per cent, and the 1933 sample 86 per cent of ITR. The number of 'heads of shops, etc.' for 1930 and 1933 are guesses based on the assumption that this category remained the same as a proportion of ITR (15 per cent) as in 1929; [c]*Trud v SSSR* (1936), p. 304.

4A (i) DIRECTORS

At the end of the NEP period, the great majority of heads of enterprises were red directors. They were typically party members who had joined the party in the revolutionary period or during the civil war, and had typically at one time held posts outside industry—in party, military, trade union or soviet organisations. In 1929, according to information based on a sample of 1162 directors, 73 per cent had joined the party between 1917 and 1921.[7] In Leningrad *oblast* in that year, 69 per cent of directors had once held 'responsible positions' in party, military and other official organisations at the time of the civil war.[8] A majority of red directors had once been workers, and most had little if any formal education.[9]

In the mid-1930s this was still the dominant 'profile' among enterprise heads. Table 5 indicates that between 1934 and 1936 most directors were party members of pre-1922 vintage, and that they had at one time been manual workers.

TABLE 5: *Enterprise directors: party membership and social background*

	Party members (per cent)	Date of recruitment into party (per cent). Before 1917, 1917–21, 1922–8, 1929 or later				Former industrial workers (per cent)
1929[a]	85	10	73	17	–	67
1934[b]	98	12	67	18	3	64
1936[b]	96	9	59	24	8	62

Sources: [a]*Inzhenerno-tekhnicheskie Kadry* (1930), pp. 21, 40–1, 46–7 (sample: 1162 directors); [b]*Kadry tyazheloi promyshlennosti* (1936), p. 166f (samples: 1934 and 1936: 457 and 799 directors respectively).

In the mid-1930s, again, most directors had a background of work outside industry. In 1935, out of 495 directors in heavy industry, 48 per cent had served with the Red Army during the 1917–21 period, and 25 per cent had been in other official posts at that time. Out of the same sample, about 50 per cent had been working in official party or trade union positions in the period 1922–28.[10] The impression given by these figures can be supported by information on heavy industry directors between January 1934 and March 1937, gathered by Granick: about 80 per cent of his sample, admittedly a small one, had achieved success in fields other than industry.[11]

It seems fairly clear, then, that in the period under review, as during the NEP, enterprise directors were for the most part people transferred from the political apparatuses to industrial management. A majority also still had little if any formal training. In this respect, however, there was a certain change in the picture. Technical considerations were now becoming more important and where possible people who had technical as well as political and administrative credentials were being promoted to the top jobs in industrial enterprises, especially in the priority heavy industry sectors. People already in managerial posts, or who had been singled out as suitable candidates for managerial jobs in the future, were encouraged to get technical training, and some special provisions were made for this.

First, a system of industrial academies was set up. The first was established in Moscow in 1927, for the 'further education' of economic administrators and enterprise managerial personnel.[12] By 1930 a network of these institutions had appeared in a number of major cities, and recruitment was extended to party, trade union and soviet officials.[13] The original intention was to provide a fully fledged higher technical education, but the great majority of students reached a much more modest level. Most of the graduates—there were about 2200 between 1930 and 1935—were sent back to industry, or were sent there for the first time, to take up jobs as directors, chief engineers or shop managers.[14] By April 1936, sixteen per cent of a sample of 608 heavy industry directors had gone through these courses.[15]

A second type of special provision was made by singling out people who had already made their mark in official jobs outside industry and sending them to higher technical institutes. As in the case of the academies, the explicit intention was to recruit industrial managers who would be both politically dependable and technically competent. This project was started in the early 1920s, and in the mid-1930s some of the most well-known managers in heavy industry were those who had once been political activists and had then been through higher technical education in the 1920s.[16]

In 1928, the party authorities proposed to expand this scheme through the so-called 'party thousands' programme. Non-industrial officials, together with those who already had industrial experience, would be recruited into higher technical institutes and thereafter posted or reposted to managerial positions at different levels of the hierarchy. According to the programme, 1000 were to be sent in

1928–29, 2000 in 1929-30, and 3000 in 1930–31. The criteria were as follows: if the would-be recruit was a former worker, then he or she must have been active in the 'social organisations' for at least three to four years, and must have had at least five years experience in production. For those who were not former workers, the requirement was at least six to seven years of responsible party, trade union, soviet or economic work.[17] How far this programme was implemented is not clear, though it is known that 'thousands' were still being recruited in 1930–31.[18] No mention has been found of recruitment in 1932 or later, so one can probably assume that the programme was dropped after 1931, perhaps in connection with other changes in higher education in 1932–33.[19]

The effect of these changes on the educational profile of directors was as follows. In 1934 23 per cent, and in 1936 29 per cent of heavy industry directors had a higher education, in addition to those who had been through industrial academies. By 1936 about ten per cent of directors had graduated before 1921, about one-third during the NEP, and the rest after 1928.[20] It is not possible to say what proportion were party thousands, since in the early 1930s some people who already had a higher education were transferred from offices above enterprise level into production.

4A (ii) CHIEF ENGINEERS

Throughout the period under review, there was a marked contrast between the profile of the chief engineers and that of enterprise heads. At the end of the NEP the chief engineers were typically old generation specialists; they were non-party, came from 'employee' families, and had had a regular higher education. By the mid-1930s, the old *spetsy* were well outnumbered by the new generation specialists who had graduated or started working in industry after the revolution. But, as the information in Table 6 indicates, the chief engineers were still usually distinct from the directors according to criteria of party membership and social background; in 1936 only a quarter were party members (and a far higher proportion than in the case of the directors were recruited after 1921), and most were of 'employee' origin.

The chief engineers were also distinct from the directors in terms of formal training and past experience. The vast majority, in heavy industry at least, had a higher technical education—87 per cent in 1934 and 90 per cent in 1936. In 1936, 33 per cent of chief engineers

TABLE 6: *Chief engineers: party membership and social background*

| | Party members *(per cent)* | Date of recruitment into party *(per cent)* | | | | Social background | | |
		Before 1917	*1917–21*	*1922–28*	*1929 or later*	*Workers*	*Peasants*	*Employees*
1929[a]	4	–	–	–	–	–	–	–
1934[b]	27	1	46	42	11	10.8		89.2
1936[b]	25	1	34	35	28	7.1	0.6	92.3

Sources: [a]*Inzhenerno-tekhnicheskie Kadry* (1930) p. 46; [b]*Kadry Tyazheloi Promyshlennosti* (1936) pp. 166f (1934 sample: 240; 1936 sample: 670)

Note: 'Social background' is an inclusive term that refers either to parents' occupation or to the person's own previous occupation.

with higher education were pre-1918 graduates, 38 per cent had graduated in the years 1922–28, and 29 per cent after 1928.[21] A certain proportion of chief engineers were 'red', that is they had previously occupied political positions outside industry. But typically they were regular graduates from technical institutes who had made their careers exclusively in industry.

4A (iii) SHOP HEADS

The profile of shop managers in the mid-1930s was more diverse than that of either directors or chief engineers. In 1934, as indicated in Table 7 below, about 40 per cent were party members, the great majority having joined after 1921, and about 50 per cent were workers by background.

TABLE 7: *Shop heads: party membership and social background*

| | Party members *(%)* | Date of recruitment into party *(%)* | | | | *Former workers (%)* |
		Before 1917	*1917–21*	*1922–28*	*1929–34*	
1929[a]	29	–	–	–	–	33
1934[b]	41	1	28	45	26	–
1935[b]	–	–	–	–	–	50

Sources: [a]*Inzhenerno-tekhnicheskie Kadry* (1930), p. 47; [b]*Sostav Rukovodyashchikh Rabotnikov* (1936), pp. 18–19.

As far as formal training is concerned, a sample survey of 250 shop heads in heavy industry in 1935 yielded the following information: 55 per cent had a higher education, 15 per cent had a secondary education, and 30 per cent were *praktiki*. The *praktiki* were mostly ex-foremen with lengthy experience who had been promoted after 1929. Of those with a higher education, 39 per cent had graduated between 1922 and 1928, and 44 per cent between 1929 and 1935.[22] By 1935, then, only 17 per cent of engineer-shop heads were old generation *spetsy*. The sample is a small one, and our guess is that a larger sample would have yielded a higher proportion of *praktiki* at this time. However, in the present context it is more important to note two points. First, that shop managers had a diverse background, comprising

(a) people promoted up the enterprise hierarchy without 'stopping off' for training on the way;

(b) shop-floor workers who had been marked out as people of capacity and sent to workers' faculties and technical institutes;[23]

(c) regular graduates from institutes who had no work experience before getting trained;

(d) red specialists, like the party thousands, political activists who were commandeered to the industrial front, after stopping off for some education.

The second point to note is that with the exception of category (d), which can have formed only a very small proportion of shop managers, shop heads had made their careers in industry alone.

4B ENGINEERS

The information available on engineers—those with a higher technical education—does not usually allow one to draw up separate profiles for those in managerial and technical positions; but it is worth taking this category as a focus of attention. It was the engineers among the old specialists who provided the main political target after 1928, and the post-1917 generation of engineers were being counterposed to them in the prevailing political rhetoric. It is therefore of interest to get a picture of the pattern of expansion of the 'new' professionals.

Given the very rapid rate of expansion of the ITR as a whole, the number of engineers as a proportion of ITR, as Table 8 shows, was declining over most of the period under review.

TABLE 8: *Categories of ITR in Soviet industry (per cent)*

	Engineers	Technicians	Praktiki
1927 (October)[a]	30	30	40
1929 (October)[a]	24	27	49
1933 (November)[b]	15	19	66

Sources: [a]A. Beilin (1935), p. 120; [b]*Sotsialisticheskaya Stroitelstvo* (1935), pp. 524–5.

However, the absolute rate of increase was striking, as the figures in Table 9 indicate.

TABLE 9: *Engineers in Soviet industry*

	Industry as a whole	Industrial enterprises	Heavy industry enterprises
1929 (October)	24200[a]	14000[c]	
1931 (January)	–	–	20300[c]
1933 (November)	60000[b]	45200[b]	34800[d]
1934 (November)	–	–	42700[d]

Sources: [a]A. Beilin, p. 120; [b]*Sots. Stroitelstvo* (1935) pp. 524–5; [c]A. Beilin, p. 321; [d]Ibid., p. 327.

This rate of growth was made possible, in the first instance, by transferring students to much shorter courses, thus quickly accelerating the output of graduates from higher technical institutes after 1929. At the same time, higher technical education was rapidly expanded and reorganised, with a feverish recruitment drive starting in the autumn of 1929. In 1932–33, courses were again made longer, but the increase in recruitment made possible a continuing rapid expansion thereafter. These changes are reflected in Table 10 below.

With the expansion of higher technical education, there was also a 'proletarianisation' of the student body. This was already happening during the NEP, but took a leap forward after 1929, aided by admission quotas discriminating in favour of ex-workers.[24] The effect can be seen in Table 11.

It should be emphasised that most of those within the 'worker' category were former workers by occupation. Only a small minority of post-1929 recruits to higher education were children of workers who had no previous experience of industry. For example, in

TABLE 10: *Output of graduate engineers: industrial vtuzy*

1926/27	3030
1927/28	3280
1928/29	4450
1930	18230
1931	11606
1932	10331
1933	4354
1934	11224
1935	22492

Sources: V. Shmelev (1931), p. 5 (1926–29 figures); *Kadry Tyazheloi Promyshlennosti* (1936),
p. 26. (1930–35 figures);
Note: 1926–29 figures cover all industrial *vtuzy*, 1930–35 heavy industry *vtuzy*; the increase
after 1929 is therefore understated in relation to industry as a whole.

TABLE 11: *Students in higher technical education: social background*

	Total (ooos)	Workers	Peasants	Employees	Others
1923/24	53.4	17.5	16.0	34.9	30.8
1924/25	48.8	27.3	16.9	39.4	16.4
1925/26	46.1	31.3	16.4	39.6	12.2
1926/27	53.3	33.3	14.6	42.8	9.3
1927/28	53.5	39.1	14.9	40.5	5.5
1928/29	55.8	43.7	15.2	35.8	5.9
1930	57.5	64.5	9.6	22.3	3.6
1931	78.9	66.7	7.3	21.2	3.0
1932	114.5	69.4	7.3	20.3	3.0
1933	132.6	66.2	7.2	25.0	1.6
1934	116.7	66.2	6.8	24.6	2.4
1935	121.1	60.5	5.4	33.4	0.7
1936	108.5	57.2	6.7	35.5	0.5

Sources: A. Beilin, p. 75 (1926–9 figures); *Kadry Tyazheloi Promyshlennosti*, p. 24 (1930–6
figures).
Note: 1926–9: all industrial *vtuzy*; 1930–6: heavy industry *vtuzy*.

Leningrad between 1930 and 1933, students with a worker
background ranged from 51 to 57 per cent of the student body; but
of these only six to eight per cent were workers' children who had
no previous work experience.[25] The change in the composition of
the student body involved mainly, then, a social movement *within*
not *across* generations.

How the social composition of graduates from higher technical education compared with the composition of recruits is not known. Throughout the 1920s the dropout rate, mainly for financial reasons, was much higher among worker-students than among those from other social backgrounds,[26] and it can be guessed that this was also the case during the early 1930s. The worker recruitment drive certainly made itself felt: in October 1929 the proportion of ex-workers among employed engineers was about eight per cent, by November 1933 about 23 per cent.[27] This proportion may also have increased later, reflecting the recruitment of 1930–32. But it is also clear that the great majority of engineers in the mid-1930s were still regular graduates with 'employee' backgrounds who had not worked in industry before getting their training. The effect of positive discrimination was thus to modify but not radically to undermine the advantages of children from non-worker backgrounds in higher education. These advantages can only have been reinforced by the shift away from positive discrimination towards a renewed emphasis on academic criteria in recruitment to higher education after 1932.[28]

To complete this brief review of the statistical information, it should be noted that the proportion of party members among engineers increased considerably in the early 1930s, though starting from a very low level. The changes between 1927 and 1933 are shown in Table 12.

TABLE 12: *Engineers: party membership (per cent)*

October 1927[a]	2.1
August 1929[b]	5.2
May 1930[c]	8.1
November 1933[d]	19.5

Sources: [a]*Inzh. Trud* (1930), no. 11, p. 321; [b]A. Beilin, p. 152; [c]*Sostav Rukovyashchikh Rabotnikov*, p. 12; [d]*Sots.Stroitelstvo* (1935), p. 526.

This increase was not all accounted for by the influx of former workers into the ranks of the engineers. The proportion of party members among engineers with a worker background was higher than among engineers as a whole. But party members were drawn from all social categories.[29]

4C   THE 'NEW' TECHNICAL INTELLIGENTSIA

From the pieces of information that have been presented, it is clear that the Soviet technical intelligentsia in the mid-1930s was quite heterogeneous in terms of social background, party membership, training and previous work experience. The new cadres were not all drawn from the working class, nor recruited wholesale into the party. Again, there was no single path of entry into or advancement within managerial and technical jobs that was clearly dominant. What sense, then, can be attached to the notion of the Soviet state creating its 'own' intellectuals in production? We shall not pretend to have an adequate answer to this question. But some suggestions can be made that may be relevant to tackling it.

First, although the political and career backgrounds of the ITR were diverse, political credentials were clearly important for a successful career. It was shown that in the early 1930s, as in the 1920s, the top enterprise managers were people with, broadly speaking, the same background as the officials of the political apparatus itself. Previous experience as an official of one or another agency of the state was a great advantage, and sometimes a prerequisite, for access to the top jobs.

But it was also shown that managers below the level of director did not usually have that background, since they had made their careers in industry alone. What then was 'new' about the new generation in this case, or in the case of the technical staff engineers? In the prevailing political imagery, a worker background and party membership were presented as two key symbols of political identity. This can be seen not only in numerous political speeches and party resolutions, but also is implicit in the information contained in Soviet social statistics in this period; these particular social facts were considered to be important by Soviet statisticians and their masters. But what their importance is, is not self-evident, although the habit of simply reproducing such statistics and thereby taking over the unwritten assumptions underlying them, gives the appearance of self-explanation. Having said that, we shall nevertheless venture a few remarks about these social indicators.

To take party membership first. It was seen that party saturation among the ITR increased quite rapidly over the period, though the range of saturation was wide between different jobs. Undoubtedly a party card was often important for promotion. Beyond the evidence of saturation itself, this point is also suggested by complaints that non-party people were being passed over for promotion at the lower levels of the managerial hierarchy for no 'good' reason. Thus in 1931 Stalin was saying that 'some comrades often push aside non-party comrades who have ability and initiative and put party members at the top instead, although they may be less capable and show no initiative'.[30]

In assessing the significance of party membership one should distinguish, though, between joining the party as an act of political engagement and joining it as the 'natural' thing to do in making a career in industry. One can find some misgivings about this. Many ITR, said one party source, joined the party less for reasons of political commitment than 'to keep up with their comrades or for careerist reasons'.[31] In the case of the red managers, taking a managerial job followed an earlier party commitment—though the earlier choice may itself have been 'careerist'. For the new generation managers and engineers who began their work in industry, joining the party was more likely to occur after they had already worked for a time in ITR posts. The remarks of a young shop manager (an engineer), who had joined the party in 1932 after two years in middle management, may be revealing in this respect: 'Joining the party seemed to us (myself and other managers who took the same decision) perfectly natural. After all we were working well, giving all our energies to the tasks assigned to us . . . a non-party person can in any case work in a party-minded way'.[32] This statement suggests a rather non-committal stance, which was certainly distant from an earlier image of *partiinost*. Our conjecture is that it was typical of the managers and engineers who joined the party in the early 1930s. Such an outlook was, however, no less 'loyal' for being less committed. The managers who later suffered most during the purges of the late 1930s were in fact the red managers who had started their careers as political activists, and those who tended to replace them were the new generation specialists who had never been so politically engaged.[33] Thus it turned out that in the political environment of the late 1930s the more neutral career path was also politically the safer one.

The recruitment of specialists with a proletarian past was another key symbol in the image of a new, politically more dependable technical intelligentsia. In the case of line management, our impression is that a worker background was an advantage and that the most rapidly promoted were those who had at one time been at the factory bench, had later gone to technical institutes and thence made their way up the managerial hierarchy. But this cannot be backed up without more information. It may be simply that the press, when providing biographical data—which was not very often—focused on this type of career path as the most politically impressive and the most consonant with the image of pro-letarianisation. Still, with a rapid expansion of every type of managerial and technical position in industry, the scope for moving up the occupational hierarchy was considerable. Former workers had no monopoly, but the opportunities were there, both for experienced *praktiki* without formal qualifications and for workers who were ambitious enough to study.

But to gauge the political significance of social mobility in this context, as opposed to merely stating that it happened, is much more difficult. One needs to know far more about what impact the process had on those who experienced it. It could be guessed that the broad prospects in principle available to workers, together with a political *milieu* that brought approval to this route into the ranks of the technical intelligentsia, gave those who could succeed along this path much to be thankful for—always assuming that to gain the title of manager or engineer was seen as a desirable step up in the world. The point would not be to make a reductionist connection between a family or occupational past and a certain political outlook. Rather, it was the process of promotion itself, and the contacts with political officials that this involved, that one might expect to encourage political conformity. But these points are not obvious, and need to be further investigated.

Rather than dwelling on the significance of party membership and social mobility, it may be more fruitful to consider how political and professional stances among the younger generation were affected by the particular political environment in which they were being trained and promoted. Let us consider first the effect of the campaign described in the last chapter. Although it was the old generation who appeared in this context as the main enemy, the campaign was addressed to the technical intelligentsia as a whole, and some of the younger specialists trained or promoted since 1917 also came under attack. The image of the young engineers conveyed in the press did not suggest that they were usually thought of as paragons of Soviet virtue. In 1929 an ITS official suggested that the recent graduates were least of all interested in socialist construction and that their only ambition was to get a soft spot for themselves.[34]

Another ITS organiser complained that among the new engineers 'the desire for an undisturbed life and an intolerance of self-criticism takes precedence over the revolutionary duty to struggle for the industrial-financial plan'.[35] One enterprise party official sought to explain this in terms of the social origin of the engineers who had graduated in the 1920s: they were mostly petty bourgeois—children of 'employees' (*sluzhashchie*), richer peasants and urban *meshchanstvo*—so that 'they bring with them the characteristic traits of philistinism: individualism, political neutrality, panic at difficult moments . . .'.[36] But one can also find the complaint that 'under certain conditions specialists with a worker background can turn out philistine, politically illiterate, bureaucratic, careerist'.[37]

Again, there was the accusation that many younger graduates had fallen in with the 'corporate ethic' of the older generation.[38] They often had no interest in 'public opinion' (*obshchestvennost*) in the enterprise, and often 'could not see the point of the social organisations'.[39] According to one report, they 'still see themselves as members of an intelligentsia caste and at production conferences behave like inhabitants of Olympus'.[40]

It can be seen from these strictures that the young specialists were not immune from political criticism, and that the tension between political demands and professional self-images did not disappear just because the young specialists were of the post-revolutionary formation. But the attack on the old generation did have the effect of encouraging internal divisions within the technical intelligentsia. This consequence was briefly discussed in the last chapter, but it may be further considered in the light of its specific effects on conflict between the generations.

Soon after the Shakhty arrests, Ordzhonikidze (the then head of Rabkrin) addressed a meeting of engineering students. The Shakhty affair, he said, 'has forced on our attention the problem of young technicians, young engineers and the commanding staff (*komandny sostav*) in general in all branches of our economy', since 'it would be absurd to think that the old *komsostav* as a whole could be defenders of the proletarian dictatorship'. Since support was now to be given to the youth, 'some conflict between the new specialists and the old will of course occur. But the party and the Soviet power have firmly decided to open the gates wide for young red specialists'.[41]

The effect of this official posture was to sanction political infighting within the technical intelligentsia, providing an opportunity for young specialists to join in the attack on the older generation and to make public declarations of their loyalty to the Soviet power and the general line. They were also encouraged to challenge the claims of the older engineers to a special professional competence, thereby helping to undermine professional solidarity. Only days after Ordzhonikidze's statement a resolution of an ITR conference urged young specialists 'not to hesitate before criticising the "authorities" among the technical personnel, to get rid of the prejudice that it is awkward to point out the mistakes of a colleague'.[42] There were frequent reports of conflict between older and younger specialists, which according to one ITS official sometimes led to 'sharp antagonisms'.[43] From one side it was said that 'the red specialists from the youth often meet an openly hostile response from the old specialists'.[44] On the other side the old generation were said to be bitter because of the attitude among the youth that 'we tolerate the old ITR, until we have our red specialists'.[45] It was this sort of posture which brought the following complaint from Rykov in 1929: 'to approach the question of the specialists scornfully, underestimating the importance of the old specialists and overestimating the abilities of the new, is harmful . . . this sort of dismissive attitude towards people, who should be valued by us at their full worth, is a complete misrepresentation of the present economic situation and is very dangerous'.[46]

But the political environment encouraged a 'dismissive attitude', in the sense of a challenge to established professional authority. In April 1929, a group of young engineers wrote collectively to the VSNKh paper demanding among other things an end to the 'caste spirit' of the engineers. They should be taking initiatives in discussing questions of technical reconstruction, and actively cooperating with workers at production conferences. Only then would the engineer become a 'real leader of production (*proizvodstvenny vozhak*) in the shop'. All this meant a re-education of the ITR, 'freeing them from bourgeois-intellectucal prejudices' and from traditional 'engineering ethics'.[47] One observer—a self-proclaimed progressive engineer—greeted this letter as a sign of important changes in outlook among the youth, who were now demonstrating their 'willingness to unite organically with proletarian public opinion and to take up their proper place in the struggle for a socialist transformation of the economy'. The reconstruction of the economy was 'by no means sufficiently understood in a socialist sense', but 'psychologically, and even ideologically, there has been some improvement among the engineers'.[48] At a conference of mining engineers and technicians in the Ukraine in 1929, a number of delegates demonstratively removed their engineers' cap and badge, demanding that these should be abolished as a sign of a separate caste.[49] In a similar spirit an engineer in the metal industry proposed to tackle indifference among ITR to socialist competition by surrounding the guilty people with 'such an atmosphere that they will feel that they are not ours, not Soviet'.[50] At the 4th VMBIT plenum in 1930, some delegates demanded that there should be a 'final break with the "monopoly" of knowledge which has remained up the present the possession of a small caste of bourgeois technical intelligentsia'. The young engineers, it was said, must launch a 'furious criticism of the "authorities" of technical thought'.[51]

The motives for all these declarations were no doubt diverse. Some may have made them because, as one correspondent said, they were 'afraid of compromising themselves by associating with the old specialists'.[52] But also, according to another observer, the young engineers had been encouraged to 'settle accounts for careerist reasons'.[53] A sense of career frustration comes through quite strongly in the press. Young engineers said that they were not being given sufficiently responsible positions, that they were often put in 'harmless' jobs in the enterprise administration rather than in production jobs which would in turn be a passport to further promotion.[54] They said that directors did not trust them,[55] or even that they were being 'persecuted' by directors, in league with the old specialists.[56] In April 1929, a speaker at a session of the Moscow Congress of Soviets said that 'we have many of our own engineers now finishing *vtuzy*, who are given nothing important to do', and that 'we pay too much attention to the old specialists'.[57]

Such complaints seem to belong mainly to the early phase of industrial expansion in 1928–29. Once that expansion got under way there was no lack of career opportunities for young engineers. Under conditions of a 'famine' in managerial and technical cadres, formal training—however hastily acquired—was a major asset. There was apparently a certain resistance to the promotion of recent graduates from technical institutes in the early 1930s, especially from red directors and *praktiki*.[58] But this does not seem to have seriously deterred their advancement. Early in 1933 Ordzhonik-idze, while defending the movement of engineers into managerial positions, said that 'it is essential that we reach a situation where the engineer who has graduated from a *vtuz* does not immediately become a big boss (*bolshoe nachalstvo*) in the factory. Let him first work as assistant to a foreman and then he will start climbing higher . . .'.[59] But the comment suggests that rapid promotions were not in fact uncommon.

There was plenty of criticism of the new generation of specialists, especially those who had graduated after 1928, because of their low level of technical preparation and alleged inability to cope with the new machinery.[60] But again, with the rapid expansion and reconstruction of industrial production the leaders of industry had to be satisfied with what they could get. The young specialists could thus readily form the impression that they were indispensable. Early on in the campaign, a leading party official, addressing an audience of engineers, spoke of the 'unobjective impudence (*nakhrap*) to be found among some young comrades'.[61] In 1932, a government leader spoke to a similar audience about the 'excessive self-confidence of the youth',[62] and in 1933 an ITS official was calling for a more self-critical approach by young engineers and an end to 'superficiality and know-all-ness (*vseznaistvo*)'.[63] This self-esteem, as is shown below, was not incompatible with insecurity in the job. But the cadres famine, and the political conditions in which the new generation specialists were trained and promoted, may well have given them the sense that they were the legitimate beneficiaries of industrial expansion.

4D   CONCLUSIONS

The picture that has emerged from Chapter 3 and the present chapter may be stated, in very broad terms, as follows. One of the major effects of the changing pattern of state activity in Soviet reconstruction was an attempt to redefine—and 'politicise'— intelligentsia roles in order to establish a closer link between the activity of the intellectuals and the currently interpreted interests of the state. It was this that defined the 'class struggle' between the state and the bourgeois specialists and the attempts to rally the support of the 'old' and 'new' generation to the general line. The clash between the defenders of the public interest and the pursuit of private interests is here manifested in a conflict over the extent and limits of authority to be established on the basis of claims to professional competence and specialised knowledge.

In what sense did the processes described—the attack on 'apoliticism' and 'corporatism', and the forms of recruitment to the expanding managerial and technical positions—create the conditions for a more organic relationship between the technical intelligentsia and the state? Very briefly, the upshot of the discussion is that some sense can be given to the notion that the Soviet state created its 'own' technical intelligentsia in production. But this cannot be read off from a table of social statistics. It was the result of a process, of changing political conditions, and of rapid personal advancement made possible by the industrial expansion. The campaign against the older generation encouraged political infighting within the technical intelligentsia and a challenge by the youth to the professional dominance (the 'monopoly of knowledge') of the older generation. At the same time, the 'famine' in cadres and the importance of political credentials made it possible for the new specialists to advance rapidly within the industrial hierarchy. They could get the sense that they were the legitimate beneficiaries of an industrial expansion in which it was the state that exercised the patronage.

But the following provisos should be added. First, the challenge to professional authority, and the political infighting, were effects of the attempt to impose a political redefinition of intelligentsia roles, but this did not transform the conditions—the social division between mental and manual labour—in which professional self-images and identities are established. We shall return to this point later.

Second, the importance of political criteria and demonstrations of Soviet loyalty in the process of advancement did not mean that only one type of career path was favoured. In the early 1930s someone who had once been a political activist was at a great advantage in entry to the top managerial positions. But those who had started their working lives in industry were also able to make quick careers, and in the late 1930s—under the rapidly changing political conditions at the time of the great purges—it was people with this background who were to step into the decimated ranks of the red technical intelligentsia.

5 The Work Situation: Pressures from Above

So far, the relationship between the technical intelligentsia and the Soviet state has been explored by examining the political attack on professional neutrality and by looking at some of the sources and consequences of recruitment to the expanding managerial and technical positions. Underlying the changes described was a major shift in the pattern of state domination. This transformation was an effect of the struggle to establish a particular form of political control over production in the course of industrialisation. To consider in greater depth the impact of this shift on the technical intelligentsia, attention will now be focused more closely on the work situation of enterprise managers and technical staff. Their position was defined by the emergence of a system of directive or 'command' planning and by the activities of a variety of agencies which were instructed to assist in carrying out plans and overcoming obstacles in the way of industrial expansion.

The discussion starts with a few general remarks about Soviet planning as it evolved in this period. It then goes on to consider the position of the technical intelligentsia within the hierarchy of industrial administration, and the role of the party and coercive agencies in relation to managers and technical staff. What may seem to be a disproportionate amount of attention is given to the coercive apparatuses. Part of the reason for this emphasis is to throw more light on the developments discussed in Chapter 3. But there is also the assumption that an understanding of the coercive agencies is of special importance for an analysis of the changing forms of state domination in this period.

5A INDUSTRIALISATION AND PLANNING

The period under review was one of very rapid industrial growth, which meant a heavy emphasis on investment in the capital goods sector (the production of the means of production) at the expense of consumer goods, and involved a massive programme for the construction of new plants and the reconstruction of existing ones. The process was state-initiated and was shaped by a highly centralised administration of production. The quantitative aspects of this development, and the technical features of the planning process, are not considered here.[1] Nor will we discuss the rationality or otherwise of the Soviet pattern of economic development. The discussion is restricted to an examination of certain relationships in which managers and technical staff were involved as a result of the form of state direction which became established.

The assumption will be that the type of planning adopted was not a method for providing an orderly coordination of the production processes of different economic sectors. Rather, it was a method for establishing priorities—the development of heavy industry and the corresponding infrastructure—in order to achieve a short-cut expansion of industrial production. It seems that directive planning must always remain imperfect, given the constraints of limited knowledge and given the fact that plans are not self-executing.[2] But in this period of 'primitive' accumulation, the central authorities had to contend with an exceptional degree of uncertainty in a rapidly changing environment. Industry was in a state of recurrent crisis, which was both cause and consequence of a system of 'taut' planning. According to a statement in the party journal, 'experience shows that the tempi of work, the degree of struggle with inadequacies in production closely correspond to the amount of tautness (*napryazhennost*) of planned tasks . . . this is the operational significance of a taut plan in the struggle to improve production'.[3] But if taut planning could be explained on these grounds, it also helped to reproduce the conditions that had given rise to it. Systematic shortages of supplies and frequent halts to production threatened to undermine the industrialisation effort, bringing campaigns to remedy the situation and thereby reinforcing the concentrated attention on priorities.

These features, together with others that will come up in the course of discussion, made the rhetoric of battle quite appropriate. The party, according to the image that it projected, was engaged in a war on the industrial front in which success or failure in meeting production targets in the priority sectors became a matter of life or death for the state. Within the organisational framework that emerged, managers at enterprise level had a certain autonomy in the implementation of plans, and could up to a point protect themselves against the consequences of outside intervention. But in the early years of Soviet industrial expansion there was a high rate of failure which brought a definite insecurity for the technical intelligentsia. The insecurity was greater for ITR lower down in the hierarchy, and was especially evident between 1928 and 1931. But at no time in the period under study could it be said that a stable set of expectations attached to managerial and technical positions.

5B   THE ITR IN THE INDUSTRIAL HIERARCHY

In the period between 1928 and 1935 Soviet industry underwent a number of reorganisations out of which the administrative structure of the 'command economy' emerged. This process did not bring about a revolution in the mode of production in the sense that collectivisation revolutionised the agricultural sector. But important changes took place. A detailed account of the reorganisations will not be given, since what is said later does not depend on it. But some comments are necessary.

Two sorts of changes after 1928, which seem to have been in fundamental tension with one another, may be singled out to begin with. First, a greater emphasis was given to the need for a 'definite degree of independence' for the enterprise, which was to be the 'basic unit for the administration of industry'. This formulation, to be found in a party directive of December 1929,[4] followed the logic of a decision in June 1927 to increase the powers of the enterprise in relation to the trusts, and was closely bound up with the attempt to bring cost accounting (*khozraschet*) principles into the administration of industry at enterprise level.

Secondly, the emphasis shifted from plans as 'prognoses' and as 'control figures' to plans as detailed production programmes that were legally binding on the enterprise. By contrast with the previous provision of a 'general framework', the industrial-financial plan (*promfinplan*) had now, according to one legal expert, a 'direct and obligatory operational significance for the enterprise' which meant a 'full and unconditional recognition of the principles of the binding nature of the plan'.[5]

Thus the enterprise was quasi-independent in legal status but since the plan was legally binding, independence here was to be understood only as a necessary condition for implementing production tasks determined by state agencies at above-enterprise level. This was the formal position throughout the period under study (it remains basically unchanged up to the present day), although there were a number of organisational changes at above-enterprise level. Of these the most significant were the increasing transfer of planning functions from VSNKh to Gosplan, and internal transformations within VSNKh itself. The latter involved setting up new industrial 'associations' (encompassing the trusts), 'sectors' and 'chief departments', and in early 1932 establishing the Commissariat of Heavy Industry (NKTP) to replace VSNKh, with other industrial sectors transferred to other commissariats. Basically what was involved was a process of division and subdivision to cope with the increasing complexity of planning and administration, and correspondingly a more important role for the central planning authority as a coordinating agency for industrial production.[6] For the purposes of the subsequent discussion it is sufficient to note that the enterprise remained the primary unit in a hierarchy that extended from central planners through VSNKh or commissariats and one or more intermediate levels down to the enterprise.

According to the formal position, enterprise autonomy was limited to the further disaggregation of plans that had been worked out already at above-enterprise level, which included detailed instructions as to quantity, quality, assortment, use of materials, size of labour force, average wages, etc. It has been argued by Granick—in our view convincingly—that the enterprise administration, while subject to continuous and often zealous guidance from above, achieved a greater measure of autonomy in practice than was suggested by the formal situation. His evidence relates to the period 1934–41, but broadly speaking his conclusions seem to be valid for the years after 1928.

First, plans were in practice neither comprehensive nor precise, and it was not expected that they would be precisely fulfilled. Hence the emphasis on over-fulfilment of plans, which would have been incompatible with a closely integrated design. Secondly, where managers were snowed under by detailed instructions from their superiors, many instructions were ignored, and would in any case have to be if they were mutually conflicting. Basically managerial incentives were geared into the plan through the use of an index of gross output; the overriding importance of this criterion meant that other indicators like cost reduction and quality of production were quite secondary. Again, the pursuit of production targets entailed using initiative in recruiting labour, in producing goods that 'belonged' to other departments, and in securing scarce supplies. This demanded a flexibility that did not exist on paper, and informal relationships between directors and their superiors or between directors in different enterprises could be decisive in establishing the conditions of success. Illegalities—the expenditure of resources for unplanned uses—were endemic in the pursuit of these objectives, but where an enterprise was doing reasonably well according to the prevailing criteria, or could satisfy its superiors that it was, the higher agencies were not likely to enquire too closely into the methods used to get results.[7]

Thus, the immediate control exercised by directors over production set certain limits to the power of the central authorities to determine its course. Planning became more detailed in the course of the industrialisation drive after 1928, but the bargaining power of enterprise directors seems to have been greater at the end of the period under study than at the beginning. By 1933–34, at any rate, compared with 1928, one detects a greater confidence among directors in resisting the more extravagant production targets,[8] in ignoring threats of punishment,[9] and in making public their protests about lack of scope for managerial initiative.[10]

In a more restricted sense than this, one could also speak of a certain autonomy for those involved in the technical direction of the enterprise. The party leadership began worrying about this at the time of the Shakhty affair. According to a resolution of the April 1928 party plenum, 'in many enterprises the role of the executive (*khozyaistvennik*) is still that of a *bad commissar* . . . instead of really administering the enterprise, his role becomes that of "general management". Instead of checking the work of specialists and systematically learning through mutual work with them, executive-communists . . . often develop a blind faith in their [the specialists'] work'.[11] The object of the criticism was to call into question the NEP relationship between the commissar director and the engineers who were left alone in the day-to-day running of production. The theme often cropped up over the next few years, and untutored managers were urged to get some technical education so that they could exercise a more convincing authority over their subordinates.[12] In the course of a well-known pronouncement to a managers' conference in February 1931, Stalin had this to say on the matter:

Ten years ago we had the following slogan: 'Since communists don't yet properly understand the technique of production, since they have still to learn how to administer the economy, let the old technicians and engineers . . . manage production, and you, communists, don't interfere in technical matters . . . '. Now it was time to finish with the stale view that we should not interfere in production. It is time we mastered another, new idea corresponding to the present period: *interfere in everything*.[13]

It thus appears that the engineers—old and new—had their own limited area of power, the kind of power which accompanies the exercise of technical functions that remain mysterious to the outsider and therefore beyond direct control. But nothing of great moment follows from this, since it seems to have been rare for subordinate ITR to come into open conflict with their superiors. The director had the power of hire and fire over the ITR, and their careers could depend on what the director said about them. But also, as will be shown below in detail, the ITR in more modest positions were themselves very vulnerable to criticism if anything was going wrong in production.

On occasion directors did come into conflict with their ITR, not with line managers, but with technical staff who were in a position to criticise the enterprise administration, for example by revealing spare capacity or subquality production. In 1928–9 some aspiring engineers in departments of 'rationalisation' were making an issue of the fact that there were 'extra reserves' that were not being utilised. But the specialists were not thanked for this discovery by their directors; on the contrary, the matter got into the press because the specialists said they were being victimised for their initiatives.[14] Cases were reported in which directors even came to blows with engineers over this question.[15] It can be inferred that line managers did not appreciate this sort of 'assistance' because it could be used as an argument for further increasing production targets, thus making it more difficult to fulfil the plan.

There was, then, strong pressure on the ITR to go along with instructions even if they did not like them, knowing that the plan was more important than any narrowly technical considerations. According to an ITS report the ITR had taken up a 'careerist' stance in relation to the enterprise administration, acting by the principle 'be obliging to everyone, and especially to the bosses (*nachalstvo*)'.[16] By 1931, the department of rationalisation had been nicknamed the 'house of rest',[17] and other staff departments that had a potentially critical function—especially quality control—were being criticised in the press for apathy and oversight. Where quality control engineers had the temerity to protest about low quality output, they too were likely to find themselves victimised. Cases were cited of 'shameless persecution of the quality control department', in which engineers had been forced to resign,[18] and there were other complaints in the press about directors who were stifling 'legitimate technical criticisms' by specialists.[19]

One can conclude from this brief discussion that there were definite limits to the power exercised over enterprise directors within the industrial hierarchy, that technical skills formed the basis for a modest influence in the enterprise, but that the subordinate ITR usually supported their superiors even if there were underlying tensions between different sections of the managerial and technical personnel.

However, gaining a partial autonomy in the implementation of plans was conditional on success according to the prevailing criteria. Yet in this period of primitive accumulation the rate of failure was high, and this had important consequences for the degree of security in managerial and technical jobs. This is partly reflected in the high rate of turnover among managers.[20] High turnover was an index of the readiness of the higher industrial administration to come to a rapid decision about the capacities of this or that manager,[21] and also an index of the activities of 'outside' agencies in the industrial arena. In the rest of the chapter, we focus attention on the latter issue, making an attempt to identify some of the sources of security and insecurity in managerial and technical jobs by examining the role of the party and of the coercive agencies in relation to the ITR in production.

5C   THE ROLE OF THE PARTY

Party officialdom, apart from its role in formulating policies and priorities at the centre, also supervised industrial production through its central and local organisations and through the party cells at enterprise level. The primary organisations (the cells) are dealt with in Chapter 6; the discussion here concerns solely central and local organisations.

Party activities in the industrial arena can be seen as a result of the fact that it was impossible to ensure the self-execution of economic plans. Party interventions provided one means of trying to correct distortions and identify trouble spots which might otherwise have remained concealed because of the covering-up tactics of industrial managers. But the job of the party organisations was ambiguously defined. On the one hand they were told to exercise concrete supervision; on the other hand, they were told not to interfere in 'operational' matters concerning production: that is, they should not violate 'one-man management'.

In the 'normal' course of events, the party organisations played a somewhat passive role in relation to industry. Thus in 1928 a Central Committee resolution complained that party supervision often boiled down to 'general declarative resolutions' and that there was 'no active struggle for the elimination of defects'. This was explained in the resolution partly by the excessive centralism of industrial administration, partly by lack of technical competence, partly by 'family-mindedness'.[22] The last failing, as a later party resolution explained, involved a 'conscious covering up of defects' in production.[23] This phenomenon has often been discussed in accounts of Soviet management, from the 1930s up to the present day. It can be explained basically in terms of the fact that in industrial regions the performance of local party officials was judged by their own superiors according to the success of industrial enterprises within their domain. Local officials were therefore inclined to let managers get on with the job and to tolerate 'defects' (and irregularities) if these were seen to be a necessary price to pay for getting satisfactory results.

However, in the early period of Soviet industrialisation there was no lack of production crises which encouraged party organisations to become more active. When enterprises were lagging seriously behind, especially in priority sectors, local party officials came under pressure from their superiors to find remedies. If the situation was serious enough, party organisations could become involved in a campaign in which central and local officials entered into details of production or began to use more actively their powers of transferring, dismissing and appointing managerial and technical personnel. In this situation, managers and engineers might be shifted around or penalised with some impunity, and were less likely to get support from local officials who were themselves subject to threats and sanctions if they failed to carry through the changes demanded. Party as well as managerial careers could be made and unmade in these circumstances; the local 'family circles' were consequently broken up. This contributed to the high rate of managerial turnover, which can thus be seen as an index of the forces militating against the development of firm local barriers to central authority.

In the period under review, the most noisy party campaigns were in connection with the coal and metallurgical industries. Because of the critical importance of those sectors in building up an industrial base, they were given much attention by the party. By examining these examples one can get some idea of the possible impact of party intervention on the ITR.

Coal production did not begin to preoccupy the party only in the early 1930s, but it was at this time, in connection with attempts to technically restructure coal mining, that it became the object of special attention. Despite—perhaps because of—an attempt to rapidly mechanise coal production during the first Five-Year Plan period, and despite a rapid increase in the labour force, output began falling in 1932. Party organisations were urged to remedy the situation. In August 1932, the Donetsk *obkom* warned managers and district party officials that 'the party judges and will judge only according to the quantity of coal produced',[24] and berated managers for their slavery to outdated methods of direction and production. In January 1933, Ordzhonikidze sent out a NKTP order demanding that coal trusts in the Donbass and the North Caucasus send him personally the names of heads of mines and chief engineers who were underfulfilling the plan; these were to be regarded as occupying their posts temporarily and were to be transferred if their work did not improve 'within one month'.[25] Soon after, the party and industrial press began publishing blacklists of managers who were failing to meet targets, and in April 1933 the Central Committee passed a resolution singling out managers who 'attempt to cover up their helplessness and bureaucratism by means of prattle about "unrealistic" plans'. Where processes were being mechanised a different type of management was needed. Among other things, the Central Committee proposed that the 'best ITR' should be moved from the trust offices to important positions in production, as mine managers, chief engineers and section heads.[26]

The proposed changes were resisted.[27] Some of the existing managers—who were *praktiki*—were told that they would now have to work as assistants. The 'old men', it was reported, were offended.

One was quoted as saying: 'let them try to work without us, let's see if these new engineers can increase output', and another: 'here come the Varangians who are going to impose their way of doing things on us'.[28] The mine administrations, and the Donetsk obkom itself, were accused of dragging their feet, and the obkom, in a telegram from Stalin, Molotov and Kaganovich, was told to 'go all out for self-criticism and checking of fulfilment in all mines and pits without exception', and to 'unconditionally punish all those who smell remotely of sabotage'.[29] In the face of such pressure, resistance was broken down, party officials and ITR were dismissed and changes in production methods were pushed through.[30]

The case of the coal industry was one example of what was described as a 'regrouping of the ranks of the technical intelligentsia in production' in 1933, with the intention of establishing a more 'scientific' approach to management.[31] The other main sector involved was metallurgy where changes in personnel were also pushed through in the face of resistance from managers and local party organisations.[32] New people were sent in as directors and shop heads in order to improve output and to put an end to 'rule of thumb' methods.[33] One of the newcomers said that 'the Achilles heel of the majority of the old leaders of metallurgical factories is their inability and unwillingness to struggle in a Bolshevik way for a high technical culture in the everyday life of the factory'; his aim was to 'break the old structure'.[34] Other replacement managers spoke in a similar vein.[35] These instances show that when party officials at the centre meant business they were able to assert their dominance through the use of powers of dismissal and appointment and to push local officials into a more active stance in relation to industry. But the definition of a good party secretary was ambiguous: one who kept a close eye on production but did not meddle. Although the local party organisations were usually criticised by the party centre for offering too little rather than too much guidance to industry, they might also deviate in the other direction, which left them open to the charge of interfering in operational matters and 'undermining one-man management'. For example, in the course of the Donbass campaign, while some raikoms were being accused of bureaucratic sabotage of central directives— that is, doing nothing—others were being criticised for excessive 'interference in production details'. In reply to this last criticism, one raikom secretary explained that conditions in the Donbass had encouraged party organisations to emphasise 'petty economic questions': 'party officials are frightened to let go the threads of economic work, since they will then lose the ground under their feet'.[36]

Similarly, when party officials put pressure on managers and shop ITR, or were instrumental in getting them replaced, this in one set of circumstances was defined by the central party authorities as part of a legitimate shake-up, in another set of circumstances was labelled as the persecution of specialists. Thus, a Central Committee resolution on the Nizhegorod auto factory in April 1932 complained of the 'complete absence of one-man management and undermining of economic leadership by the raikom and shop party organisations, anti-*spets* attitudes and persecution of administrative and technical personnel'.[37] In another case, commenting on a similar Central Committee resolution on the Beloretsk party organisation, the party journal criticised the raikom secretary for 'giving orders of an operational character to shop managers, above the heads of the directors'.[38]

In the case mentioned, production was in serious trouble and the local party officials were trying not to 'let go the threads of economic work'. The reason for a more interventionist stance was basically the same as the reason for a more *laissez-faire* approach at other times. The form of activity or inactivity depended upon a judgement about what was in the best interests of economic success or the appearance of it. But the judgement of higher party organs about whether the local party was helping or hindering production was based on more general criteria, since the central authorities had a wider set of interests to protect. The 'private' interests of local officials did not necessarily coincide with the interests of the state as defined by central officials. Hence a type of local party activity that was defined as a virtue in one set of circumstances could become a vice in another.

5D THE ITR AND THE COERCIVE STATE APPARATUSES

The form of political control over production was determined not only by the activity of the party organisations. There was also a role in the production arena for the agencies of law and order: the procuracy, the courts and the political police. In the period under review in this study there was a marked expansion in the scope of activity of the coercive apparatuses and in the use of the criminal law. This was an effect of the struggle to defend the interests of the state against the variety of private interests that were seen to be sabotaging it. Alongside an often violent confrontation with the peasantry, the agencies of the state were engaged in a 'war' to secure a firmer hold over industrial production and to implement centrally established priorities. The greater use of the criminal law in relation to industry after 1928 was one consequence of these efforts.

The conditions under which Soviet industrialisation took place brought a rapid rate of economic growth, but also had certain systematic disruptive effects—for example, a cavalier use of machinery, a high proportion of spoiled goods, neglect of industrial safety measures and a high rate of industrial accidents. These disruptions were to a large extent a result of managers' efforts to fulfil short-term gross production plans. But they could also prevent those plans being met. In that event, enterprise managers and technicians might become the target of attempts to pinpoint responsibility—or find a scapegoat—for the failure to meet the demands of the state.

Those held responsible might be regarded as simply the victims of honest error, or as negligent. On the other hand, they might be labelled as criminally negligent, or as saboteurs or as wreckers with counter-revolutionary intentions. How they were likely to be labelled depended on the political conjuncture. What was to count as negligence, sabotage or counter-revolutionary wrecking? This question could not be answered *a priori*, because there were no unambiguous criteria by which to judge whether such misdemeanours had occurred. The answer depended on a current political definition of the situation.

To explore the impact of the coercive agencies on the work situation of managers and technical staff, the period from 1928 to mid-1931 is discussed first; it had certain specific features which were closely connected with the campaign against the old generation technical intelligentsia discussed in Chapter 3. This is followed by a discussion of the period between mid-1931 and 1935.

5D (i) 1928–31

It was seen in Chapter 3 that in the three-year period following the Shakhty affair the technical intelligentsia became involved in a campaign in which one section was depicted as a counter-revolutionary force. This image was made concrete in the 'political' charge of wrecking. In the case of the ITR, charges of wrecking were always connected with alleged misdemeanours that had affected production. The use of the criminal law in relation to industry was not in itself new.[39] But it is clear that developments after the Shakhty affair led to an increase in the industrial activities of the coercive agencies.

Hard information for this period is difficult to come by, but a few figures may be quoted, dealing first with the ordinary judicial process, reflecting the activity of the procuracy and courts. According to sample data published by the Commissariat of Justice covering 38,348 ITR, between September 1927 and September 1928 1648 criminal actions were started. Of these, 50 per cent were connected with 'production errors and omissions', 20 per cent with 'violation of safety regulation' and 30 per cent with 'other errors'.[40] On this evidence a VMBIT report said that 'the work of the ITR is accompanied by the risk of being brought to trial in a criminal capacity to the same extent that the work of a painter involves the risk of falling from a roof or that of a carpenter of injuring himself with a hammer'.[41] This seems an understatement on the basis of the figures given. But the proportion of ITR affected was higher than this in some industries and regions. According to a survey by the Mineworkers' Union, during 1928 fifteen per cent of ITR in the mining industries were tried on criminal charges related to their work.[42] In the Shakhtino–Donetsk okrug, where the specialists involved in the Shakhty affair had worked, arrests were very heavy and the okrug party secretary said at one point that 'we were left without specialists in production'.[43] In this area 60 per cent of the members of the ITS were said to have had charges brought against them between May 1928 and May 1929.[44] By mid-1931, according to a recent Soviet source, some 50 per cent of ITS members in the Donbass (which included the Shakhty district) had been involved in one criminal action or another.[45]

Two points should be made at this juncture. First, the proportion of specialists involved seems to have been exceptionally high in the Donbass. This could be explained by the importance here of coalmining, an industry that not only had priority but was also especially prone to production crises. If this is correct, then it may not have been fortuitous that the specialists first singled out for a show trial were employed in that sector. Secondly, the fact that a criminal charge was brought was not a guarantee that it would stick. According to the sample survey already cited, covering the

year September 1927 to September 1928, one-third of ITR brought
to trial were acquitted, and an unspecified proportion of sentences
by local courts were reversed on appeal.[46] During 1928, in one
district in the Urals, actions were started against 414 specialists, of
which 32 per cent were dropped at the investigation stage, while 21
per cent of those tried were acquitted.[47] In 1929 in the Moscow
region, 28 per cent of actions brought against 'specialists and
executives (*khozyaistvenniki*)' were called off during investigation,
and 54 per cent of those who came before the courts were
acquitted.[48] Unfortunately, there is no information available on
sentencing policy in this period. Basically, the choice will have been
between varying periods of corrective labour 'with deprivation of
freedom', and corrective labour 'without deprivation of freedom'.
The latter sentence was in effect a fine, involving a deduction of up
to 25 per cent of salary while remaining at one's place of work.

The evidence cited so far relates to cases dealt with by the
ordinary judicial agencies, excluding those processed only by the
political police. Some of the cases investigated by the GPU later
came before the courts. This was the position, at any rate, with the
show trials of the Shakhty, Promparty, and Menshevik specialists.
But the 1928–31 period had specific features connected with the
separate activities of the security organs in the industrial sphere,
directed at alleged counter-revolutionary wrecking. The GPU does
not seem to have exercised any direct influence on the administration of the enterprise, although the 'special section' may already
be found in an enterprise organisation chart by 1930.[49] But through
its agents on the spot, it was evidently on the lookout for production
problems that might indicate a case of politically motivated
sabotage.

It is not known just how extensive the activities of the GPU were,
though it was indicated in Chapter 3 that a wide range of industries
were involved. A Soviet source suggests that 'two to three thousand'
of the old engineers turned out to be wreckers.[50] According to a
Menshevik source within the Soviet Union, by early 1931 some
seven thousand engineers were 'sitting'—a term that was usually
taken to refer to customers of the security agencies.[51] A western
observer said that the GPU was very active at the time of the
Promparty affair and that 'nobody [of the engineers] regarded
himself above suspicion . . . thousands were sent on administrative
exile to distant parts of the country'.[52]

Once in the hands of the security organs, the most likely outcome was that a specialist would continue to work, either in prison, or in 'administrative exile', or possibly on the spot in his own enterprise or office. A system developed in which the GPU hired out specialists in its charge on particular projects, thereby stopping up some of the gaps created by the numerous arrests.[53] Thus in 1931 an industrial official stated that prisoner-specialists were being used 'where they cannot do any harm'. 'They will work,' he said, 'because we know that any engineer who knows his business well cannot remain without work.'[54]

Whether or not an enterprise came under the scrutiny of the political police doubtless depended on how seriously production had been disrupted. In a perhaps typical case the chief engineer and some fellow specialists at the 'Hammer and Sickle' plant found themselves under arrest because, according to the plant newspaper,

> they deliberately tried to put a brake on the development of the factory, dragged out the process of re-equipping the rolling mill shop, tried to raise production costs and to reduce production of high quality steel . . .they tried to create disorder, to encourage accidents and idling on the job and spoiled goods . . . these wreckers hoped to spread panic and despondency among the workers and thus to dampen their enthusiasm for socialist competition.[55]

The specialists in question were thus being blamed for a whole range of problems that had given rise to a crisis situation in the plant. In November 1929 Kaganovich explained to a party conference that 'the task of the wreckers has been to infiltrate our planning and administrative organs and industrial enterprises, and to carry out their work in such a way as to disrupt the normal course of the economic life of the country by creating constant crises, now in one branch of the economy, now in another'.[56] In February 1930, Kuibyshev found an 'indissoluble link . . . between the work of wreckers and the degree of plan fulfilment'.[57] At the time of the Promparty affair, an editorial in the industrial paper said: 'At a time when industry and the whole country is experiencing a severe famine in coal, metal, electrical energy, and disorganisation in the transport sector . . . we cannot but ascribe the extreme seriousness of these problems to wrecking activity.'[58]

From these indications it can be inferred that a catalogue of the more serious problems of Soviet industry was also a catalogue of the crimes of the specialists. But the concept of wrecking was a flexible one. Problems which in quieter times might have been attributed to mismanagement or not blamed on individuals at all, in the special circumstances of the war on the industrial front could readily assume the dimensions of a crime against the state. A party official stated the case plainly in 1929: 'In our days the wrecker is not only he who is directly connected with a counter-revolutionary organisation but also he who consciously works with indifference, under all sorts of pretexts ignoring the directives of the party.'[59] Thus there could be no clear boundary between 'political' and 'non-political' crimes, nor between crimes considered appropriate to the judiciary and those appropriate to the security agencies.

It is interesting to note in this context that some western engineers who were working in the Soviet Union at this time, accepted the claim that wrecking in the GPU sense was going on. For example, referring to the situation in 1930, an American engineer (working in the asbestos industry) wrote: 'that there is a great deal of premeditated sabotage going on in Russia is obvious to most of the American specialists with whom I have discussed the matter. Certainly not all the mistakes or slowing down of tempo can be attributed only to red tape, lack of practical experience, or ignorance.'[60] In similar vein, a chemical engineer made the following comment: 'It must be realised that two factors have done much to disrupt, delay and interfere with industrial operations. One is deliberate, subtle sabotage and the other is ignorance. There is no doubt that a great deal of sabotage occurred, of shirking, complacent idling, following current events but doing as little as possible . . . '.[61] These responses show, not that the observers in question accepted the image of an organised counter-revolutionary conspiracy, but that they interpreted wrecking in accordance with just the same fuzzy criteria as the party official quoted above.

5D (i) (a) *Responses to Insecurity*
Further light may be thrown on the impact of the coercive agencies by considering some of the responses of the ITR to their position. After the Shakhty affair, specialists became very nervous. In August 1928, an editorial in the VSNKh daily said that 'the Shakhty affair has had a significant impact on . . . the consciousness of the vast majority of our specialists . . . there is much gloom among those who were least of all thinking of counter-revolution'.[62] At the end of the year an ITS survey of a wide range of industries concluded that

there was a 'lot of depression among the ITR'.[63] In March 1929, at a Leningrad conference of ITR, engineers in metallurgy were expressing the 'bitterness which has accumulated over the past year'.[64] The chances of arrest, together with very big workloads and long hours, were shattering the nerves of many specialists.[65]

The ITR responded to the situation, as might be expected, by trying to insure themselves as far as they could against possible criminal charges. One way was to leave production altogether and try to find a quieter job. In a letter to the ITS journal one finds the following outburst from an engineer: 'It is impossible to work like this any longer. You have to flee from production; maybe the pay will be less but at least life will be quieter. At the moment I am constantly under a sword of Damocles. Everyone curses you, from every side criticism and threats. Whatever you do, you'll get tried. And don't expect any gratitude from anyone'.[66] Jobs in enterprises, which were already regarded unfavourably by engineers during the NEP because of difficult living and working conditions and lack of cultural facilities away from the bigger cities, became even less popular. The option of leaving production work altogether can have been open only to a few. But many specialists did take jobs in other enterprises in the hopes of finding less pressure elsewhere. There can be no doubt that the pressures discussed contributed to the high rate of turnover among ITR in this period, although a full explanation of turnover would be more complicated.[67]

A further effect of the threat of sanctions for failure was to strengthen the 'bureaucratic' tendency to cover every action with authorisation from above. An ITS official complained that too much blame was being put on engineers for inevitable mistakes and said that they were being turned into 'petty bureaucrats' instead of 'creators of the production process'.[68] The ITR were 'attempting to avoid doing anything that could evoke the slightest censure'.[69] A German engineer remarked that Russian specialists were 'afraid to reveal any kind of initiative, they always remain within the framework of the given task, however absurd the task'.[70] In the recollections of Kravchenko, this was explained by one chief engineer as follows: 'When the centre makes mistakes, we suffer but keep our mouths shut. In fact, we must thank our stars if we're not blamed for their blunders . . . there are plenty of offices for watching over us but not many for helping . . . we use up more time worrying what this one or that one will think than in actual engineering . . . ' In the view of this specialist such an approach

was the only rational one in the circumstances: 'honest' engineers
were fools.[71]

These reactions were unintended consequences of a punitive
response in the face of production problems. The intention of the
political leaders, reflected in numerous official injunctions, was for
managers and technicians to abandon conventional attitudes to
technology, to create, to innovate, to be 'revolutionaries' in
technique. In December 1929 Bukharin, addressing himself to an
audience of young engineers and technicians, outlined an extravagant picture. The new specialists, he said, should be 'free from
conservative traditions . . . [should] work with new tempos, using
all the experience of foreign countries, be brave innovators, pioneers
of new techniques, imbued with revolutionary perspectives in
construction'.[72] This was all very fine, but if things went wrong the
specialists might be blamed. This led one party leader to remark
that 'we sometimes push people around needlessly' and that this
often led to a 'stupid waste of the initiative and energy of the
specialists'.[73]

In an insecure environment, then, the ITR responded in a
classically bureaucratic manner, if we understand bureaucratic
here to mean sticking to a conservative interpretation of the rules
and passing the buck where possible onto someone else. This was a
kind of power strategy, a measuring out of participation, which was
perhaps the only strategy available to the ITR. It was a power game
of the weak, attempting to negotiate an area of security in
unfavourable circumstances.

If these observations are correct, then a problem arises about how
to explain the undoubted rapid technical change in industry in the
early years of Soviet industrialisation. It is not being denied that
there was some scope for technical initiative from below. But the
conclusion must be that it was not the rank and file technical
intelligentsia who provided the main impetus for the technical
transformation. Rather, the impetus was given by political officialdom itself. Through its punitive form of direction the party
leadership tended to reproduce the conditions of its own dynamic
and transformative role, and thereby also to preserve its dominant
position in the power game. Though lacking in technical skills itself,
political officialdom, in struggling against 'bureaucratic' apathy
and routine, became the chief agent of technical change.

5D (i) (b) *Sources of Support for the ITR*

The elements of insecurity in the position of the ITR in 1928–31 were a result of the way in which the agencies of the state confronted some of the disruptive consequences of industrial expansion. But there were also countervailing pressures resisting these interventions, especially from officials in VSNKh and the intermediate levels of industrial administration, and possibly also within the party apparatus itself. They were able to justify their resistance on the same grounds as the agencies of control justified their intervention: namely, that they were defending the best interests of socialist construction.

The matter came out into the open at the 16th Party Conference in April 1929, when there was an argument about the activities of the control agencies in relation to industry. The discussion concerned the role of the Workers' and Peasants' Inspection (RKI), which seems to have played a very minor part in investigations at the enterprise level.[74] But the occasion was important as an indication of responses within the industrial apparatus to inquisitive outside agencies. The spokesman for the industrial officials was Birman, then chairman of the Yugostal trust. He condemned the multiplication of controls and investigations and the punitive attitude of RKI officials. Engineers in the trust offices were sometimes obliged to sit all day, 'like dentists', receiving one RKI inspector after another; there was a 'type of employee, an inspector who sometimes considers his chief service the uncovering of a crime . . . Some of these inspectors consider themselves unlucky if they do not disclose a crime of some sort'.[75] The kind of tensions that surfaced on this occasion were not often revealed in the press, but there were some hints. In November 1929 it was reported that economic officials were making appeals on behalf of arrested specialists.[76] In June 1930, as already mentioned in Chapter 3, the RKI was having a hard time persuading industrial officials that wrecking 'really existed'. Again at the time of the Promparty affair, it was admitted that 'some communists and executives' were protesting about the loss of specialists because 'we cannot do without them'.[77]

On occasion specialists could expect support lower down in the hierarchy, from enterprise directors. An American participant observer reports that directors did sometimes speak up for their subordinate ITR, and cites a case in August 1930 when several specialists in his plant (an asbestos mill) were arrested by the GPU for counter-revolutionary activities, on exceptionally flimsy grounds. As a result of intervention by the director and a supporting statement from the American himself, a heavy sentence—the case had been passed on to the courts—was reduced to one appropriate to a 'slight degree of malfeasance'.[78] But this case seems to have been unusual. Investigations were started when the enterprise was in trouble: in this situation, directors were themselves under pressure from higher up, possibly with their own position threatened. In that event, they were unlikely to come running to the assistance of their subordinates, especially if the latter had been marked out as politically suspect. On the contrary, the temptation was to pass the buck downwards when the enterprise was under attack for lagging production. In October 1929, in the course of a trial of twenty managerial and technical personnel from the 'Red Profintern' plan, the director acting as witness absolved himself from blame for failure on the grounds that technical matters were 'not my business'.[79] In the same year a worried mine manager in the Donbass addressed the following threat to his subordinates: 'I hereby warn all technical personnel that no justifications will be taken into account. The slightest deviation from the *promfinplan* will be regarded as direct aid to the class enemy . . . '[80] Two years later it was observed in the Commissariat of Justice journal that 'judicial practice shows that some managers try to put the blame for plan failures onto specialists',[81] and cases were even cited in which directors themselves had been instrumental in initiating accusations of wrecking against ITR.[82]

It was, then, in the higher reaches of officialdom, not at the enterprise level, that any direct pressure in favour of a less punitive stance towards the technical intelligentsia was making itself felt. The consequences, if not the mechanisms, of this influence can be seen if one looks at the shift in the party line in 1931.

5D (ii) 1931–35

In June 1931, as was seen in Chapter 3, there was a change in party policy in relation to the technical intelligentsia. The old generation specialists, according to Stalin's injunction, were no longer to be regarded indiscriminately as potential wreckers. An indication of this change in course had already reached the judicial agencies in May, in a Commissariat of Justice circular sent to the regional procuracies. It was said that the procuracy organs, in carrying out their task of supervising the fulfilment of the industrial-financial plan and struggling against phenomena that were preventing the 'normal course of production', had adopted an incorrect approach to executives (*khozyaistvenniki*) and specialists in production. Un-warranted charges, excessively long investigations and unjustified measures of repression had led to a 'purposeless harassment of specialists, tearing them away from their duties, sometimes denuding production of needed specialists . . . [such methods] not only cannot assist the fulfilment of planned tasks, but bring damage to the fulfilment of the plan which is difficult to remedy'. Criminal actions should be brought 'exclusively in cases of deliberate and malicious official and economic crimes, and in cases of a clearly negligent and unconscientious attitude to work'.[83] This was later backed up by an editorial in the judicial journal which instructed that 'by no means every case of non-fulfilment of the *promfinplan* should be regarded as a crime'. Certain 'troubles' in production 'may formally come under an article of the criminal code, but if in essence the troubles were not the result of wrecking, abuses, mismanagement or negligence, but were the result of honest error or inability to master new technical equipment, it is inappropriate to bring criminal charges . . . '[84]

Similar directives were contained in a Central Committee directive of July 1931, 'On the work of the technical personnel in enterprises'. It was essential to 'raise the authority of the engineering-technical workers and achieve a full realisation of their rights and duties in directing production'. A commission was to be set up to review previous sentences and investigation of production matters by outside bodies without the permission of the enterprise administration was to be forbidden. It was impermissible to describe as wrecking the results of an experiment which necessarily involved an element of risk.[85] All this was taken up vigorously by the industrial press, which sent out numerous appeals to allow more scope to 'production risk'.[86]

From these directives one could infer, even if no other evidence were available, that the use of the criminal law in relation to industry had met with resistance, although this in itself, in the absence of a general change in the political conjuncture, may not have been sufficient to explain the new policy. The first effect of the change in course was, so it seems, to discourage GPU activities in the industrial arena. The security organs did not lose interest in industry, and there were still specialists working under GPU supervision.[87] But the role of the political police in an investigative capacity in this sphere was certainly less in the four-year period 1931–35 than in the three-year period following the Shakhty affair.

Secondly, the ordinary judicial agencies became more cautious in starting criminal actions involving ITR. The immediate impact of the change in line can be seen from the reduction in the number of such actions 'in process'. In the Moscow region, between January and September 1931, 2520 specialists were involved in 1260 cases; between October and December, 56 cases were being dealt with (in other words the vast majority had been dropped); in the Urals, the number of cases in process declined from 54 in June 1931 to thirteen in December; in the Central Black Earth region, one criminal action was started in that period, compared with an average of 40 to 50 'in the preceding months'.[88]

The change in course did not, though, mean a complete end to judicial interventions involving the ITR. The procuracy and the courts were still being told to perform their share of the work of supervising the implementation of plans, and to enforce those parts of the criminal law relating to industrial production. In the words of one legal official in early 1933: 'The judicial and in particular the investigative organs have the responsibility to give help to socialist industry by preventing and eliminating obstacles and violations which are putting a brake on the *promfinplan*'.[89] Also, party directives and the criminal law remained crucially vague on what was to count as anti-state activity or as a manifestation of the class struggle. Wreckers, as Stalin reminded the country in 1931, would remain as long as the class struggle went on, and one could not become complacent. In a statement to lawyers in February 1932, a leading party official said that it was important not to treat every misdemeanour as if it were an attack by the class enemy. But it was also important 'on no account to weaken vigilance . . . and to discover whether, in any case of violation of the law, the crime had a class content'.[90]

This injunction was directed above all to the 'fierce struggle going on around the construction of the *kolkhozy*', and also to the influence of class enemies among industrial workers who, through deliberate sabotage, 'are taking advantage of every one of our blunders in order to bring under their influence the backward groups of workers'.[91] In 1934, again, similar guidelines were being given to legal officials about the possible 'class content' of criminal activity,[92] although the worst of the war in the countryside (and the famine of

1932–33) was by then over. The struggle, then, to create a viable collective and state farm sector, and to ensure deliveries of grain to the state, meant that in the first half of the 1930s most of the attention of the procuracy and courts was focused on agriculture.

Industry, however, was not forgotten, and ITR as well as workers still had to reckon with the possibility of criminal charges being brought against them in connection with their day-to-day work. In the case of managers and technical staff, possible offences broke down broadly into two categories. The first were 'economic' (or 'official') crimes involving for example fraudulent accounting to boost the indices of production, direct barter with other enterprises, and embezzlement. The second were crimes more directly linked to the process of production itself. The remarks here will be restricted to the second type, since in this period most of the offences 'noticed' by the procuracy were in that category.

The risk involved depended on how the local procuracy and courts were interpreting their assigned task of assisting in the fulfilment of the *promfinplan*. The matter can be illustrated by looking at the activities of the judicial agencies in relation to sub-quality production (*brak*), a matter that was considerably pre-occupying central party and economic agencies in the period under review. Special attention was already being drawn to this problem in 1930, when it was said that the quality of goods was generally declining, leading in the case of producer goods to huge losses through premature depreciation, breakages and explosions.[93] By late 1933, the matter was seen as critical enough to demand a special decree which laid down severe penalties for those responsible for *brak* (at least five years deprivation of freedom), which was to be regarded as a 'serious anti-state crime'. The defence industry was singled out for particular attention, and top managers (chairmen of trusts and enterprise directors) were if necessary to be made responsible.[94]

What were the repercussions of this directive? The following features of judicial activity in connection with the decree may be singled out. First, local procuracy officials were reluctant to act. According to the USSR Procurator-General, they were 'taking the line of least resistance'.[95] It was suggested that 'they [the procuracy] don't want to quarrel with the managers or other organisations' and that the economic organisations 'not only fail to give indications about concrete facts of output of poor quality goods, but in a number of cases have directly opposed the organs of the procuracy'.[96] Procurators were 'sometimes unable to overcome the direct opposition of the managers', and sometimes the latter were supported by local party officials (in the cases mentioned, raikom secretaries).[97]

Second, when sufficiently prodded from the centre, the local procuracy did start to intervene more often. But contrary to the intention of the decree the focus of attention was as much on light industry as on heavy industry, and in some regions courts were softening the impact of the directive by giving sentences under less punitive clauses of the criminal law, not involving deprivation of freedom.[98] Further, it was the ITR in the more modest positions who were tending to get the blame—again contrary to intentions. In connection with this last point, one regional procurator warned against a policy of 'bringing charges against scapegoats, leaving aside the no less blameworthy but more "responsible" people . . . The main figure among those charged has so far [up to February 1934] been the foreman. The technical director they try to avoid if possible, while the director, even against all common sense, has in a number of cases been directly shielded'.[99] The matter can be clarified by looking at the situation somewhat later on. According to figures based on 243 actions, by November 1934 the positions of those charged were as follows: 39 per cent were 'directors, deputy directors and chief engineers', 17 per cent were shop heads, 18 per cent from the quality control department, 19 per cent foremen, seven per cent 'others' (including workers).[100] The available evidence suggests that in the first category it was far more likely to be the chief engineer than his boss who got the blame.[101]

The judicial agencies were carrying out their assignment, then, by concentrating their efforts on managerial and technical staff in more modest positions. As a result, local procuracy officials began to be criticised by their superiors for 'pursuing numbers', for 'purposeless harassment of specialists' and incompetent investigations.[102] The procuracy was not making enough use of expert advice; it was hopeless for them to try to sort out the reasons for *brak* on their own since 'a clear and exhaustive account of the causes of *brak* in a confused organisational situation and in complex technological conditions sometimes demands a long and detailed study of the production process'. Over the period December 1933 to September 1934 there was a continuous increase in the proportion of sentences either reversed or changed on appeal. In 1934, 747 actions—

probably involving twice that number of people—were started in the RSFSR; 163 people were finally convicted.[103]

A similar pattern can be observed with judicial involvement after industrial accidents and injuries. In late 1931 it was said that the accident rate in industry was increasing (figures were not given), that only a small proportion of funds earmarked for safety measures were actually spent on them, but that both the labour inspectorate and the procuracy were reluctant to pursue this question.[104] In January 1933 a directive of the Heavy Industry Commissariat put responsibility for industrial accidents squarely on the heads of production units or servicing units who had failed to take possible measures to prevent them; directors or chief engineers were responsible for injuries if these had occurred as a result of violation of safety regulations.[105] After this the judiciary became more active, but it was mostly lower-level ITR or workers who were penalised. Also, among the ITR penalties were heavier the more modest the position occupied. In 1933–34 (the exact period is not given) in the Prokopievsk district in Western Siberia, 94 people in mining were charged, mostly in connection with violation of safety regulations: there were twelve mine managers, six engineers, ten section heads, 16 technicians, 31 foremen, 19 workers.[106] During the first nine months of 1935, out of 137 people charged in the Donetsk region, there were five heads of enterprises, fourteen 'responsible ITR', 27 foremen and 81 workers. The chances of getting a 'deprivation of freedom' sentence as opposed to corrective labour without deprivation of freedom were greater for 'responsible ITR' than for enterprise heads, and greater for foremen than for 'responsible ITR'.[107]

In connection with the Prokopievsk example, which was said to be 'not untypical', the district procuracy officials were now accused of the 'crudest violation of procedural norms', leading to unfounded charges against managerial and technical staff. The procuracy believed they were helping production but in fact they were disrupting it. 'To this day,' wrote a senior procuracy official, 'the courts and the procuracy do not fulfil the duties placed on them by the party and government in connection with the defence of the rights and interests of the specialists.'[108] Later, in 1935, the emphasis shifted back again in injunctions from the centre. The procuracy had an 'unserious attitude' to questions of safety at work, when in a number of regions, in metallurgy, coal and other industries accidents and injuries were on the increase. The very high proportion of successful appeals meant that people had a 'feeling of certainty that one will go completely unpunished in this category of case'.[109]

From these indications it is apparent that the judicial agencies, like the party organisations, were under conflicting pressure both to *intervene* and to avoid *meddling*. If they adopted a *laissez-faire* policy then they were letting criminals get away with sabotaging the plan; if they deviated in the other direction then they were preventing honest managers and engineers from getting on with their job. There was no clear definition of what was to count as legitimate intervention. How far the ITR were protected from outside intervention did not depend on their ability to defend an abstract set of legal rights, although it was for ignoring the 'rights and duties' of the ITR that the coercive agencies were sometimes criticised. Rather, it depended on whether this or that definition of what was best for the production effort would prevail.

There can be little doubt that in the period 1932–35 the industrial managers, including those at enterprise level, established a stronger position in relation to outside agencies than was the case between 1928 and 1931. They were better able to defend their own criteria of what was good for production and to resist or neutralise procuracy interventions when these occurred. This change, together with the less conspicuous role of the political police in the industrial arena gave the technical intelligentsia as a whole more security.

But since this security depended on the amount of influence that could be wielded, the ITR in the lower positions were *less* protected from the consequences of the use of criminal sanctions. They had less influence with the agencies of control and could be pushed around with greater impunity. Further, the underlying uncertainty in the position of the ITR as a whole in relation to the criminal law meant that even those in the top jobs were not fully secure. After 1935 the political situation was quickly changing, with a renewed attack on sections of political officialdom and further shifts in the balance of power between different parts of the political apparatus, affecting especially the role of the security organs. In this situation the sources of protection broke down, as the subsequent mass arrests of industrial managers—just one of numerous groups of officials and non-officials decimated during the 1936–8 purge—made brutally clear. Also, in this transformed political situation it was possible again to redefine ordinary crimes of production as political ones. In November 1936 Vyshinsky in this spirit instructed the local procuracies that 'all criminal cases of major conflagrations, accidents and output of poor quality products be reviewed and studied with the aim of exposing a counter-revolutionary and saboteur background in them'.[110]

It is not being argued here that the post-1935 purge of industrial managers—or of anyone else—can be read into the earlier political situation. The point is rather that throughout the 1930s the conditions under which the technical intelligentsia might establish a more secure position, namely an unambiguous definition of 'rights and duties', were lacking. In the absence of those conditions, the degree of security would remain subject to the shifting relations between officials and the changing definitions of crime.

The cyclical aspect of law enforcement, with the successive criticism of law and order agencies for intervening too little and too much in the industrial arena, was one of the effects of this ambiguity. At the same time, the cycles reflected a pervasive tension between the pressure towards 'certainty' (or socialist legality) and the pressure towards procedural flexibility.[111] In late 1934 it was suggested by one legal writer that violations of socialist legality would be easier to combat if a distinction was drawn in the law between malfeasance and crime, so that relatively trivial cases would not come under the criminal law.[112] But this was rejected by another writer on the grounds that 'often what was regarded by us in one social-political situation as a socially dangerous act, under changed circumstances ceases to be regarded as such, and the converse'. He was therefore against 'turning our legal code into some sort of dogmatic collection of eternally established norms of social order'.[113] While this conception prevailed—and it did prevail—the tension between legality and flexibility, or between law and terror, would remain unresolved.

5E   CONCLUSIONS

The object of this chapter has been to identify further features of the relationship between the technical intelligentsia and the state by examining some of the pressures from different political agencies that managers and technical staff faced in their work situation. The main conclusions that emerge from the discussion can be briefly stated as follows.

(1) The enterprise administration was able to gain a certain restricted autonomy in relation to the higher industrial agencies, at least in determining the means by which the effort to meet production targets would be made. But this restricted autonomy, in the sense of a relative freedom from detailed interference in the running of the enterprise, was conditional on keeping up a good record according to the prevailing criteria. If an enterprise got into trouble, then a more zealous form of intervention could be expected.

(2) A variety of agencies—not only the planners and industrial administrators—had jurisdiction over the activities of the enterprise ITR, since these agencies were being instructed to play their part in overcoming obstacles to the implementation of plans. This has become a familiar point in discussions of past and present Soviet industrial organisation, but still merits emphasis. The principle of one-man management, in the sense of a clear division of spheres of competence, was negated in practice, especially in conditions of battle against frequent disruptions of the production process.

(3) The punitive element in political control over production loomed large, and the boundaries between administrative and legal sanctions, or between ordinary and political crime, was blurred. Those held responsible for production failures might be seen as mistaken, or as ordinary criminals, or as class enemies. How they were labelled depended on changing criteria for certain types of misdemeanour, or on changing interpretations of vaguely defined criminal offences.

(4) The ability to circumvent pressures from superiors and from agencies of control depended on how much influence a manager had with those officials who were in principle in a position to exercise sanctions. It did not depend on an appeal to certain abstractly formulated rights. To some extent subordinate ITR, even if they lacked connections, could gain protection from their superiors in the industrial hierarchy. But in the case of directors, the high rate of turnover and the temptation to pass the buck downwards militated against this kind of solidarity. Again, the ITR had certain resources of measured participation as a way of protecting themselves against criticism. But this was a defensive strategy from a position of weakness.

6 The Technical Intelligentsia and the Workers

This chapter considers the work situation of the technical intelligentsia as it was defined by the pattern of relations between ITR on the one hand, and the workers and mass organisations of the enterprise on the other. An attempt is made to get a picture of the extent and limits of ITR authority over workers, what kinds of managerial style were adopted, and the role of trade union and party officials at the enterprise level in relation to ITR. For the most part, attention is focused on line managers, since they were the most important figures with whom workers needed to establish a relationship. But technical staff are also considered in this context, since the field of action of some staff functions was of direct significance from the point of view of production workers.

The changes in the pattern of these relationships in the late 1920s and early 1930s must be seen in the light of an attempt by the agencies of the state to impose a work discipline on a rapidly growing body of workers, mostly recruited fresh from the countryside, and to gain workers' compliance in periodic speed-ups of production. Broadly speaking the strategy of the state in this situation was a dual one: it was both 'corporate' and coercive. The corporate strategy had in turn a dual aspect. On the one hand, it brought a more thorough subordination of the trade unions to the state, so that they were unable or unwilling to offer any organised resistance to the severe material deprivations with which workers had to cope during this period. On the other hand, the party leadership encouraged the growth of a material differentiation between different categories of workers, which was institutionalised in shock-work (*udarnichestvo*).

But there were limits to the effectiveness of a corporate strategy, especially in a period of generally declining living standards. If institutionalised forms of struggle between workers and employers could be eliminated, workers' individual response to their situation were a source of far greater uncertainty. The state had to contend, for example, with a rapid labour turnover and high rates of absenteeism, which reflected individual reactions, and sought to overcome this by passing stringent labour legislation in order to keep workers on the job.

An analysis of these different strategies and their effects on the position of the Soviet workers needs a separate study and will not be attempted here.[1] But it must be remembered that relations between workers and the technical intelligentsia developed within the context of continuous efforts by the state to secure a more predictable and more productive workforce. In what follows, the discussion first takes a look at the changing balance of power within the 'triangle' of management, trade union organisation and party cell. This balance affected the boundaries of managerial authority at all levels of the enterprise hierarchy, and also the extent to which technical staff might be subject to criticism from below. The second part examines some of the conditions determining the more immediate relations between ITR and workers.

6A   THE *TROIKA* AND ONE-MAN MANAGEMENT

During the NEP the enterprise *troika* ('triangle') of management, trade union committee and party bureau was weighted in favour of management, since the trade union and party organisations by and large supported or acquiesced in managerial efforts to raise labour productivity and to tighten up work discipline. But the trade union retained a certain independent influence in relation to management, while the party organisation apparently did not become very active until the end of the NEP period.[2] By the mid-1930s, there had been a further major shift in the alignment of forces. The *troika* had in effect been reduced to a *dvoika* (a 'twosome') of management and party. The two-year period 1928–29 was especially important in establishing the conditions for that change, and this phase will be considered first.

6A (i) THE *TROIKA* 1928–29

The first years of the Soviet industrialisation drive were a time of intense activity for the enterprise party and trade union organisations. They were thrown into a feverish agitation, which gave them more to do than at any time in the six or seven years following the introduction of the NEP. The agitation was initiated by the party leadership, as part of the struggle on the industrial front, and its main purpose was evidently to produce a wage–effort bargain that would be more favourable to the state. This activity was not then basically in contradiction with the interests of state and management in securing a more productive and predictable workforce. But the organisations, on the basis of the influence they still possessed, were able to give the agitation a critical edge. This, in the context of heavy demands on enterprises to increase output and reduce production costs, gave rise to pressure from the industrial and party establishment to curtail the powers of the trade unions and to strengthen managerial authority at all levels of the enterprise hierarchy.

During 1928–29, there were two main specific complaints about the enterprise organisations in the VSNKh press. First, it was said that the trade unions, especially at the shop level, were interfering in 'operational' decisions by ITR, especially foremen and shop heads; this led to conflicts, for example, over transfer of workers between jobs, over piece-rates and over penalties for violation of labour regulations. Because of trade union interference, workers were often not carrying out orders, and if conflicts got to the Assessment and Conflicts Commission or the courts, they were often decided in favour of workers.[3] The trade unions were trying to get a cheap popularity with the workers,[4] the organisations frequently took the side of workers who had violated labour regulations,[5] and some managers thought that all decisions concerning penalties were a matter for the cell and factory committee.[6]

The second complaint was over the question of rights of appointment of managerial and technical personnel at the shop level. After 1927, the formal position was that the director had the right to appoint all subordinate ITR, while technical directors and shop heads were delegated to nominate their own subordinates.[7] The decisions were formally subject to consultation with the trade unions. Trade union and party officials had in practice retained an influence over the choice of shop ITR, especially foremen, but on occasion over shop heads.[8] A VSNKh official said that 'all practice shows that the main point of disagreement [between management and unions] is the question of selection and appointment of the leading administrative-technical apparatus of the enterprise'.[9] At the 4th VSNKh plenum, Kuibyshev claimed that there had been a 'return to the electivity' in the choice of ITR and that the formula 'public opinion is against him' had become typical.[10] On the other hand, the role of 'public opinion' in this matter may have been taken for granted by the factory committee and the cell. Thus, a resolution of the cell bureau at the Hammer and Sickle plant complained that 'the administration understands incorrectly the question of promotion of shop administrations; this has led in a number of cases to the direct appointment of promotees from above, bypassing the shop party and trade union organisation and the workers'.[11]

An interventionist approach by the enterprise organisations was encouraged by a number of changes in this period. It was given a major impetus by the campaign for 'self-criticism'. This was launched in April 1928, when Stalin encouraged the rank and file to speak up against alien or incompetent administrators, and reminded officials that the working class was the master (*khozyain*) of the national economy.[12] In industrial enterprises it was the party and trade union organisers and the enterprise press that played the key role in the campaign. Kravchenko, then on the editorial board of his plant newspaper, states that there was much scope at that ime for attacks on the factory administration and exposés of faults in production:

> [we wrote about] unconscionable waste and spoilage of goods. Mechanics who showed no proper respect for their tools and machines. The high cost of unit production in our plant, as compared with similar plants in Sweden or America. The unpardonable attitude of comrade So-and-So towards the workers. Bad quality in current output. How a certain process could be 'rationalised' . . . The insufferable housing conditions of the workers who lived in the barracks.[13]

The self-criticism campaign as such was shortlived, its peculiar democratic features not lasting beyond 1928. Only two months after his April speech Stalin was explaining that self-criticism should be aimed at eradicating 'petty-bourgeois indiscipline', not at debunking the Soviet power, demoralising managers and weakening the construction effort.[14] Thus cold water was likely to be poured over democracy if it got out of hand. But there were other elements in the situation which encouraged interventions by the enterprise organisations, in particular the suspicion that surrounded the ITR after the Shakhty affair. The party and trade union officials played their own part in initiating criminal accusations against specialists. They joined in the effort to worm out the alien elements and to demonstrate their revolutionary vigilance, and perhaps to direct attention away from their own share of responsibility for production failures, by singling out the technical and managerial personnel who had earned their disapproval.

The effectiveness of this criticism from below will have depended on whether the party or trade union officials had the support of their superiors outside the enterprise.[15] But there were certainly many complaints by ITR of hostile treatment.[16] The case of the metallurgical plant at Nadezhdinsk may serve as an example, though possibly an extreme one. According to engineers at an ITS meeting in December 1928, the background to the conflict was the attempt by shop heads to rationalise and reduce costs, which had met with a 'blank wall of mistrust'. Technical progress had allegedly ceased because of persecution for unavoidable errors, and the procuracy was being brought in; the shop head was a 'pebble' in the hands of the '*spets*-baiting' shop bureau; it had taken on the role of an extraordinary commission telling everyone what to do; the shop head could promote no one because his suggestions were rejected by the bureau; members of the party cell criticised ITR in front of the workers; the attempt to economise was regarded as 'exploitation of the workers'; the mood of the ITR was 'close to panic'.[17] By contrast, a trade union source described the meeting as typical of the engineers' overreaction to criticism; excesses sometimes occurred, but 'the specialists in enterprises, in their mass, are not able and often do not want to work in a situation of proletarian self-criticism'.[18]

The political climate in which the specialists found themselves contributed, then, to certain quasi-populist currents in this period. But it did not prevent a realignment of forces within the *troika*. In 1929 a number of political directives made it clear that the party leadership was prepared to back up management on the points of contention mentioned earlier. In January a VSNKh directive on the rights and duties of managerial and technical personnel gave the director—and by delegation shop managers—the right to appoint subordinate ITR without trade union involvement.[19] In March, a government decree gave more powers to enterprise management in imposing penalties on workers for infractions of work rules—

decisions were still to be subject to appeal to the Assessments and Conflict Commission, but this was not to prevent the decision being carried out.[20] The Central Trade Union Council published a circular defending this measure and instructing trade union officials not to interfere in the struggle for work discipline.[21] Then in September the Central Committee brought out a decree, 'On measures to improve the administration of production and to establish one-man management', which contained a more general attack on the 'direct interference by party and trade union organs in the operational-production work of the enterprise administration' and spoke of the need to 'concentrate in the hands of heads of factories and plants all the threads of the administration of the economic life of the factory'. Directors and shop managers were to carry out 'all necessary measures to strengthen production discipline'. The trade unions, though given the customary instruction to 'put forward and defend the everyday cultural-material and economic needs of the workers' and to participate energetically in production conferences, were told in unequivocal terms to keep out of 'operational' matters and to concentrate on organising the 'production activity' of the workers.[22]

The September 1929 decree was published after what one VSNKh official described as a 'bitter argument' with the trade unions,[23] and after the party had carried out a major purge of the trade union apparatus.[24] To judge by a few hostile comments which found their way into the Soviet press, the decree did not get an enthusiastic reception from enterprise trade union and party officials or from workers. At the Hammer and Sickle plant, some workers were saying that it was 'nothing but a suppression (*zazhim*) of the workers', others predicted that 'within a year the workers will be completely pressed down (*sovsem pridavlyat*)'.[25] The party journal quoted the following remarks: 'One-man management gives more rights to the *spetsy*, among them there are alien elements and they can use their rights to carry on wrecking work'; 'one-man management puts the workers in bondage . . . the Bolsheviks are turning their backs on democracy and self-criticism'; 'the director will now do what he wants'; 'the working class was boss (*khozyain*) only in '18–'19'.[26] Another party source acknowledged the generally hostile response by the enterprise organisations and workers' correspondents. At a meeting of workers' correspondents in a Samara factory it was said that 'now all the activists will fly from the factory, like corks from a bottle';[27] one party secretary remarked that 'they want to return to the old ways (*vostanovit' starinku)*',[28] another spoke of the impending 'suppression of self-criticism'.[29] A union official at the Krasny Vyborshchets plant was reported as saying: 'now all my work in the shop will break down. Now the shop committee will not be able to . . . defend the economic needs of the workers, influence the placing and transfer of workers, etc . . . Inevitably, the authority of the shop union bureau will be given a hard blow'.[30]

One-man management as a principle of administration was not a new theme in the Soviet context. As indicated in Chapter 2, the question of one-man versus collegial management was the subject of an important debate in the party during the civil war. But the focus of the issue had shifted. Before, the argument had been over whether there should be a collegial administration at the enterprise level, in the sense of a formally institutionalised collective management. This argument had already been decided by 1921. The question now was how far the more limited institutional constraints on managerial authority, embodied in the *troika*, would continue to work.

It was now argued that the need for a 'single will' in management was especially important given the new conditions brought by reconstruction. One party official wrote that 'the extreme complexity of economic work in existing enterprises, which we are furthermore systematically expanding, rationalising and reconstructing . . . brings out in a particularly acute way problems of improving the organisation of production, a merciless economy of resources, a maximum increase in the productivity of labour and the strictest labour discipline'.[31] The emphasis here was on the *economic* reasons for further bolstering the authority of the one-man manager. But one could also find the argument—in our view far less convincing—that there was a direct link between *technological* conditions and organisational 'needs'. Bukharin can be taken as a spokesman for this conception:

The strengthening of the principle of one-man management is itself called forth by the growth of new technique: the variety and at the same time the unity of the technological process, on the basis of the conveyor-continuous method of labour, demands the exceptional coordination . . . and harmony of this process, a strictly defined regime, and a many-centred administrative power is in principle *incompatible* with this new technical basis;

therefore the director of the factory, the head of the shop, the foreman are . . . the all-powerful leaders (*polnovlastnye rukovoditeli*) of the factory, the shop, the production section.[32]

The assumptions underlying these attempts to justify a further strengthening of managerial authority did not pass entirely unchallenged. For example, in October 1929 a certain Gegechkori (a trade union official) was attacked in the trade union press for syndicalism, after suggesting, in connection with a discussion of production conferences, that 'as the worker becomes a master of industry, the power of the manager dissolves (*rastvoryaetsya*), becomes superfluous'.[33] In 1932 one Ozerov published a pamphlet entitled 'The Soviet worker—organiser of production' which took at face value the notion that new forms of labour organisation (the shock brigade in particular) should give workers on the shop floor an organisational as well as an executant role in production. In Ozerov's view, the struggle for greater productivity was 'above all a struggle for a greater organisational role for the worker . . . '. Production conferences were the first step in an extension of worker participation but the worker could not be an organiser unless he was also a planner and not limited to his machine-tool. All this was given short shrift in the managerial press, which had the following comment:

Not to see the decisive role of the dictatorship of the proletariat, to ignore *this basic* organisational role, and in particular the organising role of the Soviet leader (*rukovoditel'*) in production, and to attribute to it a secondary organisational importance because the workers are participating in the administration of production—this means either not knowing or ignoring the ABC of Marxism–Leninism, and in the best case it means trying to make an immediate transition from the present stage to communism.[34]

In November 1932, we find a party member writing to *Pravda* with the following suggestion:

Before the October revolution the power in the shop belonged to the head and deputy head of the shop. Their actions were always carried out in such a way that the worker was made to feel their power. Now, in the 15th year of the dictatorship of the proletariat, these positions must be abolished, without awaiting the not-far-distant times of the world revolution. Their existence reduces the self-respect of working people, hence—away with them, and put all responsibility for the shop on a shop committee, which must consist of people working there.[35]

This letter was only cited in a critical article, and as might be expected, the sentiments expressed were seen as ominously syndicalist. But the fact that the sentiments found their way into the press and were thought worthy of comment, suggests that the notion of a one-man hierarchy had not yet acquired complete legitimacy, and that in this sense the argument about forms of organisation in a post-capitalist society was not yet closed.

However, if the conventional assumptions might be challenged at an abstract level, the actual trend was undoubtedly towards a strengthening of managerial authority and a shift in the relative positions of the three 'points' of the triangle. We shall try to see what this shift involved by looking first at the trade union, and then at the party after 1929.

6A (ii) THE TRADE UNION 1930–35

After the publication of the one-man management decree, the trade union officials did not immediately step in line. In 1930, there were frequent complaints that the decree was being undermined or ignored by both the enterprise organisations. A Central Committee directive on the metal-working industry in April 1930 said that the 'vast majority' of party and trade union committees had done nothing to implement the directive.[36] At the 16th Party Congress in June Stalin explained that 'we can no longer tolerate our enterprises being turned from production organisms into parliaments'.[37] In February 1931, a few directors were still complaining about trade union interference, and one said that the management of his plant was being distorted by the 'worst trade union methods from the Tomsky era'.[38]

But after 1930 one reads very infrequently in the managerial press about 'violations of one-man management' by the trade union organisations, which nearly always appear as second fiddle to the party. It must be assumed that the trade union organisation declined quite rapidly as a separately identifiable force that management needed to reckon with. Theoretically, the trade unions preserved their status as defenders of the material interests of the workers and guardians of the Labour Code. But to have acted out this formally assigned role in opposition to the immediate interests of production as defined by managers or by the party, would have been seen as sabotaging the plan. There was therefore little that the trade unions could do in a defensive capacity.

In January 1933, Ordzhonikidze, in a rare reference to the unions, had this to say:

> One cannot make out what the trade union organisations are doing in the factory. Yet the trade unions must concern themselves with what the workers are eating, with their living conditions . . . We have completed a five-year plan, are building socialism, have built large-scale industry, but you can't say this to a worker who is sitting in cold barracks—he will throw every curse at you (*ko vsem chertyam poshlet*).[39]

Referring to the situation at Magnitogorsk in 1933, Scott wrote in similar vein:

> The shop committee had little significance to most of the workers. It organised poorly attended meetings, addressed by trade union functionaries who talked on the construction programme for Magnitogorsk, the 2nd Five-year plan, the international situation. Also when the workers had been sick or hurt they took their slips to the chairman to be okayed. That was all. The administration meant a good deal to the workers. It hired and fired, gave them their orders, paid their wages. The party meant a good deal too. You could get a room through the party, get a new job, lodge complaints . . . The shop committee, however, did none of these things . . . it was almost dead. It did nothing to help defend workers against bureaucratic and over-enthusiastic administrators, and to ensure the enforcement of labour laws. . . . [40]

In 1934 the standing of the trade unions in the eyes of its members seems to have improved a little, in connection with the transfer of social insurance functions from the Commissariat of Labour (abolished in 1933) to the trade union apparatus.[41] But no sign has been found of any change in the alignment of forces within the *troika*. According to Kravchenko's recollections of the metal-working plant at Nikopol in 1935, the trade union chairman 'had more title than power. Since the trade union functionaries could not open their mouths, let alone make decisions, without permission from the Party, they were generally men of no importance . . . the chairman's influence was so negligible that any high official could afford to ignore him'.[42] With due allowance for colouring, our guess is that the situation was not dissimilar elsewhere.

The weak position of the trade union officials did not mean that violations of the labour code—for example, the use of illegal overtime and the neglect of safety precautions—would be entirely ignored. It has been shown already that in the case of industrial accidents the (usually less influential) ITR would often get the blame for neglect. But managers might on occasion be called to account in connection with other matters immediately affecting workers' interests. In one case managers were criticised because they 'are not interested in and do not know in what conditions the workers live, how their daily needs are satisfied',[43] in another because they were 'buried in technical and production questions at the expense of the workers'.[44] In a further instance Pyatakov, deputy Commissar of Heavy Industry, berated local party organs for having allowed management to 'completely ignore the living person on whom depends the fulfilment of the plan'.[45] But it is safe to infer that these criticisms appeared in the press when the enterprise was seriously lagging behind production targets and when managers had for this reason lost the support of their superiors. In the case mentioned by Pyatakov the connection is indeed explicit.

The only instance of a well-publicised dispute between the trade union and the industrial establishments in the 1930–35 period is instructive in this context. In December 1934 and again in April 1935, the Central Trade Union Council sent inspecting teams to the Red Profintern engineering plant in Bezhitsa. It published very critical reports on working conditions, especially on illegal overtime and absence of labour protection, which the trade union officials on the spot had been powerless to prevent. The managerial press responded by accusing the union of sabotaging production just when 'for the first time in years' the plant had overfulfilled its production programme. Subsequently, the union press recanted, the Central Committee published a resolution censuring the union and labour inspectorate involved, and a number of managers (not the director) were penalised for violation of the labour laws.[46] In this case the outcome was for some time uncertain because, it seems, there was no clear support from the industrial and party establishment for a management that had a bad record. But once the record improved, the trade union intervention began to look like sabotage rather than a defence of the 'living person on whom depended the fulfilment of the plan'.

6A (iii) THE PARTY 1930–35

The position of the enterprise party organisation was structurally different from the trade union, since it was asked to act as one link in the overall chain of party supervision over industrial production. The prescribed role of the party organisation was to 'help the administration in every way in the matter of fulfilling the *promfinplan*' and to focus its main attention on the 'political leadership of the masses'. This division of functions, according to the September 1929 decree on one-man management, 'presupposes the closest link, mutual assistance and the creation of a comradely atmosphere in work, excluding the possibility of a family atmosphere and the mutual covering up of one another'.[47]

Yet if party officials had the same objective as management and the party official's own performance was to be judged in the end by the same criteria, then it could be expected that the distinction between 'comradely' and 'family' relations would be difficult to sustain in practice. In May 1932, Kaganovich was urging enterprise party officials and managers to retain their separate identities, warning them 'not to cover one another up, not to create a family atmosphere'. 'Each,' he said, 'should be in his own place and at the same time together.'[48] This formula was not in the abstract illogical, since managers and party organisers had different tasks to fulfil in the common effort to meet production goals. But the critical faculties of the party organisers were naturally blunted by the way that their role was defined. This emerged especially clearly in campaign situations when enterprise party organisers together with their superiors might suffer for having in the past tolerated mismanagement or irregularities. Thus, in the case of the Donbass campaign in 1933, the press made much fuss about party officials who were resisting the effort to shake up the administration of the enterprise and to expose previous abuses.[49]

This is not to say that managers could ignore party secretaries, nor that the latter never interfered. 'Violations of one-man management' by the enterprise party officials was an occasional theme in the press in the early 1930s. At a party conference in Kuznetsk in 1930, the regional party secretary noted that 'up till now the main figure in the shop, and the head of production, has been the secretary of the party cell . . . But the real one man manager is still hiding somewhere in the shadows'.[50] It was said that party organisers were influencing the hire and fire of managerial personnel at the shop level, that shop managers and sometimes directors did not appoint ITR without party approval.[51] In February 1931, a VSNKh official said that the question of the director's right to nominate the shop management had yet to be 'finally solved'.[52] In November 1932, à *Pravda* report complained of continuing distortions of one-man management where enterprise party officials were exerting influence in 'administrative-economic matters and in the transfer of administrative-technical personnel'.[53] The ambiguity in the position of the party secretaries is thus again apparent. They were being asked not to stand aside from production problems, but if they started to encroach on managerial functions they were likely to be ticked off for meddling.

In a similar way, party criticism of engineers and technicians which before June 1931 might have been tolerated or even regarded as healthy proletarian criticism, would later very likely be defined as '*spets*-baiting'. It was suggested in the last chapter that despite the change in course in 1931, the ITR remained vulnerable to criticism from above and to some extent to criminal sanctions, if the enterprise was failing to meet expectations. In this situation, it was also tempting for plant party officials to assist attempts to single out rank and file specialists for blame, especially since in these circumstances enterprise directors might fail to support their subordinates.

For example at the Dzherzhinsky metallurgical plant '*spets*-baiting' was said to be the 'right attitude (*khoroshii ton*)'. Engineers who had done 'good rationalising work', according to the industrial press report, were being criticised by the party secretary and trade union chairman, who were also 'trying to prejudice workers against individual engineers and technicians'; at workers' meetings they would try to discredit the ITR and gave demagogic speeches 'in defence of the working class'. The party secretary was also hostile to young specialists, of whom he said: 'Young specialists have been let off the leash . . . We must shake off the arrogance from young specialists'.[54]

In January 1932 a comrades' court at the Kompressor factory

put a group of ITR on trial, while the enterprise paper launched an attack on wrecking activity by the technical personnel and their 'hostility to the working class'. Caricatures of the ITR as capitalist sharks, with striped trousers and oily hair, appeared in the paper, together with a demand that the ITR under trial should clear out of the factory. All this was described in the industrial paper as 'the logical conclusion of a system of persecution of ITR, creating for them intolerable conditions of work and putting all the blame on them for the complete failure of the past year . . . '. Subsequently a local court condemned the way in which the ITR had been cast as scapegoats and the way comrades' court had been set up. The raikom issued reprimands to the enterprise party and trade union officials involved, and to management which had allowed it to happen.[55]

In 1933, no doubt encouraged by the atmosphere of sabotage hunting in the Donbass at the time, a mine newspaper reported that 'the organisations and the worker collective of the Batitsky pit . . . unmasked a gang of counter-revolutionaries, white bandits (led by electrical technician B.) who, getting into positions of technical leadership, made every effort to put the pit out of action'.[56] In the same year there were accusations of wrecking against specialists at the mechanical shop at Uralmash. Referring to one of the engineers implicated the party secretary had said that 'we don't fulfil the production programme because we have such class enemies as engineer T.'. Later, the raikom published a resolution condemning 'the crudest violations of the party line by the party cell and the trade union committee . . . facts of persecution of specialists . . . groundless accusations of sabotage, threats of legal actions, violations of one-man management etc.'[57] A year later a serious fire at one of the Uralmash plants again brought dire accusations from the party secretary against a group of specialists and the discovery of a 'counter-revolutionary organisation . . . carrying out diversions under the direct instructions of foreign specialists, fulfilling the directives of a foreign machine-building firm'.[58]

In another case, at the time of the campaign against *brak*, it was reported that a young engineer L. at the Moscow Utilzavod had committed suicide after harassment by party and trade union officials. The exposure of a high percentage of defective output had been followed by a mock funeral, in which a coffin was draped with the inscription 'death to *brak*, death to the defective producer (*brakodel*) L.'. At the subsequent trial the party secretary got one year's corrective labour and the trade union chairman eight months, and the chairman of VMBIT said in the course of a prosecution speech: 'although in our country there are unprecedented opportunities for our engineers to exercise initiative, it must be understood once and for all that engineers and technicians alone, with all the will in the world, cannot do everything, if the *troika* does not give them the necessary help . . . '.[59]

From these examples we would draw the conclusion that in certain situations of crisis, the rank and file technical intelligentsia were vulnerable to criticism from below as well as from above, and the familiar 'class enemy' labels might make a reappearance. But it should be remembered that the party secretaries involved were penalised for their interventions (though they must initially have had support or tolerance from higher up). Also, it should be noted that the reporting of such cases in the press was always very favourable to the ITR, giving the impression that the ITR were the humble victims of irrational attacks. One is not told much about the background to such conflicts, nor what the specialists in question may have done to warrant their unpopularity with the party organisers. Perhaps the latter had not been treated with the respect they thought they deserved? It is in this way, at any rate, that one could interpret the remark of the party secretary about the arrogance of the young specialists who had been 'let off the leash'.

The occasional attacks from below on rank and file specialists did not, in any event, detract from a general strengthening of managerial authority in the early 1930s. The party secretary could not be ignored, since his role was potentially critical. But the impression is that as managerial confidence increased in this period, so the party organisers could be more easily restrained. According to the judgement of one prominent director in 1934, there were three types of manager: those who were 'isolated' from the party organisations, those who thought that the organisations were a 'necessary evil' with whom one had to carry on 'politics' and have as little unpleasantness as possible, and those who used the party as a 'blind weapon'. But none of these descriptions suggest that party organisers were likely to come into serious conflict with managers. This director was admittedly complaining that the party secretary often regarded himself 'not as a participant in the struggle for the plan' but as a 'directive or controlling organ'. Yet the yards of resolutions passed by the party 'immediately get thrown into the archives, because nobody has time to read them, let alone fulfil them'.[60] Even when the party tried to be a controlling organ, it succeeded in being no more than an irritant.

6B   THE ITR AND THE WORKERS

So far we have considered the changing conditions of Soviet industrial production as they affected the position of the ITR in relation to the enterprise organisations. Underlying the various attempts to reduce interference from below was the struggle to improve labour productivity and work discipline in general. In the late 1920s and early 1930s these efforts were being made under unusually unfavourable conditions. The conflict which is inherent in any attempt to extract relatively more effort for relatively less reward was exacerbated by the harsh conditions in which workers were obliged to live and work. The generally declining living standards, together with a rapid expansion of the workforce with fresh workers who lacked a taken for granted approach to factory discipline, produced an exceptional degree of dislocation and strain. The agencies of the state, as we have said, sought to overcome the effects of this strain through a variety of corporate and coercive responses. But the struggle also had direct implications for those sections of the technical intelligentsia who were asked to mediate between the state and the workers as agents of discipline in the production process itself. The object of this section is to look at some of the effects of these changes on the relationship between ITR and workers.

Briefly, it will be suggested that the pressures of an industrialisation drive in 'primitive' conditions and in an economic environment of crisis, were conducive to a tough style of management. Conflicts between workers and ITR, when they occurred, took an individualistic form and workers were in no position collectively to resist decisions about conditions of labour. At the same time, it will be argued that an image of unremittingly exacting managers or of unconditional subordination of industrial workers would be unfounded.

6B   (i)   SOURCES OF CONFLICT BETWEEN WORKERS AND ITR

During the period under review, the weakening of the trade unions allowed a general consolidation of the delegated powers of managers over the workforce This change was the result of pressure to increase the productivity of labour, which could be expected to create considerable tension. To judge from the Soviet press, relations between ITR and workers were most fraught, or at least the tensions were mostly overtly expressed, in the early phase of Soviet industrialisation, especially in the years 1928–9. This was a period of upward pressure on work norms and downward pressure on wage rates and living conditions. At the same time, the ITR were then experiencing the full effects of the political suspicion with which they were surrounded after the Shakhty affair. These circumstances together seem to have encouraged an unusual amount of overt antagonism. When workers gave vent to their disaffection they might incur the charge of '*spets*-baiting'. This was a general label which could be attached to any form of action against specialists that was currently defined as illegitimate. In the context of ITR/worker relations, it referred to some form of resistance by workers to the demands of shop managers and supervisors, or else to hostile behaviour to the technical staff. In the case of the technical staff, it was most often engineers in the work study departments (usually the 'technical norms bureaux') who were incurring the displeasure of the workers. Resistance and hostility could mean criticism, or grumbling, or abuse, or in some extreme cases physical attacks on foremen, technicians and engineers.

'*Spets*-baiting' in this sense was not a new phenomenon. As noted in Chapter 2, there were frequent injunctions during the NEP urging workers to develop better relations with the ITR. But the Shakhty affair, in this respect as in others, started a new phase. As soon as the Shakhty arrests were announced, there were official cautions against *spet*-baiting. In March 1928, a leading official of the Central Control Commission said that 'the task of the party is to restrain the masses from groundless *spets*-baiting'.[61] But relations between workers and specialists deteriorated, and in September 1928 a *Pravda* editorial complained that all specialists were being treated like enemies.[62] Relations were especially fraught in the Donbass. According to one managerial press report, 'the Shakhty affair hit Donugol like thunder' and 'the old ties [of managerial and technical personnel] with the masses, supported by routine or pressure, or a chance combination of forces, have been broken'.[63] In a speech in 1929, the secretary of the Shakhty party committee said that after the Shakhty affair 'the workers didn't trust anyone, even an honest specialist, they all took the view—specialists are our enemies, so attack them all (*posemy kroi vsekh*)'.[64]

In some cases, workers became involved in violent confrontations with specialists, often after refusing to carry out an order, or after a threat of disciplinary action. Reports of physical assaults on shop ITR and work study engineers appeared with some frequency in 1928 and 1929.[65] The relative incidence of actual violence in ITR – worker conflicts is difficult to judge, but the following isolated example may give some idea: in the first four months of 1929, in the pits of the Shakhtino mine administration, 460 disciplinary actions were taken for 'refusal to fulfil the directives of the administrative and technical personnel', and 71 for 'insults to the ATP'. Four of the latter were cases of violence.[66] But one should bear in mind that the absolute level of conflicts here was probably exceptionally high. It was said in the local party paper that in the Shakhty okrug '*spets*-baiting and refusal to work have become mass phenomena'.[67]

Managerial sources tended to highlight ITR – worker conflict, as part of the attempt to clamp down on worker 'hooliganism'. A VSNKh official talked about the 'avalanche of material' on this matter which came to the notice of VSNKh every day.[68] Some trade union reports also expressed concern. According to a VTsSPS investigation into the metal and coal industries, workers, union officials and specialists all attempted to hide the extent of conflict. Specialists feared loss of support if they told the truth, while trade union organisers were trying to smooth things over to demonstrate their success in combating *spets*-baiting.[69] An official of the textile workers' trade union claimed that information about attempts on the life of ITR did not get beyond the factory gates, since the ITS did not want to make specialists even more unpopular than they were already. Four such attempts in one textile plant between March 1928 and March 1929 were said to have been concealed for these reasons.[70]

However, trade union sources usually, when dealing with worker hostility to ITR, tried to define it as salutary criticism rather than persecution. Thus, in December 1928 a trade union investigation into the position of specialists in the Ukraine claimed that 'on the whole the attitude of the workers to the technical personnel has not changed after the Shakhty affair', but 'it is true that healthy proletarian mistrust on the part of the mass of workers, understood by some ITR as *spets*-baiting, has greatly increased and has on the whole taken correct forms'.[71] An editorial in the trade union paper said that 'demoralised workers who engage in hooliganism exist in every enterprise', but *spets*-baiting was not a 'mass phenomenon'.[72]

The party and trade union organisations were sometimes charged with condoning *spets*-baiting and turning a blind eye to worker abuse of the ITR. In 1928 the North Caucasus kraikom announced that 'leaders of party cells and trade union committees who do not decisively resist the expression of hostile attitudes towards specialists, let alone support such phenomena, must be replaced by more mature cadres',[73] and the Shakhty district party committee claimed that the trade union organisations 'often don't see or don't want to see *spets*-baiting, and insults against foremen go unpunished'.[74]

The intensity of ITR – worker conflict in this period, like other manifestations of unruliness, was officially explained in terms of the influx of new workers into industry. A Central Committee directive in February 1929, 'On maintaining labour discipline', instructed that 'special attention must be given to the link between the fall in labour discipline and the influx into production of new strata of workers mostly connected with the countryside . . . The most severe cases of violation . . . come precisely from these cadres of workers . . . '.[75] This last statement may have been true, although we do not have the information either to support or refute it. But it does not get one very far. It is a sociographic statement not a sociological explanation, saying nothing about the situation that produced the conflict. It may be more promising to look at the combined effect of two sets of circumstances: first, changing conditions of work in the broadest sense, and second, the political climate created by the offensive against the old generation specialists.

Among the first set of conditions the most important seems to have been the attempt to speed up production by raising work norms. This is suggested by the frequent involvement of work study engineers in ITR – worker conflicts at this time. According to a VSNKh official it was well known that 'rate-setting' engineers were the most liable to the attacks of 'disorganising elements'.[76] In one case reported in August 1929, when a work study engineer was beaten up in a textile factory, the trade union paper commented that 'under the influence of skilful propaganda by *kulaks* and self-seekers the workers directed all their dissatisfaction with economic breakdowns and the bungling of administrators against individual honest specialists'. As a result conflicts tended to be resolved by means of 'the knife, the fist, gossip and dawdling'. But the 'bungling', it transpired, was the attempt to transfer weavers from four machines to six, which was good for neither weavers nor machines, and was also threatening some workers with redundancy.[77]

Thus worker confrontation with engineers was in this context quite understandable. It was one form of struggle—no doubt a desperate one—over conditions of work, and in particular, over how much work to do for what reward. This argument would go on in one way or another, even without collective bargaining. But in the absence of possibilities for a collective response to changing conditions at work, resistance might be restricted to isolated confrontations with individual members of the managerial and technical staff.

It was clear too that the political environment after the Shakhty affair encouraged overt ITR – worker conflict because it brought, at least for a time, an atmosphere of tolerance towards worker hostility to specialists. Workers were able to answer back in the knowledge that specialists were in a vulnerable position. There were complaints that the ITR were taking the 'line of least resistance' in matters of work discipline, which was explained by one mining engineer as follows: 'We have gained the impression that if the workers like you, that is when you turn a blind eye to production matters, then you are all right, but if not, then they remove you for an "incorrect approach to the masses" '.[78] The party therefore quickly tried to put the record straight, in the directive of February 1929: 'In the eyes of a staunch class-conscious proletarian, good engineers and foremen are those who show technical initiative and . . . strictly carry out labour discipline, who are themselves models of discipline and demand unconditional discipline from those subordinate to them'.[79]

Thus the party authorities, not for the first time, found themselves confronting the unintended consequence of other political decisions. In one extreme case, after a shop head was assaulted by a worker, a local party newspaper wrote: 'Every attempt at mob law (*samosud*) against engineers, technicians and administrators is . . . the most grave crime against the revolution, for the proletarian masses are doing everything possible to ensure harmony between physical and mental workers, regarding the latter not as their servants, but as comrades . . . The blow delivered to the engineer's head is a blow to socialist construction'.[80]

But such injunctions could not conceal the fact that the conflict between physical and mental workers was partly a consequence of the party attitude itself. The party sought to strengthen the ITR as agents of discipline, but the political attack on the technical intelligentsia made it more difficult to do so. It was seen in Chapter 3 that the specialists were being urged to abandon their professional aloofness ('caste-spirit') and to join in the common struggle for production. Part of the thrust of this attack was to appeal to *proletarian* sentiments against *intellectual* ones: the specialists did not understand the workers, did not know how to talk to them and to gain their cooperation. The resulting pressures can be seen in a resolution of the 4th Congress of engineers and technicians in April 1929:

> in our conditions the ITR is a part of the working class. But at the same time it is the commanding and organising (*organizatorskii*) staff of the proletariat in production. Every engineer and technician must find in his work a harmonious combination between these two conceptions so that neither should suffer. In no measure is the weakening of the economic administration and directing (*rukovodiashchaya*) activity of the ITR permissible . . . But at the same time the ITR must take into account the social production relations of our economy, understand the position of the workers at the present time in the production process, know how correctly to utilise the creativity of the masses . . . All this requires a break with the individualist psychology of certain groups of engineers.[81]

In some sense, then, an appeal to workers against the intelligentsia formed part of the political offensive of the late 1920s. This seems to have found a ready response among workers, for reasons that would need a wider cultural analysis to be properly understood. This was how one engineer, from the 'Red Putilovets' plant, saw it in February 1929:

> We are going along the same road, but unfortunately not side by side. The October Revolution took away the divide between the engineer and the worker, but the imprint of the past that remains on the intellectual, including the technician, has not been completely overcome. The workers regard the engineer as a 'lord'

(*'barin'*), especially those elements from the countryside . . . who are coming into the enterprise . . . '.[82]

Also it seems to have been a common view among workers that the role of engineers in production was *parasitic*. Several statements were cited in the press which expressed, in very similar terms, the idea that engineers were an 'unnecessary expense'. As one worker put it, 'engineers are a superfluous overhead. They don't do anything, but only watch over the behaviour of the workers'.[83] It may have been this kind of view that explained the references to the continuing influence of 'Makhaevshchina', that is, the idea that the technical intelligentsia was not in any way productive, but was only an agent of exploitation.[84]

'Makhaevshchina' did not receive any official support. But the political appeal to proletarian sentiment, and the forms of worker participation—at least at the beginning of the industrialisation drive—looked impressive enough to be taken at face value by many specialists, and to offend some self-proclaimed professionals who had no desire to 'identify' with the proletariat. One engineer was reported to complain that the Soviet power had brought in the 'justice of the masses' by introducing wall newspapers, production conferences and other forms of worker participation.[85] Another specialist, while enthusiastic about the industrialisation effort, had this reservation: 'one cannot forgive the proletarian dictatorship for the humiliating conditions it has imposed on engineers and technicians . . . At a meeting a workman will get up and shout and gesticulate "we workers . . .". It is perfectly obvious that the man is an ignorant fool . . . yet one can't answer him, for he is the boss'.[86] In similar vein, an interview with an engineer in 1930 elicited the following remarks: shock-work was a good idea, but 'if tomorrow a shock-worker gets up before the mine committee or the party cell or before the raikom and starts trying to direct us, then not a trace will be left of these feelings. Uncultured workers don't have the right to teach me my job'.[87]

There was, then, a certain tension between the demand for a subordination to the ITR as agents of discipline, and on other hand the quasi-populist appeals to workers that formed part of the attack on the professional self-esteem of the technical intelligentsia.

6B (ii) MANAGERIAL AUTHORITY AND MANAGERIAL STYLES
1930–35

After 1929, there were far fewer reports of ITR – worker conflict of the kind described above. They did recur, and these cases were apparently connected with attempts to increase labour productivity by changing established patterns of work. This was especially clear in 1933, in connection with the revision of work norms in that year. It was reported that 'revision of quotas met with considerable resistance from class-hostile elements, grabbers, and loafers. Numerous sorties of class enemies have been recorded, directed at hampering fulfilment of the plan to increase productivity. These sorties were of various kinds: now threats against technical norms bureaux employees, now clever showdowns, sabotage of timekeeping, propaganda against quota revision etc . . . '.[88]

Thus the attempt to extract more effort from the rapidly growing body of industrial workers met with some resistance. But the impression is that during the first half of the 1930s the relationship between management and workers became less overtly fraught and that there was less questioning of managerial decisions. The evidence for this is in part purely negative: the relative absence of discussion about the problem in the press. But some more positive indications may also be found. In November 1932 a trade union official was able to claim that 'by and large the conditions under which the engineer or technician can feel that he is master *(khozyain)* in the shop . . . have been created'.[89] In 1934 a shop manager wrote that although 'three to four years ago' it was common for workers to answer back and argue with supervisors, this was no longer the case.[90] In the same year, at a conference of heavy industry managers, one director said in this connection that 'recently the role of the director has been very greatly strengthened and his authority has increased',[91] while another said that shopheads too had become 'leading central figures'.[92] In February 1935 a prominent manager said that 'if in the distant past the daily struggle for elementary discipline was at the centre of our work, now this work has been significantly eased, because the struggle for discipline is being carried out by the working masses themselves'.[93]

If manager – worker conflict became less visible by the mid-1930s, this change could be accounted for in a number of ways. Partly it could be explained by the role of the law enforcement agencies. They were now giving more backing to managers in disputes over dismissal—though there were still complaints that the courts were being too lenient in such cases.[94] Moreover, the changes in the *troika* meant that party and trade union organisations were themselves playing a more active role in bringing pressure to bear on deviant workers, and could no longer to the same extent act as a channel of appeal against managerial decisions. Also, the change in policy towards the technical intelligentsia in 1931 may have made it more difficult to challenge the authority of the ITR.

But these explanations are insufficient, since to leave it at that would be to rest on the assumption that manager – worker conflict was simply suppressed by exercising sanctions for deviant behaviour. This does not take into account the fact that there was a pattern of managerial indulgence which modified the consequences of the efforts by the state to raise labour productivity. This pattern of indulgence, which was quite compatible with a rough and 'rude' managerial style, can be inferred from the criticisms to which managers were themselves subjected by the central authorities. For example, managers were not enthusiastic when under pressure to revise work norms. On occasion there was tension here between engineers working in the rate-setting departments and line managers, with the latter defending existing norms. But usually, it was said, the 'technical norms' engineers became 'instruments' in the hands of management and did what they were told.[95] In connection with the revision of work norms in 1933 there were complaints about overspending on wages, and dire warnings to managers against any such attempts to 'plunder state funds'.[96] Clearly, management was not necessarily keen to force through a change in the wage – effort relationship if this meant holding down the earnings of workers.

This reluctance need not be seen as altruistic. It was partly a reflection of the shortage of labour and the fear that norm revision would create difficulties in maintaining a stable labour force. Further, the job of revision was very complicated, and the possible reduction in labour costs may not have been sufficient to spur managers into action.[97] But also, as already suggested, managers had to face informal pressure from workers to keep the norms down, and this pressure could not be entirely ignored.

Managers were also criticised for not making use of all the administrative rights to which they were entitled in the struggle against various infractions of work regulations, especially in connection with absenteeism.[98] It appears that there was to some extent a tacit acceptance of poor discipline, since managers often saw it as more important to hold onto labour rather than create further uncertainty through dismissals.

The managers did not, then, always meticulously carry out their role as agents of discipline. In April 1931 Ordzhonikidze complained to a meeting of ITR at the Stalingrad tractor factory that the ITR were 'trying to make everyone happy': 'If in such a lax factory one works on the basis that everyone should be kept happy, nothing will come of this. Here we need strong leadership. One must go and say: "Go to your place and work". Today a worker will swear at you, but in two days he will himself see the results of his action'.[99] In 1934, he was speaking in similar terms to a group of engineers just graduating from the Industrial Academy:

> You must, comrades, bring a cultured method of work into our factories . . . and a decisive struggle . . . against lax discipline . . . Very often we [*khozyaistvenniki*] and sometimes even our engineers think like this: order, discipline, culture . . . this is a matter for the bourgeoisie. We are all workers, we have a workers' power, why should we push people around ['*chevo nam lyudei tyanut*'] . . . this is the prattle of people who understand nothing . . .[100]

It is doubtful that the instruction to bring a more 'cultured' method of work into Soviet factories had much effect. In some cases the new generation engineer – managers, with more education and a more professional self-image, did try to follow this injunction. For example, in the case of the Donbass campaign of 1932–3 already discussed, one of the major tasks of the engineers who were sent in to revive metal and coal production, was to improve labour productivity by introducing a more rigorous labour regime. They proposed to do this by bringing more culture into manager – worker relations. One engineer complained in 1932 that 'swearing (*ruganie*) has been turned into a system and must be replaced by technical directives (*technicheskie ukazaniya*)'.[101] In 1933 another engineer explained that the model manager was 'a leader, a teacher of the workers who at the same time is able to learn from the workers himself . . . an experienced, hard administrator, and a real organiser of the worker masses . . . '. But, he said, 'pressure isn't enough, one must make people use their heads (*malo nazhat', nado i pomozgovat*)'.[102] In 1934, Pyatakov (deputy Commissar of NKTP) was asking for a similar change: 'formal subordination' was a necessary but not a sufficient condition of work discipline; only if the manager had 'mastered technique' would he be really authoritative for his subordinates, since he would then be able to 'explain and clarify an order'.[103]

What we see here is an appeal for a more cultured approach to management—that is, less *ruganie*—as a means of securing a more effective control over the labour process. What was wanted was a style of management that would be both less rude and less permissive: 'cultured' workers were those who accepted managerial decisions as rational, and therefore needed to be neither browbeaten nor indulged. But for the most part this remained, we suspect, an exhortation that did not correspond to an actual shift in managerial style. The atmosphere of the 'war' on the industrial front remained conducive to 'pressure' rather than 'using one's head'. A quieter style of management would have to await quieter times.

6C CONCLUSIONS

The relations between the technical intelligentsia on the one hand and the workers and mass enterprise organisations on the other, were shaped within the context of a 'primitive' state-dominated accumulation in which continuous efforts were being made by the state to secure a more disciplined and predictable workforce as a condition for increasing the productivity of labour and meeting the pressing production targets embodied in the plan. This had major consequences for the role of managers and of the mass organisations, for the manner in which conflict between workers and ITR was expressed, and for the styles of managerial direction.

To begin with, there was a change in the balance of power within the *troika* of management, trade union and party, whereby the triangle was in effect reduced to a twosome (*dvoika*) of management and party. During the NEP the trade union organisers had, by and large, acquiesced in managerial efforts to raise labour productivity. But managerial decisions could be successfully challenged. In 1928–29, under the heavy pressure of demands to increase output, raise work norms and reduce production costs, there were protests by the industrial establishment about trade union interference in 'operational' decisions, and in the appointment of ITR at the lower levels of the hierarchy. As a result, the attempt to 'concentrate all the threads of administration' in the hands of management was now taken a stage further. This change was officially justified either in terms of the need for a 'merciless economy of resources' or—and this was a different argument—in terms of changing technological conditions which were incompatible with a 'many-centred administrative power'.

The assumptions underlying these arguments did not go without challenge, but the actual trend was undoubtedly towards a strengthening of managerial authority in relation to the trade unions. The role of the enterprise party organisation was differently defined, since it was asked to act as one link in the chain of party supervision over industrial production. The party had a potentially critical role which meant that it could not be ignored in the sense that the trade union could. But enterprise party officials did not usually come into conflict with management: since they were asked to assist in the implementation of the plan, it was difficult to give a real content to the distinction that they were asked to maintain between 'comradely' and 'family' relations.

The strengthening of managerial authority did not mean, however, that there was an unconditional subordination of workers to the ITR. First, although the possibilities of a collective response to management demands were excluded, this could not eliminate workers' individual reactions to their situation, some of which took the form of the various phenomena labelled as '*spets*-baiting'.

Second, if manager–worker conflict was less visible after 1930 than in the earliest phase of industrial expansion, this was not simply due to the suppression of conflict through the exercise of sanctions. There was also a pattern of managerial indulgence, quite compatible with a rough style of direction, which brought complaints against managers that they were not doing enough to implement changes in work norms, that they were overspending on wages and generally being lax with unruly workers. Managerial behaviour in this context therefore modified the drastic effects of the 'merciless economy of resources' on the conditions in which workers lived and worked.

Third, the ITR remained to some extent vulnerable to criticism from below. The conditions under which they might be subjected to this pressure were not a result of the workers' choice. It was likely to occur when managers and technicians were under criticism from above because the performance of the enterprise was consistently failing to match up to expectations. But the existence of this potential lever meant that the party leadership was able to retain a link with the workers over the heads of its managerial representatives.

7 Material and Symbolic Privileges

In this chapter we shall try to get a picture of the relative material position of the technical intelligentsia as compared with the industrial workers, and later add some remarks on the hierarchy of 'social honour'. The question of distribution of income and other material rewards is not to be confused—though it often is—with an analysis of social or power relations, which have been the main object of this study. The two sorts of phenomena (distributive and relational) may of course be closely connected since, for example, the pattern of income distribution is likely to depend on the power of a group to defend a certain standard of living, or to establish the criteria by which certain types of work will be better rewarded than others. But a statement about relative living standards is not a statement about social relations.

The available evidence from which to construct an account of the material position of the technical intelligentsia—whether in monetary or non-monetary terms—is unfortunately slender. Still, the information is sufficient to show that in the early 1930s material distribution increasingly favoured the ITR as against manual workers, although 'ITR' and 'workers' were both umbrella categories within which there was in turn a considerable differentiation.

7A MONETARY REWARDS

During the NEP period, monetary income differentials between workers and ITR seem to have increased by comparison with the civil war period, but so far as is known not to any great extent. The figures in Table 13 give some indication of the change between 1924 and 1926, in three selected industries:

TABLE 13: *Monthly earnings of shop managers and workers in transport specialised machine tools and metallurgy*

	Average monthly earnings of heads of shops and departments (chervonets rubles)	No. times greater than the average earnings of	
		unskilled workers	skilled workers
1924	148.8	4.6	1.4
1925	166.7	4.8	1.7
1926	235.6	5.2	2.4

Source: *Vestnik Truda* (1927) no. 2, p. 26.

In the chemical industry, between 1918 and 1927, the relative change as between 'workers' and 'engineers' was as follows (Table 14):

TABLE 14: *Monthly earnings of workers and engineers: chemical industry*

	Workers	Engineers	No. times greater than workers' earnings
1918 (pre-revolution rubles)	7.3	10.8	1.5
1925–26 (chervonets rubles)	62.6	153.0	2.4
1926–27 (chervonets rubles)	72.0	200.0	2.7

Source: *Inzh. Trud* (1929), no. 8, p. 229.

Between 1926 and 1928, as shown in Table 15, the earnings of heads of shops and departments in relation to manual workers' earnings, changed in the following way (in selected industries):

TABLE 15: *Average monthly earnings of heads of shops and departments (per cent of average workers' earnings)*

Industry	1926	1927	1928
Engineering	344	320	309
Metallurgy	376	358	364
Coal	352	396	397
Textiles	408	381	379

Sources: *Inzh. Trud* (1929), no. 8, p. 226; *Trud v SSSR* (1936), pp. 110, 139, 156, 189.

These changes in the relative income of some ITR jobs, which are mentioned here only as a bare indicator of a trend, were not conspicuous, and in many cases seem to have been reversed after 1926. But after 1928 the trend towards a relative monetary privilege for the ITR became quite marked, and by the mid-1930s the enterprise ITR were considerably better off in relation to workers than they had been at the beginning of the industrialisation drive. In conditions of rationing (introduced in 1929 and fully removed only in 1935–6), with a severe overall shortage of consumer goods and with shifting non-monetary privileges, the importance of monetary differentials was necessarily limited. Direct allocation of scarce goods and benefits was in such a situation at least as important. In what follows we look at pay differentials, and in the next section go on to discuss the non-monetary material position of the ITR.

Some impression of income differentials between ITR and workers between 1928 and 1935 can be gained from Central Statistical Administration figures. Until 1932 annual earnings data are available only for ITR and employees (*sluzhashchie*) taken together. However, two special wage studies carried out in March 1928 and October 1934 enable one to compare the earnings of selected occupations within the ITR between the two years.[1] The annual figure were as follows (Table 16).

TABLE 16: *Average monthly earnings of workers ITR and employees (rubles)*

	Workers	ITR	Employees
1928	69	123	
1929	75	134	
1930	83	152	
1931	96	175	
1932	115	303	173
1933	126	341	190
1934	147	379	209
1935	185	437	234

Source: *Trud v SSSR* (1936), p. 96.

These figures are of limited value, even after 1931, since they do not differentiate within the ITR or worker category, nor between industries. On the basis of the special surveys in 1928 and 1934, covering 20 industries, a somewhat clearer picture emerges. The roughly comparable occupational categories covered are, in the

1928 study; (a) foreman (b) shop and department heads (a single figure for the two combined); in the 1934 study, (a) foremen (b) shop heads (c) department heads and chief engineers (a single figure for the two combined). The average earnings of these categories combined were somewhat higher (between seven and ten per cent) than the average earnings of ITR as a whole, and the inclusion of chief engineers in 1934 must to some extent distort the comparison. But the general trend is clear. First, one may compare the average earnings of ITR (based on an average of the selected occupations) with the earnings of skilled and unskilled workers. Five industries are selected for comparison in Table 17, including the industries with the highest and lowest differentials (ferrous metallurgy and clothing respectively):

TABLE 17: *Average monthly earnings of ITR as a percentage of earnings of fitters and unskilled workers*

| | Fitters | | Unskilled workers | |
	March 1928	October 1934	March 1928	October 1934
Ferrous metallurgy	241.7	327.7	416.1	590.6
Power stations	205.8	240.3	417.7	487.2
Coal	242.9	288.8	477.2	605.3
Rubber	135.1	167.8	210.3	346.4
Clothing	120.5	133.8	277.9	259.8

Source: M. Yanowitch, 'Trends in differentials between salaried personnel and wage workers in Soviet industry', p. 235.

Let us now look at the earnings of the separate ITR categories on which the figures above are based (Table 18), and compare these with the earnings of skilled and unskilled workers (a few figures on earnings in May 1935 are also included).

The figures so far cited indicate that the ITR/worker differential increased over the period, and that the range of ITR earnings was wider, as between different industries, than the range of worker earnings. The increase in ITR earnings was most marked in the priority sectors of heavy industry. Thus, between 1931 and 1933, the percentage increase in average ITR earnings in coal and ferrous metallurgy was 222 and 187 respectively; in textiles and canning, 155 and 139 respectively.[2] The extent of variation in earnings at the

TABLE 18: *Average monthly earnings of ITR and workers (rubles)*

	March 1928[a]	October 1934[b]	May 1935[b]
Ferrous metollurgy			
Department heads	{ 264	677	–
Shop heads		827	1139
Shift engineers	–	–	740
Foremen	175	517	525
Skilled workers	90	191	{ 209
Unskilled workers	52	106	
Power stations			
Department heads	{ 251	610	688
Shop heads		614	895
Shift engineers	–	–	707
Foremen	256	459	566
Skilled workers	123	221	{ 217
Unskilled workers	61	109	
Coal			
Department heads	{ 246	550	–
Shop heads		625	–
Foremen	145	382	438
Skilled workers	71	197	{ 213
Unskilled workers	36	94	
Rubber			
Department heads	{ 312	556	–
Shop heads		543	–
Foremen	185	312	–
Skilled workers	158	227	–
Unskilled workers	101	110	–
Clothing			
Department heads	{ 169	342	–
Shop heads		311	–
Foremen	135	226	–
Skilled workers	117	198	–
Unskilled workers	51	102	–

Source: [a]M. Yanowitch, op. cit. pp. 248–51; [b]*Trud v SSSR* (1936) pp. 105, 112, 147.

end of the period, both between different industries and within the ITR category, is suggested by Table 19 for July 1935.

The official figures on ITR earnings are broadly speaking in tune with the occasional information on individual plants that may be found in other sources. However, the official figures do not reveal the full range of variation. To take a few isolated examples. As early as 1929, in the asbestos mining industry, the earnings of engineers

TABLE 19: *Distribution of ITR average monthly ruble earnings: July 1935 (per cent)*

Industries	Up to 220	221–300	301–380	381–460	461–540	541–620	621–700	701–860	861–1100	More than 1100
Ferrous metallurgy	4.8	9.6	16.2	16.2	14.9	10.4	7.4	8.8	6.3	5.4
Coal	3.9	16.2	27.9	15.6	10.8	7.3	7.0	6.3	3.2	1.8
Power stations	2.5	11.7	20.1	21.3	16.3	11.4	6.3	6.4	3.2	0.8
Textile	14.3	23.3	24.1	15.3	10.2	5.8	2.9	2.8	1.0	0.3
Shoe	12.8	30.6	27.5	15.0	7.9	3.6	1.2	1.2	0.2	0.0

Source: *Trud v SSSR*, (1936). p. 83.

were 'up to eight times' the average worker's wage.[3] At Magnitogorsk in 1933, basic rates were approximately as follows (in rubles per month)[4]:

Unskilled workers	100
Skilled worker's apprentice	200
Skilled workers	300
Inexperienced engineer	400–500
Experienced engineer	600–800
Administrators, directors, etc.	800–3000

At the end of 1934 and the beginning of 1935, the basic rates in one of the Magnitogorsk shops were approximately as follows (in rubles per month)[5]:

Unskilled workers	120
Foremen	550
Shift engineers, master mechanics and electricians	800
Assistants to shop head	1000
Shop head	1200

The basic ITR rates were frequently boosted by bonus payments for plan overfulfilment, and were boosted by a higher proportion for the top categories within the ITR. Thus, we are told that at the Magnitogorsk shop mentioned, ITR often received two to three times' their basic salaries (in 1934–35) but only occasionally did earnings drop below the basic rate.[6] Magnitogorsk may provide an extreme instance of differentiation in earnings, because it was unmistakably a priority enterprise and because of its peripheral location. But other sources suggest that even in more centrally located enterprises, the ratio of unskilled workers' earnings to the earnings of top enterprise officials (in the mid-1930s) might reach 1 to 15,[7] or 1 to 20,[8] even as low as 1 to 80.[9] These figures do not refer to basic rates, but include incentive payments, which for the vast majority of ITR took the form of progressive bonuses, by contrast with the piece-rates which during the first Five-Year plan period had become the dominant form of wage payment for manual workers. There was some discussion in 1933 around a proposal to introduce piece-rates for the ITR, but against this it was argued that such a system would be very difficult to carry out in practice, since the engineer did not produce things, but organised the production of things.[10] Piece-rates for ITR were introduced in a few industries in 1933–34, notably in some metallurgical plants.[11] But these were exceptional cases. Bonuses, which included also the occasional windfall when projects or special assignments were completed, were the principal form of 'wage-drift' in the case of the ITR. Furthermore, it should be noted that after August 1931, income tax for salaries above 500 rubles a month was set at a flat rate of 3.5 per cent, so that almost all of the 'extras' were retained.[12]

The handsome monetary rewards for some ITR jobs did not prevent continuing complaints in the industrial press about the inadequate earnings of the ITR. Such complaints were already much in evidence in the 1928–31 period, but became more noisy after Stalin's highly publicised attack on *uravnilovka* (levelling) in 1931. This response, the possible reasons for which will be considered below, must be seen in the context of the wide variation in earnings between ITR occupations at different levels of the hierarchy, and in the context of the attempt to improve the position of the most modest ITR jobs in relation to manual labour. But it was a clear indication of the official commitment to a 'bourgeois' mode of distribution, which made possible the considerable material rewards of a managerial or engineering career. In 1928, a party official had said that 'we cannot pay the specialists as much as the capitalists do, because with us the specialists cannot be an instrument of capitalist exploitation . . . and because we do not want to create a special top stratum (*osobaya verkhushka*)'.[13] Yet the effect of the subsequent changes was undoubtedly to create such a *verkhushka*.

7B   NON-MONETARY MATERIAL PRIVILEGES

In the trend towards a greater material differentiation, access to scarce goods through a mechanism of direct allocation was perhaps as important as money. In particular, especially after 1931, the ITR had access to better housing, to special retail shops and to separate eating places. In a situation of acute shortage of consumer goods and living space, these were crucial benefits which offset, or at least softened, the impact of the material hardships of the first half of the 1930s.

The first steps in the direction of improving conditions for the ITR were taken in 1930, when a number of party and government directives placed ITR working in production on an equal footing with workers in the allocation of rations, housing space and the distribution of social insurance.[14] In these respects workers previously had a formal advantage over the ITR, though this did not mean that before this date workers had more to eat or more space to live in.

The 1930 measures were apparently not always implemented, since in November Narkomtrud complained of the 'crudest violations of party and government directives' aimed at improving living conditions for the ITR.[15] It was only in the following year, as part of the campaign against *uravnilovka*, that one detects a clear change in this respect. A party and government decree of August 1931. 'On improving the living conditions of ITR' restated, among things, ITR rights in relation to rations and living space. The decree was given more publicity than the previous measures, and was apparently more actively enforced. At a meeting in Moscow in September 1931, attended by officials from the procuracy, economic organs, local soviets and housing and supply agencies, ITS representatives complained that there was still a '*spets*-baiting' attitude in the housing trusts and supply organs, and the Moscow procuracy asked to be informed about violations of the August directive.[16] In December 1931 a Commissariat of Justice official said that 'we must bring all the force of revolutionary law down on those who try to undermine the policy of concern for specialists with a "policy" of infringement and bureaucratic pettifoggery'.[17] In 1932 (but not later) one may still find complaints in the press that in some areas local officials were adopting a 'formal approach' to the 1931 decree.[18] But violations were publicised and guilty officials were brought to trial.[19]

In addition to these measures, in 1931 and 1932 restricted shops and eating places were introduced for the benefit of ITR,[20] and credits were assigned for the construction of cooperative housing for specialists.[21] Not all of the funds allocated for ITR housing were in fact used, but it was reported that by 1934 living conditions for ITR had very much improved, and that by 1934 separate eating arrangements for specialists had been introduced in almost all enterprises.[22] Special stores for ITR were apparently abolished in 1935, when rationing of most goods was abolished, although such stores were retained for top party and state officials.[23] But by that time the relative improvement in ITR salaries clearly gave specialists an advantage when purchasing goods at 'commercial prices' in the open stores.

Non-monetary advantages, like monetary ones, were unequally distributed between different categories within the ITR. The position of the top managers and engineers seems often to have been quite luxurious compared with the workers or even the rank-and-file ITR. Kravchenko, who progressed from the factory bench to some of the highest managerial positions, writes: 'My standards of life were modest, even bleak, when compared to those men in my position in America. But in Nikopol, Taganrog, Pervouralsk or even Moscow they were so far above the average, so remote from the working class level, that I seemed to live in a world apart'.[24] At Magnitogorsk, the director, sub-directors and chief engineers (together with the party and police chiefs) lived in opulent multistorey houses, while the manager of a shop would typically live in a three-room flat, and the majority of the workers in barracks.[25] There seems little doubt that Magnitogorsk, again, provided an extreme case of differentiation. But it may be seen as symptomatic of a trend which was especially striking in the context of an overall decline in living standards in the early 1930s.

Some of the changes in the relative material position of the ITR in the first six to seven years of Soviet industrial expansion have been outlined above. The problem then arises how to account for these developments. This is a difficult question which needs more investigation than has been possible in the present study. The suggestions that immediately come to mind may look platitudinous. That does not make them wrong, but they need more demonstration.

First, one may to some extent account for the changes in terms of the scarcity of technically qualified people. Even in the absence of a free labour market, there were apparently strong 'market' pressures towards greater differentiation in wage and salary scales.

Second, there is no doubt that the relatively high ITR earnings and other perquisites, like the rewards that went to the labour 'aristocracy' (the shock-workers), were seen as an effective incentive to stay on the job. Thus, 'abnormalities' in pay and living conditions, as well as the heterogeneity in salaries as between different trusts or even enterprises, were cited as important reasons for the high turnover among specialists,[26] and the campaign against rapid turnover among the ITR was closely linked to the official pressure for an improvement in their material position.[27]

Again, the erosion of so-called *uravnilovka* was seen as the most effective, if not the only stimulus to more productive work; continuing criticisms of *uravnilovka*, especially as between the more modest ITR jobs and skilled manual labour, often accompanied appeals for greater productivity.[28]

Material differentiation was also intended as an incentive to training, and as a means of placing the most 'talented' in the most 'important' positions. The main rationale behind Stalin's appeal in 1931 for greater differentials among manual workers, namely that 'the unskilled worker is not interested in transferring to more skilled work, and is deprived of perspectives of advancement',[29] was extended to the industrial work-force as a whole. Whether or not this time-honoured justification for material inequalities was well grounded is a matter that needs pursuing. In the present context it can only be said that by all appearances such a rationale was present in the formulation of wage and salary policy.

However, references to scarcity and incentives to training or to greater productive effort seem inadequate because it is just in such terms that the better-off tend to legitimate their privileges, and because in many cases—above all perhaps in ITR jobs—the criteria for determining a greater or lesser contribution were quite unclear. It is therefore tempting to say, even if the conventional considerations retain some explanatory status, that the rulers used the political determination of income distribution in order to strengthen the loyalty of the technical intelligentsia to the state. The material privileges were, in the words of one manager, a 'gift of the state',[30] and could thus provide one sort of condition for political compliance.

Finally, it should be said that if the material privileges of the technical intelligentsia were a gift of the state, they were not a source of political influence in relation to the state. Material privilege was one of the perquisites of authority, but it was not a basis for that authority. The disjunction between material privilege and political power is perhaps most vividly demonstrated by the case of the engineers condemned for sabotage. Despite their prisoner status, they appear to have been given every material advantage, whether working directly under police supervision or leading a near-normal working life with certain restrictions.[31] They were put in cages, and were well fed inside them. One contemporary observer was so struck by the change in tone of official policy towards the specialists in 1931, in particular by the material rewards that were now promised to the technical intelligentsia that he concluded that 'the communist bureaucracy was preparing itself to share with the engineers the monopoly of power it held in the name of the working class'.[32] But such a conclusion was unwarranted. Sharing power and living well were not the same thing, and no immediate inferences could be drawn from one about the other.

7C SOME REMARKS ON 'SOCIAL HONOUR'

The change in the relative material position of the ITR was accompanied by a less tangible change in the official perceptions of the ranking of social honour. This trend was to become more marked at the end of the decade, but was already clearly visible by the mid-1930s. It involved an official effort to establish social legitimacy for intelligentsia functions, a legitimacy which they had to some extent lacked in the period since the October revolution. For one of the effects of the revolution was to downgrade the intelligentsia in the official ranking of social honour in favour of the industrial workers, and more particularly in favour of political officialdom, which continued to project a self-image as the vanguard of the working class.

The revolution had downgraded the intelligentsia not only in this sense. It had also tended to legitimate a social antagonism towards the intelligentsia, which appears to have had strong roots, in the prerevolutionary period, among the peasantry and the workers and within the party itself. The party leadership attempted to some extent to discourage expressions of hostility towards the intelligentsia after the revolution, on the grounds that the intelligentsia had a vital role to play in restoring Soviet industry and in maintaining cultural activity. In the case of the ITR, this pressure was evident in the party injuctions against '*spets*-baiting' during the decade after the revolution, which were aimed both at local political officials and at workers on the shop floor.

Such injunctions were frequently reiterated during the campaign of 1928–31. But that campaign, as we have seen, encouraged the expression of popular anti-*spets* sentiment, even if this was not usually the intention. It is only at the end of this period that one detects a clear reorientation in favour of the technical intelligentsia in the officially defined hierarchy of social honour, when the party became less ambiguous in its attitude towards anti-*spets* behaviour. Stalin's assertion in 1931 that 'the working class must create its own production-technical intelligentsia', since 'no ruling class has managed without its own intelligentsia',[33] can be interpreted at one level as a defence of the intelligentsia as a social category *per se*. It seems to have been directed against the notion that the intelligentsia as such had a questionable role in a post-capitalist society. In 1928, Stalin's assertion in 1931 that 'the working class must create its own acquire 'culture' and move into the ranks of the intelligentsia:

> There are people who are prepared to applaud our lack of culture . . . If you have managed to climb out of your lack of culture, if you have become literate and have mastered science then you are an alien, you have 'torn yourself away' from the masses, have ceased to be a worker . . . the working class cannot become a real master (*khozyain*) of the country . . . if it has not mastered science and is not able to direct the economy on the basis of science.[34]

The view criticised here still had its adherents in the 1930s. And there was still talk of 'Makhaevshchina'—'Makhaevschina', said a party theoretician in 1931, 'still has an influence among the working class', and he found it necessary to argue that the members of the technical intelligentsia had a legitimate function in socialist as well as capitalist society.[35]

One can conclude from these references that the need was felt to legitimate, as an enduring feature of post-revolutionary society, the social division between mental and manual labour. This division, in the context of industrial production, was 'inherited' from capitalist forms of organisation. During industrial expansion and technological reconstruction, western technology and western work tasks were taken over readymade. Soviet industrial expansion involved a new form of industrial organisation in the sense that a system of directive planning was established. But neither the division of work tasks nor the forms of training made it possible to challenge the customary definitions of the tasks of engineer, technician and worker. Workers were encouraged to train, and it became easier to move from one industrial job to another. But this is a separate point. The question of conditions of recruitment to the different occupations is of course different from the question of how the occupational roles were defined.

Thus the shift in the position of the technical intelligentsia in the official ranking of social honour was linked to the attempt to legitimate the social division between mental and manual labour, which if anything was reinforced in the conditions of industrial expansion. After 1931, especially, there were constant reminders that the ITR were legitimate, indeed exceptionally worthy, actors in socialist reconstruction. By the mid-1930s, industrial organisers and engineers, for all their insecurity, had attained, together with some categories of workers, something of the position of state heroes.

This shift was reinforced by the emergence of a heavily technical culture. The education system became highly orientated towards industry and technology, and the vast majority of new intellectuals in the 1930s were *technicians* in the broadest sense. Soviet culture in the 1930s embodied an ideal which in effect, if not intention, was the polar opposite of the all-round 'cultured' intellectual (the 'Renaissance man'). Bukharin, in a piece published in 1934, described the position as follows:

We now often meet people who are perfectly at home in technology and in the corresponding fields of the exact sciences, but who do not have the least idea of ancient Greek tragedy, or of 'Young Germany' or even of Pisarev, Dobrolyubov and Chernyshevsky. They are often ignorant of the most elementary historical facts. In a word, not a trace of 'classical' education is left. The hero of the day is the inventor—the technician—the shock-worker. This is the 'cultural style' of the period we are going through. . . .[36]

This tendency was indeed so strong that it also drew the cultural intelligentsia into the technical orbit: to write the industrial novels of the 1930s, writers might be compelled to acquaint themselves with technique and production. What Stalin called 'engineers of soul' became vicarious engineers in the literal sense.

The growing hegemony of a technical culture was not simply a Soviet phenomenon. All modern technical systems produce their own kinds of intellectuals whose formation is different from that of the 'literary intellectuals' of the past and is closely bound up with technical education.[37] This trend was already very marked in the West in the 1920s and was one of the sources of the fascination with technocracy as an image of the future evolution of capitalist societies. Veblen, who produced the first well-known modern version of the technocratic idea, was specifically concerned with the economic waste engendered by entrepreneurial capitalism, and proposed as a remedy a change in personnel: the professional engineer ought to be the decision-maker in modern industrial societies.[38] But the technocratic idea was also grounded in a cultural shift in which, to take Otto Bauer's formulation, ' . . . the engineer is becoming the hero of the new generation . . . traditional humanist cultural values are not in a position to compete with the technical mode of thought'.[39]

Bauer's remarks were a response to a general tendency in advanced industrial societies. Yet conditions in the USSR in the 1930s, given the rapid industrial expansion and the accompanying famine in cadres, were especially conducive to the emergence of a technical culture in which the technical intelligentsia, given the prevailing division of labour, appeared as the main beneficiaries. Stalin's slogan 'cadres decide everything' (launched in 1935),[40] was the perfect expression of this trend, and showed also the tenacity of received conceptions of the social division between mental and manual labour.

8 Conclusions

In these final remarks, the threads of the argument are drawn together and the main conclusions set out. The object of the study has been to throw light on some elements of social change during Soviet reconstruction by examining the relationship between the technical intelligentsia and the state. The general assumption at the outset was that Soviet reconstruction involved important shifts in the mode of state domination which were conditioned by the effort to establish certain forms of control over industrial and agricultural production. These processes meant putting politics in command in the sense that the transformation was the result of a state-initiated solution to the contradictions of the NEP, and in the sense that the scope of activity of political agencies was greatly extended. The emphasis, then, has been on the consequences of a process of transformation. This is not to argue that the emergence of the 'Stalinist' state in the 1930s can be accounted for solely in terms of the social upheavals involved in industrial expansion and col-lectivisation. The fact that a 'revolution from above' was possible at all suggests that in one sense 'politics' was already 'in command' in the NEP period, and by the same token shows the importance of examining the political practices of the agencies of the state in the decade following the October revolution. But the social transform-ation that began in the late 1920s created the conditions for a critical change in the position of the state within Soviet society, involving a form of generalised 'politicisation' of social relations. The central aim of the book has been to explore this point by looking at its implications in a specific context.

The process of politicisation was examined first by looking at the offensive against the bourgeois specialists after the Shakhty affair. In the political imagery of the time, this was one element in an intensifying class struggle against the enemies of socialist con-struction. The rhetoric of class conflict was taken here not as a framework of inquiry but as an object of analysis. It was seen as the ideological reflection of the struggle by political officialdom to carry through a crash programme of industrial expansion, which involved on the one hand a prolonged confrontation with the peasantry and on the other hand a 'war' to secure a firmer hold over industrial production. Expressed differently, it was a struggle by the defenders of the public interest against the pursuit of a variety of private interests which were seen to be sabotaging state objectives.

In the context of the offensive against the bourgeois specialists the class struggle appeared as an attempt to browbeat the technical intelligentsia into compliance with the left turn and to challenge the intellectuals' claim to authority based on technical competence. In the prevailing imagery, Bolshevik willpower was set against professional apoliticism, and public-spiritedness against guild-like introversion. In the NEP conditions these features imputed to the technical intelligentsia had been tolerated as part of the bargain with the *spets*, but in the later transformed political environment professional neutrality or grumbling began to look like subversion.

Perhaps the key element in this clash was the tension generated by the extravagant production targets which characterised the early period of Soviet industrial expansion. The 'Bolshevik' plans were met with widespread scepticism from the technical intelligentsia. The specialists were in no position effectively to defend their conception of what was rational against the perceived irrationality of the plan. But in conjunction with other elements in the situation—especially the search for a scapegoat for economic disruption—the conditions were established for a thoroughgoing attack on the technical intelligentsia. In this campaign it was the old generation specialists who bore the brunt of the attack, a section of them being depicted as class enemies in league with western governments and intelligence agencies. The charges of wrecking made this accusation concrete and allowed the coercive apparatuses of the state to appear openly as the chief instrument for the defence of socialist construction. The offensive was also presented as an attempt to win over the old generation specialists ideologically to the current party line. But since the main form of persuasion was frankly coercive, it is not surprising to find that the effect of efforts to politicise the bourgeois specialists was often the opposite of that intended.

Together with this campaign, the form of recruitment of new specialists to the rapidly expanding managerial and technical positions was seen as a vital means by which to establish 'representatives of the state' in production, or in Stalin's image, as a process by which the working class was to establish its 'own' technical intelligentsia. Rephrased in Gramscian terminology, the official conception was that the Soviet workers' state would create an organic intelligentsia in production. This seems to have been understood in two different—though not mutually exclusive—ways. First, there was the notion that since this was a workers' state—the state 'represented' the proletariat—then if managers and technicians acted on behalf of the state they must also 'belong' to the working class. Second, there was the idea that specialists would belong to the working class by virtue of being recruited from a working class background.

The first notion depends upon an assumption about the class nature of the Soviet state which needs to be examined through a concrete analysis of the relationship between the working class and the political agencies which spoke in its name, and an analysis of the position of industrial workers in relation to the technical intelligentsia 'representing' the state in production. In so far as the study can contribute to a discussion of this question, the conclusion must be that it is misleading to speak of a technical intelligentsia 'organic' to the working class. In the second, much more restricted sense, it would be appropriate to speak of the technical intelligentsia 'belonging' to the working class in so far as workers by occupation or their children were able to enjoy upward social mobility. On this point, it was suggested that the opportunities for advancement within the occupational hierarchy in industry were indeed great and that this could serve as one sort of link between the working class and its 'representatives'. But just what the political effects of social mobility were would need more investigation.

The general conclusion on this issue is as follows. The concept of an emerging organic technical intelligentsia has some validity. But as used here it refers not to the relationship between the intelligentsia and the working class, but to the political and professional self-images which emerged within the technical intelligentsia in relation to the state. A number of features are important in this connection. First, the offensive against the specialists encouraged the younger generation to join in the attack and to demonstrate their loyalty to the party and the current political line. In this sense the campaign was effective in breaking down professional solidarity. Second, the very rapid expansion in managerial and technical positions created a severe shortage of cadres which made it possible to advance quickly through the hierarchy, with the state dispensing the patronage. Third, although the political and career backgrounds of the technical intelligentsia were quite diverse, political as well as narrowly technical considerations were manifestly important for making a good career, and in the case of the top jobs the people occupying them in the first half of the 1930s had broadly speaking the same background as the officials of the political apparatus itself. Finally, it can be said that the material privileges which went with the job, because they were a 'gift of the state', could serve to reinforce the sense of identification with the established political order. The attack on 'levelling' (*uravnilovka*), as well as establishing wider material differentials among industrial workers, also helped to create a 'special top stratum' within the technical intelligentsia. The departure from the principles of the Paris Commune, to which Lenin had referred in 1918, was now taken to greater lengths, for the professed reason that the requirements of productivity dictated it. There may have been some substance in this, but there is reason to be sceptical; in the case of the ITR, at any rate, there was no clear way in which the criteria for a greater or lesser contribution could be determined.

The relationship between the technical intelligentsia and the state was, however, far more complex than the notion of organic intellectuals in production can suggest. First, the challenge to professional authority was limited in an important way: it did not take the form of a challenge to the social division of labour within which occupational identities were reproduced. Indeed, the need was felt to legitimate the social division of labour as an enduring feature of post-revolutionary society, and to accord the technical intelligentsia the kind of social honour which it had to some extent lacked during the 1920s. Thus, in the case of the new generation technical intelligentsia, the tension between political demands and professional self-images could be expected to persist, even if the new specialists were encouraged to reject some of the values associated with corporatism or 'caste spirit'.

Secondly, the importance of political criteria and demonstrations of Soviet loyalty did not mean that only one type of career path was favoured in the early 1930s. Those who had started their working lives in industry, together with the red managers and technicians who had once been political activists, were able to advance quickly up the occupational ladder. In the late 1930s, under the rapidly changing political conditions during the 'great purge', it was in fact those specialists who did not have a politically active past who were the more rapidly promoted, and the red technical intelligentsia who suffered the most from the onslaught.

Finally—and this is the key point—an analysis of the relationship between the technical intelligentsia and the state does not get very far without a close examination of the work situation of enterprise managers and technical staff, and of the way their position was affected by the activities of different political agencies in the arena of production.

The conclusions reached in this context can be stated as follows. The position of the technical intelligentsia in Soviet industrial enterprises was defined by the emergence of a system of directive or 'command' planning, which could not provide an orderly coordination of different production processes, but was a method for concentrating resources on priority sectors—the development of heavy industry and the corresponding infrastructure—in order to achieve a short-cut expansion of industrial production. The development of command planning in the USSR did not bring about a revolution in the mode of production in the sense that collectivisation revolutionised the agricultural sector. But there was the important change that plans, as well as becoming more detailed, acquired a 'direct and obligatory significance for the enterprise'. At the same time—especially in this period of 'primitive' accumulation—the central planners had to contend with an exceptional degree of uncertainty in a rapidly changing economic and technological environment. Industry was in a state of recurrent crisis, with systematic shortages of supplies and frequent halts to production threatening to undermine the industrialisation effort. If the disruption was serious enough party campaigns were started to remedy the situation, thereby reinforcing the concentrated attention on priorities.

Within this setting, the enterprise administration, while subject to detailed and often zealous guidance from above, was able to achieve a restricted autonomy in relation to the higher industrial agencies and planners, at least in determining the means by which the effort would be made to meet production targets. The immediate control exercised over production by the enterprise directors set limits to the power of the central authorities to determine its course. At the same time, within the enterprise administration itself, a certain power attached to the exercise of technical functions, although it was rare for ITR subordinate to the director to challenge decisions that were made in the interests of plan fulfilment or the appearance of it.

But this restricted autonomy exercised by the enterprise administration was conditional on keeping up a good record according to the prevailing criteria. If an enterprise got into trouble because— for whatever reason—production was lagging, then a more active and detailed intervention could be expected from above, not only from industrial administrators and planners, but also from other political agencies which were given jurisdiction over the activities of the enterprise ITR and were instructed to assist in overcoming obstacles in the way of plan implementation. In the early years of Soviet industrial expansion the rate of failure was high, and this had important consequences for the degree of security in managerial and technical jobs. In this context particular attention was given to the role of the party and coercive state apparatuses. In 'normal' times the local party organisations played a rather passive role in relation to industry. But in crisis situations local party officials came under pressure from their superiors to find remedies. In this event managers and technical staff might be pushed around with some impunity, and with the break-up of local 'family circles', managerial and party careers could be rudely interrupted.

In the response to disruptions in the production process, the punitive element loomed large, and the ITR were likely to get the blame if things were going seriously wrong. Furthermore, the boundaries between administrative and legal sanctions, and between ordinary and political crime, remained blurred. What was to count as honest error, or negligence, or counter-revolutionary sabotage, depended not on an unambiguous definition of these misdemeanours but on a current political assessment of the situation and on shifting definitions of crime. This point becomes very clear if one looks, for example, at the change in the party line towards the technical intelligentsia in 1931 and the consequences of this for the role of the procuracy and the political police in the industrial arena. A technical 'mistake' which had once assumed the dimensions of a crime against the state could in a different political situation take on the modest appearance of an honest error or not be blamed on individuals at all.

The ability to circumvent pressures from the coercive agencies depended on how much influence a manager or member of the technical staff was able to wield. The ITR lower down in the hierarchy tended to wield less influence and were therefore less protected from the use of criminal sanctions. The rank-and-file specialists did have certain resources of measured participation as a way of protecting themselves against criticism. It was just this that gave rise to the complaints that the specialists were behaving 'bureaucratically', by trying to avoid doing anything that might incur censure. But this was a power strategy from a position of weakness. It was an attempt to negotiate an area of security in unfavourable circumstances.

This 'bureaucratic' apathy was an unintended consequence of a punitive response in the face of production problems, and raises the question of how it was possible in these circumstances to carry through a rapid technical transformation in Soviet industry. It was not denied that there was some scope for technical initiative from below. But the conclusion must be that it was not the rank-and-file technical intelligentsia that provided the main impetus for a technological transformation. The main impetus came from party officialdom itself. In its struggle against the consequences of apathy and routine, the party leadership tended to reinforce the inertia that it intended to eliminate. It tended therefore to reproduce the conditions of its own dynamic and transformative role. It was the party, not the technical intelligentsia, which became the chief agent of technical change.

In trying to identify the sources, extent and limits of job security for the technical intelligentsia, it was stressed that the period between 1928 and 1931 had specific features. These were closely linked with the political offensive against the old generation specialists, and the consequent active role of the political police in the arena of production. Between 1932 and 1935 the ITR were more secure because the managers were better able to defend their own definition of what was good for production and to resist or neutralise outside interventions. This may have reflected a long-term trend towards greater managerial bargaining power. But the subsequent purges of the technical intelligentsia in the late 1930s, when the sources of protection broke down at almost all levels, also made clear the underlying insecurity of the technical intelligentsia as a whole. It was not argued that the post-1935 purge of industrial managers (or of anyone else) could be read into, or predicted from the political situation of the early 1930s. The point was rather that where it was not possible to appeal to clearly defined 'rights and duties', the degree of security would remain subject to the shifting balance of power between the officials of different political agencies, and to the changing definitions of crime.

As well as offering some indications about the sources of security or insecurity in ITR jobs, these conclusions may also help to clarify the extent and limits of 'control' exercised over the technical intelligentsia by the agencies of the state. The extension of the scope of activity of political agencies which characterised the reconstruction period was not the same as successful 'control'. It was suggested earlier that the latter notion requires the assumption of a 'Weberian' bureaucratic rationality in which the activities of subordinates are determined by the application of clearly established general rules to particular cases. It is not of course denied that certain elements of a bureaucratic mode of domination in Weber's sense were present: for example, the ITR were evidently part of an administrative hierarchy, and they were selected not elected. But in other key respects—for example, the notion that bureaucratic rule means 'calculability' and predictability, and involves clearly defined spheres of competence for each category of official—the role of political agencies in relation to the technical intelligentsia was clearly at odds with the bureaucratic image.

First, on the question of 'calculability'. The intervention of outside political agencies helped to ensure that certain priority sectors were not forgotten. But the role of these agencies was determined within the context of a continuous effort to confront the failure of particular enterprises to meet the established targets, or to cope with the disruptive consequences of previous political decisions. Thus there was rather a series of rescue operations than an exercise of bureaucratic calculation.

Secondly, a clear definition of spheres of competence ('rights and duties') was absent. This indeed appeared to be a necessary condition for the rescue operations to take place. The local party, the procuracy or the security organs might intervene in the production arena under instructions to assist in the implementation of plans. They might then find themselves under criticism from the centre for 'undermining one-man management' or 'ignoring the rights of the specialists'. But given the constant need to correct distortions in the implementation of plans, there could be no *a priori* formulation of what was to count as legitimate intervention. Thus 'one-man management' was in this context necessarily negated in practice.

It can be concluded from this that the form of state domination of the early Stalinist period did not require a Weberian bureaucratic rationality in order to work. The notion of state domination or of 'politics in command' refers to the position of the state apparatus in the totality of social relations, and especially to the role of political agencies in relation to production, which involved a 'unity' of political and economic direction. But the manner in which this domination was secured—and the corresponding unity between the political and the economic—testified to endemic tensions between the agencies of the state and the technical intelligentsia, and between different sections and levels of the political apparatus itself. The central party authorities were involved in a continuous coordinating effort in the face of the tendency for the practices of local political officials and managers of production to conflict with the currently defined general interest.

While faced with a variety of pressures from above, the ITR also stood in formal authority over the industrial workers, and were asked to act at the enterprise level as agents of discipline in the production process. The ITR had considerable delegated powers in an organisational environment that was conducive to a tough style of direction and reduced to a minimum the possibilities of a collective response to management demands. The one-man management principle, in the context of manager–worker relations, was strengthened by a shift in the balance of power between the three 'points' of the triangle of management, trade union and party organisation. The arguments in favour of a one-man authority were not put forward for the first time at the end of the 1920s. We have shown that the question of one-man as against collegial management was the subject of an important debate during the civil war. But after 1928 the focus of the issue shifted. During the civil war it was a question of whether a collective form of administration should be retained, and by 1921 this issue had already been decided— against some opposition within the party—in favour of the 'single will'. Later it was a question of how far the more limited institutional constraints on one-man authority, embodied in the *troika*, would continue to work. During the early 1930s, with the weakening of trade union authority, the *troika* was in effect reduced to a *dvoika* of management and party. But the party officials at enterprise level—who unlike the trade union organisers had a certain standing in the enterprise—did not usually come into conflict with management and could only give the appearance of being 'controlling organs'.

The weak position of the trade union officials did not mean that violations of the labour code would always be ignored. But these violations would be 'noticed', and managers or technical staff called to account, when they had already lost the support of their superiors for other reasons: namely, when production was lagging and the enterprise was consistently failing to meet production targets. Thus workers' interests were defended when failing to defend them was seen to threaten the fulfilment of the plan.

We also argued, however, that the image of an unconditional authority or of unremittingly exacting managers, is misplaced. On the one hand, the exclusion of collective forms of struggle could not eliminate workers' individual responses to their situation. The argument over conditions of work, and over how much work to do for what reward, would go on in one way or another, even without collective bargaining. On the other hand, there was a certain pattern of managerial indulgence which modified the consequences of the effort by the state to increase the productivity of labour. There were informal pressures against high work norms which managers could not or did not wish to ignore, and the ITR were being told to be less 'lax' with unruly workers. Also, the ITR were to some extent vulnerable to criticism from below. At the time of the political offensive against the old technical intelligentsia, such criticism was indeed encouraged, since a quasi-populist appeal to the workers against the specialists formed part of that offensive. There was therefore some tension between the attempt by the party to bolster its legitimacy with the working class and the demand for a subordination to the ITR as agents of discipline in production. This quasi-populist phase did not last long, but the ITR could still under particular conditions be subjected to criticism from below. The situations in which this might occur—when managers or technicians were under attack from above—were not determined by the workers themselves. But there was a complexity in the relationship between the state, the technical intelligentsia and the workers which is not conveyed by the image of an unconditional authority.

The different elements in the position of the technical intelligentsia that have been identified were effects of a change in the pattern of state activity conditioned by the effort to carry through a crash programme of industrial expansion. The Soviet state was engaged in a 'war' on the various production fronts which involved major shifts in the role of the state in society and thereby a transformation in the pattern of social relations. The object of this study of enterprise managers and technicians has been to illuminate some of the consequences of that change, as well as to give a convincing characterisation of the social position of the technical intelligentsia during the early Stalinist period. It has become apparent that this position was complex: the technical intelligentsia was a 'representative' of the state and a victim of the state, an object of domination and an agent of discipline in the labour process, insecure and socially privileged.

These ambiguities were effects of the particular mode of state domination which characterised the early Stalinist period. We also believe that the transformations that Soviet reconstruction involved had profound long-term consequences for the development of the Soviet state, and that the role established for the technical intelligentsia in this period was in some key respects formative. But to demonstrate this would require a different sort of study from the one attempted here. The present effort is intended as an analysis of a historically specific set of social relations, and has therefore a more restricted purpose. But it is hoped that some understanding has been gained of a critical phase in the history of the USSR.

Notes

CHAPTER 1

1. A summary statement of this view can be found in I. Deutscher, *The Unfinished Revolution* (1967), Chapter 2. Deutscher is basically following the concept of 'combined development', especially as presented in Trotsky's *History of the Russian Revolution*, for example

> In order to realise the Soviet state, there was required a drawing together and mutual penetration of two factors belonging to completely different historic species: a peasant war—that is, a movement characteristic of the dawn of bourgeois development—and a proletarian insurrection, the movement signalising its decline. That is the essence of 1917 (Ibid., vol. 1, p. 64).

2. This theme is briefly explored in M. Lewin (1975), Chapter 4.
3. The best general account of war communism is still E. H. Carr (1952).
4. L. Trotsky (1961), pp. 169–70.
5. This story is told in detail in M. Lewin (1968), and in E. H. Carr and R. W. Davies (1969).
6. See for example Stalin's comments on the increasing importance of the state apparatus, at the 17th and 18th Party Congresses in 1934 and 1939 (Stalin (1976), pp. 737f. and 927f.).
7. M. Lewin, 'Society and the Stalinist state in the period of the Five Year Plans', *Social History*, no. 2 (1976).
8. M. Fainsod (1958) provides a rich documentation for an analysis of the conflicts between different sectors and levels of the political apparatus in the 1930s.
9. See, for example, Friedrich and Brzezinski (1956).
10. See for example Schneider (1969), pp. 109–10.
11. In *Capital*, vol 1, Marx (1970) has this to say: 'An industrial army of workmen, under the command of a capitalist requires, like a real army, officers (managers) and servants (foremen, overlookers) who, while the work is being done, command in the name of the capitalist' (p. 332); in *Theories of Surplus Value* it is stressed that not only the 'direct worker by hand or machine' but also 'the foremen, engineer, manager, clerk etc., in a word, the labour of the whole personnel required in a particular sphere of material production . . . add their aggregate labour to the constant capital and raise the value of the products by this amount' (Marx (Moscow, n.d.) pp. 398–99).
12. Carr and Davies (1969); Granick (1954); Azrael (1966). Unfortunately, this book was completed before the appearance of the very thorough study by K.

Bailes, *Technology and Society under Lenin and Stalin* (Princeton, 1978). This deals with some of the same issues that are considered here, although the theoretical questions raised in the present study are different in certain important respects.

CHAPTER 2

1. Lenin, *Sochineniya*, vol. 36, p. 137.
2. An account of strike action by different sections of the intelligentsia is given in S. Fedyukin (1972), p. 42ff.
3. For one of numerous accounts, see P. Avrich, 'Workers' control', *Slavic Review*, vol. 22 (1963), p. 47f.
4. For Lenin's conception of state capitalism—workers' control, see 'The current tasks of the Soviet power', *Sochineniya*, vol. 36, pp. 178f.
5. The decree is closely examined in P. Avrich, *op. cit*; see also E. H. Carr, *The Bolshevik Revolution*, vol. 2, p. 72ff.
6. For example, the situation at the Putilov works: The four engineers who headed the main subsections of the plant (artillery, engineering, carriage and metal production) refused the directorship offered after the resignation of the former director, and as a result the chairman of the factory committee took over as head of the plant. But while some engineers were being arrested for their refusal to cooperate, others promised to assist the factory committee (*Istoriya Kirovskóvo Zavoda* (1966), pp. 11–12, 15).
7. In the period between October 1917 and June 1918, in one-half of cases where nationalisation of individual enterprises took place, the reason stated was 'sabotage' by the owner, that is, actions which amounted to a refusal to carry on production. The other nationalisations were accounted for by the special importance of the enterprise to the state (M. Dobb (1966), pp. 84–5).
   The period of 'spontaneous' takeovers was described by a speaker at the first All-Russian Congress of Sovnarkhozy in May 1918, as follows:

   Those who work in these enterprises can say that the fault did not lie only in the workers, in the fact that the workers took to 'holding meetings', but in the fact that the personnel of the enterprises, the managing staff, folded its hands because the old stick had fallen from them—the stick with which it used to drive the workers—and it had none of the other means which the western European bourgeoisie has of making the worker work . . . All these conditions confronted the working class with the insistent task of management, and it had to be taken in hand. Of course, the working class took it in hand clumsily. That is understandable. They chased out the old directors and technicians, perhaps because these people had treated them badly in the past, though cases are known of kindly treatment by decent managing personnel in enterprises (*Trudy i-vo Vserossiiskogo Syezda Sovetov Narodnogo Khozyaistva* (1918), cited in E. H. Carr, *The Bolshevik Revolution*, p. 76).

8. This point is also made by Azrael (1966).
9. The social origin of students in five higher technical institutes in 1914 was as

follows (per cent): hereditary nobility, 9.7; personal nobility and functionaries, 14.8; clergy, 2.3; 'honoured citizens and merchants', 14.0; petty-bourgeoisie and guilds (*meshchane i tsekhovye*), 31.6; cossacks, 1.0; peasants, 21.1; others, 4.9 (A. Beilin (1935) p. 62). Beilin notes that 'peasants' were peasants by passport, who had in many cases left the land and taken up urban occupations, such as artisans or traders.

10. The first trade union for engineers, the All-Russian Union of Engineers (VSI), which incorporated most of the existing societies of engineers, was set up in March 1917, and until the end of 1918 was the main representative body of the higher technical personnel (*Inzkenerny-Trud* (1928), no. 2, p. 60). Subsequent forms of trade union representation for engineers and technicians are discussed below. The proceedings of the January 1918 conference are in *Zanyatiya Pervoi Moskovskoi Oblastnoi Konferentsii* (1918).

11. Grinevetsky in ibid., pp. 32–40.

12. Sattel in ibid., p. 47.

13. Grinevetsky in ibid., pp. 32–40.

14. Several speakers were highly pessimistic about the future of Russia at the end of the war, predicting the transformation of Russia into a German, English or American colony. There was some discussion about what should be done in this event, one speaker suggesting that small-scale Russian capital should be transformed into corporate capital, a change for which the support of the engineers would be essential (see statements by P. P. Yurenev, S. I. Krichevsky, K. G. Shindler, A. M. Berkenheim, ibid., pp. 43–5). Bardin (1938, p. 53) notes that before the revolution some engineers were in favour of a considerable measure of nationalisation of industry as a means of protection against foreign capital.

15. Ibid., p. 39.

16. Ibid., pp. 47–8.

17. Lenin, *Sochineniya*, vol. 35, p. 197.

18. Lenin, *Sochineniya*, vol. 36, p. 137.

19. Yu. Larin (1925), p. 10.

20. In May 1918 representatives of the VSI took part in discussions with the government on the question of nationalisation, discussions which were described by one VSI participant in the following way: 'we protested so energetically against the idea of nationalisation, and defended this protest so brilliantly, that at one time there was reason to believe that even the initiators of the idea were reconsidering it . . . however, under the pressure of pre-conceived ideological positions, this hesitation evaporated . . .' (*Otchet o Zanyatiyakh 2-i Moskovskoi Oblastnoi Konferentsii*, p. 20).

21. For a brief account of the role of the old specialists in enterprise administration during the civil war, see Larin, *op. cit.*, p. 39f. The arrangements varied, but by the time of the 10th Party Congress in March 1921 a fully collegial system at enterprise level was uncommon. According to Shlyapnikov at that time, the directorate of the enterprise was usually the head of the enterprise together with the factory committee, the formal head being either an old specialist or a Red Director (*Desyaty Syezd RKP*, p. 366).

22. Grinevetsky cited in *Voprosy Ratsionalizatsii* (1925), p. 29.

23. Remarks of Evreinov, that engineers had remained at their posts during the civil war, 'tolerating hunger and all kinds of attacks', because 'we loved

Russia, loved our people, and were committed to production' (*Stenograficheskii Otchet* (1923), p. 30).

24. Lenin, *Sochineniya*, vol. 36, p. 272.
25. Yu. Larin (1925), p. 15.
26. Lenin, *Sochineniya*, vol. 38, p. 18.
27. Ibid., p. 165.
28. Lenin, *Sochineniya*, vol. 36, p. 331.
29. The party programme is translated in Bukharin and Preobrazhensky, *The ABC of Communism* (ed. E. H. Carr), see the section on the specialists, p. 342f.
30. Most of these propositions can be found in various statements by Lenin during the civil war. In May 1918 he commented:

> I cannot recall a single socialist work or the opinion of any prominent socialist that I know which in dealing with the future socialist society, points out the concrete practical difficulties that will confront the working class upon the seizure of power when it takes up the task of converting the whole vast sum of culture, knowledge and technique which has been accumulated by capitalism and which is historically necessary for us—of converting all this from an instrument of capitalism into an instrument of socialism (*Sochineniya*, vol. 36, p. 382).

An interesting analysis of this problem can be found in Bukharin's article 'Burzhyuaznaya revoliutsiya i revoliutsiya proletarskaya' in *Pod Znamenem Marksisma*, nos. 7–8 (1922), p. 63f.

31. The writings of W. Machajski provide one example of a radically anti-intelligentsia stance. His argument—or part of it—was that the intellectual roles of manager and engineer were wholly exploitative under capitalist conditions; if bourgeois specialists were recruited to work for the Soviet state, they would simply form, together with the socialist intelligentsia, part of a new ruling class, acting as parasitic agents in the extraction of surplus value (A. Volskii (W. Machajski) (1968), pp. 380–1, 395f, writings of 1918). The view that the technical intelligentsia was in no way productive—to be contrasted with Marx's position—later acquired the Bolshevik label 'Makhaevshchina', in honour of Machajski (see Chapter 6, p.   ).
32. Lenin, 'The current tasks of the Soviet power', *Sochineniya*, vol. 36.
33. *KPSS v Rezolyutsiyakh*, vol. 2, p. 168.
34. N. Bukharin (1920), pp. 41–2, 49, 66, 115–6, 119.
35. For some left communist arguments, see N. Osinsky (1918), pp. 24–38; the democratic centralists were vocal at the 9th Party Congress in April 1920: see, for example, *Devyaty Syezd RKP* (1960), p. 115.
36. *The Workers' Opposition*, pp. 2, 18–19.
37. This issue has been brilliantly discussed in H. Braverman (1976), and in other recent discussions of the capitalist labour process, to a large extent sparked off by Braverman's contribution. It would be worth while to re-examine the early Bolshevik disputes about forms of organisation in industry in the light of this important debate.
38. Trotsky, *Sochineniya*, vol. 21, p. 100.
39. Lenin, *Sochineniya*, vol. 40, p. 213.
40. Lenin, *Sochineniya*, vol. 42, pp. 156–7, 339.

41. *KPSS v Rezolyutsiyakh*, vol. 2, pp. 406, 427.
42. The survey is summarised in A. Beilin (1935), pp. 133–53. It included metallurgical plants in the south and in the Urals; engineering plants in Leningrad, Moscow and the Ukraine; two large military plants; mines under Aznneft and two large coal mines; textile plants in Leningrad and Moscow; chemical plants.
43. Ibid., p. 136.
44. *Iz Istorii Sovetskoi Intelligentsii* (1966), p. 219.
45. A. Beilin (1935), pp. 152–3.
46. In October 1929, about 28 per cent of foremen were party members, and about 75 per cent former workers (*Inzhenerno-Tekhnicheskye Kadry* (1930) pp. 36–7, 46–7).
47. *Inzh. Trud* (1928), no. 2, p. 61f.
48. *Stenograficheskii Otchet Rabot 1-go Vserossiiskogo Syezda Inzhenerov* (1923), p. 33.
49. *Inzh. Trud* (1928), no. 2, p. 63.
50. *Inzh. Trud* (1932), nos. 13–14, p. 34.
51. Tomsky in *Stenograficheskii Otchet . . .* (1923), p. 34.
52. *Vestnik Inzhenerov* (1922), nos. 1–3, p. 43.
53. Evreinov in *Stenograficheskii Otchet . . .* (1923), pp. 29–30.
54. *Vsesoyuzny Syezd . . .* (1924), pp. 13–33.
55. Ibid., pp. 32–3.
56. Ibid., p. 333.
57. Sokolova in *Iz Istorii Sovetskoi Intelligentsii* (1966), pp. 178–9.
58. Dzherzhinskii, *Izbrannye Proizvedeniya.*, vol. 2, p. 214.
59. E. Rozmirovich in *NOT, RKI i Partiya* (1926), p. 60.
60. Lunacharsky (1924), p. 61.
61. Carr and Davies (1969), p. 381.
62. Ibid., p. 382.
63. *Predpriyatiye* (1924), no. 6, p. 12.
64. See Ordzhonikidze, speech to 15th Moscow Party Conference, *Stati i Rechi*, vol. 2, p. 29.
65. Carr and Davies (1969), p. 351f.
66. Ibid., p. 824.
67. *Pravda* (15 January 1925).
68. *VKP v Rezolyutsiyakh*, vol. 2, p. 269.
69. *Direktor* (1971), p. 217.
70. *Torgovo Promyshlennaya Gazeta* (31 March 1926).
71. *Torg.-Prom. Gaz.* (17 February 1926).
72. *Predpriyatiye* (1926), no. 5, pp. 5–6.
73. *KPSS v Rezolyutsiyakh*, vol. 2, p. 322.
74. Ibid., pp. 226f.
75. Ibid., p. 319.
76. *KPSS v Rezolyutsiyakh*, vol. 2, p. 235.
77. *Predpriyatiye* (1924), no. 3, p. 79.
78. Ibid., p. 11.
79. Ibid., p. 80.
80. *Predpriyatiya* (1926), no. 7, p. 23.
81. For a discussion of the RKKs and of labour disputes, see Carr and Davies, op. cit., p. 563f. In 1926/27, one-third of disputes which had led to strikes

were settled in favour of workers, less than one-third in favour of management, and the rest gave divided results (ibid., p. 564).

82. For examples of such complaints, see *Predpriyatiya* (1924) no. 8, p. 10; (1926), No. 5, p. 9.
83. *Predpriyatiya* (1924), no. 3, p. 10.
84. *Odinadsaty Syezd VKP*, p. 279.
85. *Vestnik Inzhenerov* (1923), 1–3, p. 32.
86. *Predpriyatiya* (1924), no. 8, p. 10.
87. *Vsesoyuzny syezd inzhenerov* (1924), p. 12.
88. *Predpriyatiya* (1925), no. 5, p. 5.
89. *KPSS v Rezolyutsiyakh*, vol. 1, p. 344.
90. *Torg.-Prom. Gaz.* (18 June 1926).
91. Ibid.

CHAPTER 3

1. *Pravda* (10 March 1928).
2. *Pravda* (8 May 1928).
3. *Pravda* (5 July 1928); R. Medvedev (1972), p. 112.
4. *KPSS v Rezolyutsiyakh*, vol. 4, pp. 84f.
5. *Pravda* (29 March 1928).
6. *Pravda* (14 March 1928).
7. *Pravda* (17 March 1928).
8. Molotov (1928), p. 11 (speech of July 1928).
9. Speech to a meeting of ITR, July 1928. *Inzh. Trud* (1928), no. 7, pp. 295–9.
10. Address to Moscow party conference, *Torg.-Prom. Gaz.* (17 February 1929).
11. Yakovlev in *Shestnadtsataya Konferentsiya VKP*, p. 470.
12. Stalin, *Problems of Leninism* (1976), p. 339.
13. *Za Industrializatsiyu* (13 February 1930); *Planovoe Khozyaistvo* (1930), nos. 7–8, p. 5.
14. *Za Ind.* (13 February 1930).
15. *16 Syezd VKP*, p. 36.
16. *Inzh. Trud* (1929), no. 17, p. 496.
17. A. Etchin (1928), p. 5.
18. *16 Syezd VKP*, p. 319.
19. Ibid., p. 77.
20. See for example, *Pravda* editorials after the defeat of the right opposition at the 16th Party Conference (12 June 1929, 25 August 1929, 29 October 1929).
21. *Za Ind.* (7 November 1930).
22. *Pravda* (15 December 1929).
23. *Pravda* (5 February 1930).
24. Witness, for example, Ordzhonikidze's remarks about planners (and Groman in particular) in September 1929. While denying that the government wished to make any blanket condemnation of the old specialists, he said 'we must not deceive ourselves: bourgeois specialists are able with the greatest of difficulty and in rare cases to understand our ideas' (*Stati i Rechi*, vol. 2, p. 176).
25. On the Promparty affair, see *Za Ind.* (20 October 1930 and following days); also *Protsess Prompartii* (1931); Medvedev (1972), p. 118f.

26. Medvedev (1972), p. 122f; a detailed analysis of the Menshevik trial can be found in *Sotsialisticheskii Vestnik* (March and April 1931).

27. Medvedev (1972), p. 112f.

28. Ibid., p. 112. (At the time of the Shakhty affair, the Chekist in question was head of the economic section of the Transcaucasian GPU). Avtorkhanov gives an interesting and plausible account of the origins of the Shakhty case (based on a story he heard from a member of the Moscow party committee). Yevdokimov, head of the GPU in the North Caucasus, presented Menzhinsky, chairman of the GPU, with a report which alleged, on the basis of letters passed between the Shakhty specialists and former mine owners (then living abroad), that systematic sabotage was planned. But since these letters had yet to be 'decoded', Menzhinsky remained unconvinced, especially since 'he well knew his colleagues' propensity to build their careers on the basis of mythical cases'. Yevdomikov then went to Stalin, who personally authorised the arrest of the specialists. Faced with this *fait accompli*, Menzhinsky, Kuibyshev and Rykov accused Stalin of exceeding his authority, but Stalin then hinted at a Politburo session that the strings of the case led to Moscow. 'Kuibyshev beat a hasty retreat, Menzhinsky fell silent, and Rykov merely looked questioningly at Bukharin and Tomsky.' At this point Stalin's victory was 'beyond doubt' (Avtorkhanov (1959), p. 28f).

29. Ciliga (1940) pp. 153, 223, 226–7.

30. Kravchenko (1947), p. 86. It is worth noting that Trotsky, in exile, accepted all the charges against the industrial and agricultural specialists implicated in the Promparty affair, which in his view demonstrated the correctness of the left opposition's criticisms of 'minimal positions' in the years 1923–28. 'The specialists who have been brought to trial have shown what an intense struggle they carried on in the past for minimal programmes for the Five Year plan.' In the period of the struggle against the left opposition, 'the central committee was the unconscious political mouthpiece of specialist-wreckers who in turn were hired by foreign imperialists and Russian-emigrant *compradores*' (*Byulleten Oppozitsii*, no. 17–18 (1930), pp. 20–1). He responded in a similar way to the Menshevik trial in March 1931 (barring Ryazanov, who was also implicated), but in 1936 issued a retraction, admitting that 'during the period of the Menshevik trial, it [the *Byulleten*] underestimated by far the shamelessness of the Stalin judiciary and because of this took too seriously the admissions of the former Mensheviks' (*Byulleten*, no. 21–2 (1931), pp. 19–22, 35–6; no. 51 (1936), p. 15). By the same token, Trotsky might have questioned the Promparty charges, but he did not do so.

31. The confessions of engineers working in the Yugostal trust were read out by a Rabkrin official, suggesting that they had been sabotaging production over a number of years under the orders of former capitalist owners. At this point there were sceptical voices from the floor: 'And do you believe this?' 'You conducted 25 investigations during that period [when the alleged sabotage had been going on], how come you didn't notice anything?' (*16 Konferentsiya VKP* p. 485).

32. *16 Syezd VKP*, p. 319.

33. *Plan. Khoz.* (1930), no. 7–8, p. 6.

34. *VKP v Rezolyutsiyakh*, vol. 4, pp. 94–8.

35. Stalin (1976), pp. 336, 338.

36. *Za Ind.* (7 November 1930).
37. Kuibyshev, *Stati i Rechi*, vol. 5, p. 55.
38. Lunacharsky in *Varnitso* (1930), no. 2, p. 12.
39. The expression was Radek's; in an article in the ITS journal at the time of the Promparty affair, he made dire warnings to any ITR who 'refuse to put any energy into their work or who engage in counter-revolutionary whispering'; if they did not fulfil their duties they would be 'thrown mercilessly out of the door at the first opportunity' (*Inzh. Trud* (1930) no. 24, p. 173).
40. *Front Nauki i Tekhniki* (1931), no. 7–8, p. 7.
41. Cited in *Inzh. Trud* (1930), no. 5, p. 112.
42. On this see Chapter 5.
43. Shein in *Izvestiya* (25 November 1929).
44. *Trud* (10 April 1929).
45. *Torg.-Prom. Gaz.* (1 May 1929).
46. Ibid.
47. *Za Ind.* (29 January 1930).
48. *Varnitso* (1930), no. 3–4, p. 12.
49. *Za Ind.* (21 January 1930).
50. *Pravda* (23 October 1930), editorial.
51. Cited in *Byli Industrialnye*, pp. 192–3
52. *Inzh. Trud* (1929) no. 20, p. 601.
53. *Sots. Vestnik* (12 September 1931), p. 15.
54. Cited in Kravchenko (1947), p. 81.
55. *KPSS v Rezolyutsiyakh*, vol. 4, p. 85.
56. *Pravda* (29 October 1929).
57. *Za Ind.* (16 February 1930).
58. *Pravda* (13 November 1930).
59. *Inzh. Trud* (1928), no. 8, p. 349.
60. *Inzh. Trud* (1929), no. 5, p. 133.
61. *Predpriyatiye* (1929), no. 3, p. 26.
62. *Torg.-Prom. Gaz.* (15 December 1928).
63. *Torg.-Prom. Gaz.* (6 July 1928).
64. *Dinamo* (1 March 1929); *Elektrozavod* (8 February 1930).
65. *Trud* (10 April 1930); *Varnitso* (1930), nos. 3–4, p. 12.
66. *Martenovka* (4 March 1930).
67. *Sovetskii Sibir* (26 February 1930).
68. *Inzh. Trud* (1931), no. 15, p. 380.
69. *Part. Stroit.* (1929), no. 1, p. 4.
70. *Krasny Shakhtyor* (26 July 1928).
71. Rudzutak in *Torg.-Prom. Gaz.* (7 August 1928).
72. *KPSS v Rezolyutsiyakh*, vol. 4, p. 85.
73. *Inzh. Trud* (1928), no. 8, pp. 356–7.
74. Ibid., p. 355.
75. *Inzh. Trud* (1928), no. 7, p. 290.
76. *Torg.-Prom. Gaz.* (1 May 1929).
77. *Inzh. Trud* (1929), no. 1, p. 9.
78. *Za Ind.* (3 November 1930).
79. *Trud* (15 November 1930); for further details of this argument see *Za Ind.* (15 October, 2 November, and 12 November 1930); *Trud* (18 November 1930).

80. *Inzh. Trud* (1931), no. 15, p. 367.
81. See, for example, a statement by Shvernik, *Za Ind.* (31 January 1930), and by the chairman of the All-Ukrainian Council of Trade Unions, *Za Ind.* (15 February 1930); Rykov stated in February 1930 that it might 'possibly' be necessary to abolish the ITS as independent organisations; *Varnitso* (1930), no. 2, p. 19. The demand for abolition was made locally at least as early as the beginning of 1929 (see, for instance *Krasny Shakhtyor* (30 January 1929)—report on a regional conference of the mineworkers' ITS).
82. *Inzh. Trud* (1930), no. 11, p. 325.
83. *Pravda* (12 June 1930).
84. *Inzh. Trud* (1929), no. 17, p. 496.
85. *Za Ind.* (21 September 1931).
86. *Inzh. Trud* (1932), nos. 10–11, p. 310.
87. *KPSS v Rezolyutsiyakh*, vol. 4, p. 342.
88. Political circles usually concentrated on current political issues, for example, the latest party resolutions, Stalin's speeches, and the like (*Inzh. Trud* (1932), nos. 10–11, p. 310f.)
89. *Rychag* (15 February 1931).
90. *Inzh. Trud* (1930), no. 11, p. 326.
91. *Inzh. Trud* (1931), no. 3, editorial.
92. A. Etchin in *Za Ind.* (13 February 1930).
93. *Varnitso* (1930), nos. 7–8, p. 5.
94. *Za Ind.* (1 February 1930).
95. *Za Ind.* (27 April 1930).
96. *Inzhenerny Rabotnik* (1928), no. 8, p. 71.
97. *Elektrozavod* (12 August 1930).
98. *Sovetskii Sibir* (16 March, 31 May 1930).
99. *Za Ind.* (15 May 1930).
100. In four regions (Moscow, Leningrad, Georgia, Central Black Earth region) there were more than 2000 applicants from ITR in February and March 1930, *Part. Stroit.* (1930), no. 6, p. 32.
101. Ibid.
102. *Za Ind.* (14 April 1931).
103. Stalin (1976), p. 552.
104. *Za Ind.* (14 April 1931).
105. *Inzh. Trud*, and *Front Nauki i Tekhniki* (late 1931 and early 1932).
106. Rudzutak in *Za Ind.* (16 August 1931).
107. On the release of old engineers in the metallurgical industry, see *Byli Industrialnye*, p. 189. See also reports from factories on specialists formerly convicted on wrecking charges, who were now back at work, such as *Pravda* (17 January 1932); *Za Ind.* (20 January 1932).
108. *Inzh. Trud* (1932), nos. 31–2, p. 718.
109. Speech to 5th All-Union Conference of ITS (November 1932) (*Inzh. Trud* (1932), nos. 34–6, p. 795.)
110. *Pravda* (5th July 1933).
111. *Za Ind.* (28 May 1934).
112. Stalin (1976), p. 551.
113. Ibid., pp. 549–52.

114. *Za Ind.* (26 July 1933); Ordzhonikidze, *Stati i Rechi*, vol. 2, p. 600.
115. *Spravochnik Partiinogo Rabotnika*, vyp. 8, p. 376.
116. *Front Nauki i Tekhniki* (1932), no. 7–8, p. 20.
117. *Inzh. Trud* (1932), nos. 34–6, p. 790.
118. Ibid., p. 791.
119. Stalin (1976), p. 551.

CHAPTER 4

1. *KPSS v Rezolyutsiyakh*, vol. 4, pp. 84f; pp. 111f.
2. Address to Leningrad party organisation, *Pravda* (15 July 1928).
3. *KPSS v Rezolyutsiyakh*, vol. 4, p. 335.
4. Ibid.
5. Stalin (1976), pp. 546–7.
6. A. Gramsci (1971), p. 63f.
7. See Table 5 below.
8. A. Kogan (1930), p. 14.
9. See Table 1 in Chapter 2.
10. *Sostav Rukovodyashchikh Rabotnikov* (1936), pp. 15–6.
11. Granick (1954), p. 296.
12. *16 Syezd VKP*, p. 79.
13. *Spravochnik Partiinogo Rabotnika*, vyp. 8, p. 444.
14. *Kadry Tyazheloi Promyshlennosti* (1936), p. 14.
15. *Trud v SSSR* (1936), p. 309.
16. See Emelianov (1974), p. 45.
17. *Part. Stroit.* (1930), no. 1, p. 77.
18. V. Kravchenko (1947), pp. 172–3.
19. See p.   below.
20. *Kadry Tyazheloi Promyshlennosti* (1936), p. 166f.
21. Ibid.
22. *Sostav Rukovodyaschikh Rabotnikov* (1936), pp. 18–19.
23. The following cases exemplify this career-path: (1) Korobov: apprentice at a metallurgical plant before the revolution; 1922–28 studied at engineering institute; 1928–35: shift engineer, assistant to shop head, shop head; 1936: chief engineer (joined party in 1935). (*17 Syezd VKP*, p. 529.) (2) Butenko: worker; studied at *rabfak* and *vtuz* in the 1920s, graduated 1928; 1928–33: shift engineer, shop head, chief engineer (joined party 1931). (*Za Ind.*, 28 May 1934.) (3) Kartashev: worker, studied at *rabfak* and *vtuz* 1922–28; 1928–33: head of mine section, assistant head of mine, head of mine (*Sotsialistischeskii Donbass*, 18 November 1933.) (4) Sokolov: worker, received higher education in the 1920s extramurally; assistant head of mine in 1933. (*Sots. Donbass*, 7 August 1933.)
24. See decisions of July 1928 and November 1929 Central Committee plenums, *KPSS v Rezolyutsiyakh*, vol. 4, pp. 111f and 334f.
25. *Novye Kadry Tyazheloi Promyshlennosti* (1934), p. 142.
26. *Trud* (16 March 1929).
27. *Sotsialisticheskoe Stroitelstvo* (1935), pp. 518–9.
28. This shift was initiated by a government decree of September 1932 on the

organisation of technical education. It included the statement that 'in carrying out the decisions of the party and government the commissariats and the *vtuzy* and *tekhnikumy* allowed certain distortions to occur, mainly in the form of a one-sided attention to the quantitative growth of students with inadequate attention to the question of quality of training, as well as excessive specialisation, as a result of which the graduates of some *vtuzy* were often on the level of technician and not of engineer'. (*Novye Kadry* (1934), pp. 10–11.)

29. In November 1933, the proportion of engineers with a worker background in the party was 45 per cent compared with 19 per cent of engineers as a whole; but of party members who had graduated between 1928 and 1933, two-thirds were from non-worker backgrounds. (*Sotsalisticheskoe Stroitelstvo* (1935), pp. 518–9, 526–7.)

30. Stalin (1976), p. 548.

31. *Part. Stroit.* (1930), no. 6, p. 32.

32. Korobov in *Za Ind.* (28 May 1934).

33. This point would need to be explored further, but evidence of this consequence of the purge of industrial managers in the late 1930s can be found in Scott (1942), and Kravchenko (1947).

34. *Torg.-Prom. Gaz.* (1 May 1929).

35. *Za Ind.* (11 January 1930).

36. *Elektrozavod* (17 September 1930).

37. *Trud* (16 March 1929).

38. *Trud* (14 April 1929).

39. *Rychag* (5 June 1930).

40. *Stalinskii Udarnik* (10 November 1930).

41. *Pravda* (28 March 1928).

42. *Torg.-Prom. Gaz.* (5 April 1928).

43. *Inzh. Trud* (1928), no. 8, pp. 348–9.

44. *KPSS v Rezolyutsiyakh*, vol. 4, p. 85.

45. *Inzh. Rabotnik* (1928), no. 8, p. 74.

46. *Izvestiya* (14 April 1929).

47. *Torg.-Prom. Gaz.* (5 April 1929).

48. *Torg.-Prom. Gaz.* (1 May 1929).

49. *Trud* (14 April 1929).

50. *Trud* (12 June 1929).

51. *Inzh. Trud* (1930), nos. 22–3, pp. 676–7.

52. *Za Ind.* (18 May 1930).

53. *Torg.-Prom. Gaz.* (15 December 1928).

54. *Inzh. Trud* (1930), nos. 22–3, p. 675.

55. *Za Ind.* (19 June, 13 September 1930).

56. *Za Ind.* (4 October 1930).

57. *Izvestiya* (14 April 1929).

58. Ordzhonikidze had this to say on the subject in 1933:

> Without a doubt there is a certain conservatism in promoting young cadres, all the more so since there exists some jealousy, it seems, among a section of our older managers who have not kept up with the times. They reason this way: 'you promote a young engineer, and who knows, maybe

tomorrow he will replace me'. I can tell you a secret. He will, in fact, replace you. But all the better. The sooner we have engineers armed with a knowledge of technology in our plants, all the better for our industry as well as for our managers. (*Za Ind.* 22 January 1933.)

59. Ordzhonikidze, *Stati i Rechi*, vol. 2, p. 438.
60. Here are a few examples: in 1931 an ITS official wrote that 'despite the fact that the majority of our engineers are graduates of our higher technical schools, the quality of their preparation and their knowledge of production is extremely low, and this applies especially to graduates of recent years' [*Inzh. Trud* (1931) nos. 16–17, p. 500; according to a chief engineer in the metalworking industry, the new specialists were helpless when it came to a 'practical understanding of the process of production as a whole' (*Za Ind.* 27 January 1932)]; at Magnitogorsk, in 1933, the young engineers 'could not cope with the complex new equipment' [*Za Ind.* (11 September 1933)].
61. *Predpriyatiye* (1928), no. 4, pp. 13–14.
62. *Inzh. Trud* (1932), nos. 31–2, p. 718 (Chubar).
63. *Sots. Donbass* (10 January 1933).

CHAPTER 5

1. Brief accounts of the changes involved can be found in A. Nove (1972), chapters 7–8; M. Dobb (1966), chapters 10–11.
2. This point is well explored in Andrle (1976) in a first-rate study of contemporary enterprise directors in the USSR.
3. *Part. Stroit.* (1930), no. 2, p. 37.
4. 'On the reorganisation of industrial administration', *Resheniya partii*, vol. 2, pp. 136–42.
5. L. Ginzburg in *Sovetskaya Iustitsiya* (1931), no. 20, pp. 16–17.
6. A. Nove (1972), pp. 212–15.
7. This paragraph is a summary of some of the arguments in D. Granick (1954). A similar picture can be gained from J. Berliner (1957) and V. Andrle (1976) for the postwar period.
8. See for example Ordzhonikidze's remarks to the central committee *Za Ind.* (18 January 1933) and his attack on the 'rotten talk of some managers about the unreality of the plan' *Za Ind.* (21 April 1933).
9. According to Ordzhonikidze, discipline among enterprise managers had fallen and 'warnings don't work any more'—Ordzhonikidze (1956), vol. 2, p. 456 (speech to Donetsk obkom, January 1933).
10. See, for example, a variety of criticisms of 'petty tutelage' by chief administrations in *Pravda* (12 January 1934); *Za Ind.* (17 January 1934 and 20 November 1934).
11. *KPSS v Rezolyutsiyakh*, vol. 4, p. 85.
12. See, for instance, Ordzhonikidze, address to Moscow party conference (September 1929)—*Stati i Rechi*, vol. 2, p. 179; *VKP v Rezolyutsiyakh*, vol. 2, p. 273; appeal to managers and party and trade union organisations—*Za Ind.* (3 September 1930).
13. Stalin, *Voprosy Leninizma*, pp. 355–63.

14. *Inzh. Trud* (1928), no. 11, p. 492; (1929), no. 1, p. 8; no. 15, p. 445.
15. *Torg.-Prom. Gaz.* (14 May 1929; 20 December 1929).
16. *Inzh. Trud* (1929), no. 1, p. 8.
17. *Za Ind.* (20 January 1932).
18. *Predpriyatiye* (1932), no. 7, pp. 8–9; 1933, no. 22, p. 1.
19. *Inzh. Trud* (1934), no. 4, p. 101; (1935), no. 2, p. 36.
20. The following figures suggest that the rate of turnover among directors remained high throughout the period:

Enterprise directors: Turnover (per cent)

	1926^a	January 1928^a	January 1934^b	1936^b
Held post for				
Less than one year	40.1	36.4	25	35
One to three years	43.0	49.8	55	40
Three to five years	16.9	13.8	16	20
More than five years	–	–	3	8

Sources: [a]*Bolshevik* (1928), no. 8, p. 64. (1926 sample: 770 directors; 1928 sample: 766 directors). [b]*Kadry Tyazheloi Promyshlennosti* (M. 1936) p. 166f; 1934 and 1936 samples cover 457 and 799 directors respectively, in heavy industry (excluding mining and construction.)

21. D. Granick (1954), Chapter 7.
22. *KPSS v Rezolyutsiyakh*, vol. 4, pp. 87–8.
23. Central Committee plenum (November 1929), ibid., p. 342.
24. *Sots. Donbass* (17 September 1932).
25. *Pravda* (3 February 1933).
26. *KPSS v Rezolyutsiyakh*, vol. 5, pp. 91–7.
27. See, for example, Kaganovich's account in *Pravda* (13 July 1933).
28. *Sots. Donbass* (20 May 1933; 6 July 1933).
29. *Za Ind.* (24 May 1933).
30. Accounts in *Pravda* (8 July 1933; 24 September 1933).
31. *Za Ind.* (20 July 1933).
32. *Sots. Donbass* (23 July 1933).
33. *Za Ind.* (9 May 1933).
34. *Sots. Donbass* (12 May 1933).
35. Statements by new shop managers in *Sots. Donbass* (10 and 28 October 1933).
36. *Sots. Donbass* (27 December 1932; 2 January 1933).
37. *Part. Stroit.* (1932), no. 7–8, p. 63.
38. *Part. Stroit.* (1934), no. 9, p. 10.
39. At the 2nd Congress of Engineers' Sections in December 1924, there were complaints that too many criminal charges were being brought arising out of production problems (especially accidents), and an ITS report of 1927 said that between January 1925 and March 1927 there were a 'large number of conflicts' on this score (see *Vsesoyuzny syezd inzhenerov* (1924), p. 93f; *ITS s*

Dek. 1924 po Mart 1927 (1927), p. 72).

40. *Inzh. Trud* (1929), no. 8, p. 244.
41. *Inzh. Trud* (1929), no. 9, p. 272.
42. Ibid., p. 62.
43. *Krasny Shakhtyor* (6 January 1929).
44. *Krasny Shakhtyor* (4 May 1929).
45. L. Brodsky (1966), p. 73 (citing archives).
46. *Inzh. Trud* (1929), no. 8, p. 241.
47. *Za Ind.* (13 February 1930).
48. *Za Ind.* (21 June 1930).
49. *Predpriyatiye* (1930), no. 19–20, p. 29.
50. I. Trifonov (1960), pp. 160–1, cited in Azrael (1966), p. 217, n. 95.
51. *Sots. Vestnik* (7 April 1931), p. 21.
52. L. Fischer (1932), pp. 222–3.
53. See *Shestnadtsataya Konferentsiya VKP*, p. 490; *Sots. Vestnik* (8 November 1930).
54. A. Serebrovsky in *Front Nauki i Tekhniki* (1931), no. 7–8, p. 15.
55. *Martenovka* (4 March 1930).
56. Speech to Moscow party organisation, *Pravda* (26 November 1929).
57. *Za Ind.* (18 February 1930).
58. *Za Ind.* (20 October 1930).
59. *Part. Stroit.* (1929), no. 1, p. 5.
60. Rukeyser (1932), p. 233.
61. Hirsch (1934), pp. 105–6.
62. *Torg.-Prom. Gaz.* (19 August 1929).
63. *Torg.-Prom. Gaz.* (23 November 1928).
64. *Torg.-Prom. Gaz.* (27 March 1929).
65. Littlepage and Bess (1939), p. 203; Rukeyser (1932), p. 245.
66. *Inzh. Trud.* (1929), no. 5, p. 133.
67. For examples of ITR resignations because of 'abnormal conditions of production', see *Torg.-Prom. Gaz.* (23 July 1929 and the following days). High turnover was also to be explained by impatience with slow promotion, allocation to inappropriate jobs, discrimination in social services, and perhaps most important, the general shortage of specialists, encouraging offers of higher salaries from other enterprises. See, for example, *Torg.-Prom. Gaz.* (11 and 12 July 1929).
68. *Torg.-Prom. Gaz.* (17 March 1928).
69. *Torg.-Prom. Gaz.* (2 August 1928), editorial.
70. *Sots. Vestnik* (8 February 1930).
71. Kravchenko (1947), p. 81.
72. *Pravda* (15 December 1929).
73. Syrtsov, speech to a session of VTsIK, *Izvestiya* (23 November 1929).
74. The activities of RKI seem to have been concentrated on government offices and intermediate levels of industrial administration; indications of RKI initiatives at enterprise level were found in *Torg.-Prom. Gaz.* (14 December 1928); *Martenovka* (25 June 1929).
75. *16 Konferentsiya VKP*, pp. 495, 497. Birman has been described here as a 'spokesman' because, according to one of the delegates, many industrial officials 'silently agreed' with Birman, even if they did not dare to admit it openly (ibid., p. 569).

76. *Torg.-Prom. Gaz.* (27 November 1929).
77. *Za Ind.* (7 November 1930).
78. Rukeyser (1932), p. 260.
79. *Torg.-Prom. Gaz.* (1 October 1929).
80. Cited by Fedyukin (1965), p. 387.
81. *Sov. Iust.* (1931), no. 127, p. 2.
82. *Inzh. Trud* (1931), no. 19–20, p. 438.
83. *Sov. Iust.* (June 1931), no. 16, p. 15.
84. *Sov. Iust.* (September 1931), no. 27, p. 2.
85. Cited in *Leninskii plan industrializatsii* (1969), p. 157.
86. For example, *Za Ind.* (1, 3 and 10 August 1931).
87. The most publicised example was the construction of the Baltic–White Sea Canal, which involved a large number of specialists imprisoned on wrecking charges (*Pravda*, 5 August 1933). Another much-publicised GPU-supervised project was the building of the first Soviet 'blooming' by prisoner-engineers (*Za Ind.*, 6 January 1933).
88. *Inzh. Trud.* (1932), no. 13–14, pp. 338–40.
89. *Sov. Iust.* (1933), no. 1, p. 11.
90. Postyshev to the 6th Conference of Judiciary Officials (RSFSR), *Sov. Iust.* (1932), no. 6–7, p. 5.
91. Ibid., pp. 2, 5.
92. See statements to 1st All-Union Conference of Judiciary Officials (July 1934), *Za Sotsialisticheskuyu Zakonnost*, no. 7, 1934.
93. *Sov. Iust.* (February 1930), no. 6, p. 22.
94. TsIK and Sovnarkom decree (8 December 1933), *Sobranie Zakonov*, no. 73.
95. *Za Sots. Zak.* (February 1934), no. 2, pp. 14–15.
96. *Za Sots. Zak.* (January 1935), no. 1, p. 18.
97. *Za Sots. Zak.* (November 1934), no. 11, pp. 14, 16; (January 1935), no. 1, p. 18.
98. *Za Sots. Zak.* (February 1934), no. 2, p. 14; up to October 1934, out of 272 cases, the breakdown was as follows: heavy industry 27 per cent; tractor repairs 20 per cent; light industry 24 per cent; food 17 per cent; transport 5 per cent; others 6 per cent (*Za Sots. Zak.* (November 1934), no. 11, p. 18).
99. *Za Sots. Zak.* (February 1934), p. 16.
100. *Za Sots. Zak.* (November 1934), no. 11, p. 18.
101. For some examples, *Za Sots. Zak.* (December 1934), no. 12, p. 8.
102. *Za Sots. Zak.* (May 1934), no. 5, p. 42.
103. *Za Sots. Zak.* (December 1934), no. 12, pp. 5, 13.
104. *Sov. Iust.* (September 1931), no. 26, p. 18.
105. *Sov. Iust.* (March 1933), no. 6, p. 23.
106. *Za Sots. Zak.* (December 1934), no. 12, p. 20.
107. *Za Sots. Zak.* (February 1936), no. 2, p. 22.
108. *Za Sots. Zak.* (December 1934), no. 12, pp. 18, 20.
109. *Za Sots. Zak.* (April 1935), pp. 15, 17; (February 1936), p. 22.
110. Cited in R. Conquest (1968), p. 388.
111. This tension is discussed in M. Lewin, 'The social background of Stalinism' and in R. Sharlet, 'Stalinism and Soviet legal culture', both in R. Tucker (1977).
112. Ya. Berman in *Za Sots. Zak.* (1934), no. 11, p. 15.

113. A. Liberman in *Za Sots. Zak.* (1935), no. 1, p. 38.

CHAPTER 6

1. The best account to date is still, in my view, S. Schwarz (1953).
2. On the party organisations, see an *Orgburo* directive of 1927, *KPSS v Rezolyutsiyakh*, vol. 3, pp. 447f.
3. See, for example, *Torg.-Prom. Gaz.* (6 September 1928, 2 March 1929, and 15 March 1929).
4. *Torg.-Prom. Gaz.* (26 February 1929).
5. *Torg.-Prom. Gaz.* (April 1929).
6. A. Etchin (1930), pp. 21–2.
7. See Chapter 2.
8. *Torg.-Prom. Gaz.* (6 February 1929, 15 March 1929).
9. Khvostovsky in *Predpriyatiya* (1929), no. 9, p. 20.
10. *Torg.-Prom. Gaz.* (30 November 1928).
11. *Martenovka* (12 October 1928).
12. *Torg.-Prom. Gaz.* (18 April 1928).
13. Petrovsky metallurgical plant, Dnepropetrovsk (Kravchenko (1947) pp. 52–3).
14. *Torg.-Prom. Gaz.* (26 June 1928).
15. In one instructive case, an engineer (T.) in the Shakhty district was dismissed as a result of initiatives by the trade union and party organisers. He had been described by a workers' correspondent as a 'man with bureaucratic manners' and 'an exploiter who simply cannot learn to work in Soviet conditions'. After protracted efforts engineer T. was reinstated. The verdict of the district trade union council was that engineer T. was 'demanding but honest'; the problem was how to 'struggle *against* wreckers and *for* honest specialists' (*Krasny Shakhtyor*, 2 February 1929).
16. For examples see *Trud* (24 February 1929); *Za Ind.* (25 May 1930).
17. *Torg.-Prom. Gaz.* (4 January 1929).
18. *Trud* (12 January 1929).
19. *Za Ind.* (1 February 1929).
20. *Sov. Iust.* (March 1929), no. 12.
21. *Trud* (26 March 1929).
22. *KPSS v Rezolyutsiyakh*, vol. 4, pp. 310–17.
23. Khvostovsky in *Predpriyatiye* (1929), no. 9, p. 19.
24. S. Schwarz (1953), p. 180f.
25. *Martenovka* (17 December 1929)—report of a general workers' meeting.
26. *Part. Stroit.* (1930), no. 2, p. 57.
27. A. Etchin (1930), p. 5.
28. *Za Ind.* (8 June 1930).
29. *Barrikady*, 20 February 1930.
30. A. Etchin (1930), p. 5.
31. Ibid., pp. 17–18.
32. *Pravda* (4 August 1933).
33. *Trud* (3 October 1929).
34. *Za Ind.* (29 March 1932).

35. Velichko, cited in *Pravda* (15 November 1932).
36. *Za Ind.* (6 April 1930).
37. *16 Syezd VKP*, p. 44.
38. *1 Vsesoyuznaya Konferentsiya* (1931) pp. 28, 30–1.
39. *Stati i Rechi*, vol. 2, p. 458.
40. Scott (1942), pp. 31–2.
41. Schwarz (1953), p. 314; Scott (1942), p. 32.
42. Kravchenko (1947), p. 175.
43. *Sots. Donbass*, (8 September 1932).
44. *Za Ind.* (11 March 1934).
45. *Za Ind.* (29 April 1934).
46. *Trud* (14 December 1934, 11 April 1935, 23 May 1935); *Za Ind.* (20 April 1935, 23 May 1935).
47. *KPSS v Rezolyutsiyakh*, vol. 4, pp. 310–17.
48. Address to Moscow party organisation, cited in *Za Ind.*(18 January 1934).
49. *Pravda* (4 August 1933, 8 August 1933); *Sots. Donbass* (14 August 1933 and following days).
50. *Sov. Sibir* (12 April 1930).
51. *Sov. Sibir* (29 May 1930); *Za Ind.* (8 June 1930).
52. I. Kossior at *1 Vsesoyuznaya konferentsiya* (1931), p. 110.
53. *Pravda* (15 December 1932).
54. *Za Ind.* (18 January 1932).
55. *Za Ind.* (20 January 1932). Comrades' courts were set up (in their 1930s form) in 1929 and their functions somewhat redefined in 1931; the aim was to impose measures of a 'preventive and disciplinary character' on people violating rules on labour discipline; the courts could issue reprimands or small fines or raise the question of dismissal with management or the trade union; they were under the general supervision of the Commissariat of Justice and the trade unions; it was rare for them to deal with cases involving ITR (as opposed to workers) but this occasionally happened (*Sov. Iust.* (1931), no. 10, p. 14; (1933), no. 1, p. 10).
56. *Sots. Donbass* (15 September 1933).
57. *Za Ind.* (1 August 1933).
58. *Za Ind.* (23 July 1934, 27 July 1934).
59. *Inzh. Trud* (1934), no. 4, p. 125.
60. S. Birman in *Za Ind.* (18 January 1934).
61. Zatonsky in *Pravda* (10 March 1928).
62. *Pravda* (11 September 1928).
63. *Torg.-Prom. Gaz.* (5 January 1929).
64. Fedyukin (1972), p. 387, citing archives.
65. A trade union investigation of the metal and coal industries in February 1929 reported that cases of violence against specialists 'have not decreased since the Shakhty affair' (*Torg.-Prom Gaz.* (24 February 1929)). Violence was also reported, for example, in the food industry (*Torg. Prom Gaz.* (17 April 1929)); sugar industry (*Torg.-Prom. Gaz.* (28 July 1929)); chemical industry (*Torg.-Prom. Gaz.* (21 August 1929)); tanning industry (*Torg.-Prom Gaz.* (21 August 1929)). Violent deaths of engineers were reported in *Trud* (2 July 1929) ('Skorokhod' plant in Leningrad); *Trud* (26 September 1929) (sugar factory); *Trud* (26 August 1929) (textile factory in Ivanovo-Voznesensk). See

also *Predpriyatiye* (1929), no. 3, p. 25 for more examples.
66. *Krasny Shakhtyor* (11 May 1929).
67. Ibid.
68. Khvostovsky in *Predpriyatiye* (1929), no. 3, p. 25.
69. *Torg.-Prom. Gaz.* (24 February 1929).
70. *Trud* (1 March 1929).
71. *Rabota Profsoyuzov* (1929), p. 31.
72. *Trud* (1 March 1929).
73. Fedyukin (1972) p. 390, citing archives.
74. *Krasny Shakhtyor* (11 May 1929).
75. *KPSS v Rezolyutsiyakh*, vol. 4, p. 170.
76. *Predpriyatiya* (1929), no. 7, p. 24.
77. *Trud* (26 August 1929). On the effects of raising work quotas, see also Fainsod (1958), Chapter 16.
78. *Krasny Shakhtyor* (14 October 1928).
79. *KPSS v Rezolyutsiyakh*, vol. 4, p. 170.
80. *Krasny Shakhtyor* (9 January 1929).
81. *Vsesoyuzny Syezd Inzhenerov* (1929), pp. 13–14.
82. *Torg.-Prom. Gaz.* (1 February 1929).
83. *Predpriyatiye* (1929), no. 3, p. 26; other examples can be found in *Torg.-Prom. Gaz.* (7 December 1928, 11 July 1929).
84. See Chapter 2, note 31.
85. *Varnitso* (1928), no. 2, p. 15.
86. Cited by Ciliga (1940), pp. 114–15, apparently referring to 1930; the specialist was an engineer of German origin and was a member of the Leningrad Soviet.
87. *Za Ind.* (18 May 1930).
88. *Inzh. Trud* (1933), No. 6, p. 169.
89. Veinberg in *Inzh. Trud* (1932), no. 34–6, p. 801.
90. *Pravda* (27 May 1934).
91. *Za Ind.* (23 September 1932).
92. *Za Ind.* (24 September 1932).
93. Birman in *Pravda* (3 February 1935).
94. Vyshinsky in *Front Nauki i Tekhniki* (1932), no. 7–8, p. 17.
95. *Za Ind.* (12 February 1932).
96. *Pravda* (8 July 1933); *Inzh. Trud*, no. 6, p. 169.
97. These explanations are offered in Granick (1954), p. 84.
98. *Pravda* (4, 7, 9 July 1933).
99. Ordzhonikidze, *Stati i Rechi*, vol. 2, p. 306.
100. Ibid., p. 572 (speech of May 1934).
101. *Sots. Donbass* (20 September 1932).
102. *Za Ind.* (24 September 1934).
103. *Za Ind.* (24 September 1934).

CHAPTER 7

1. TsSU SSSR, *Differentsiatsiya Zarabotnoi Plat v Fabrichnozavodskoi Promyshlennosti SSSR za 1927 i 1928* (M. 1929); TsUNKhU SSSR, *Zarabotnaya Plata Rabochikh*

Krupnoi Promyshlennosti v Oktyabre 1934 (M. 1935). A summary of the figures is given by M. Yanowitch, 'Trends in differentials between salaried personnel and wage workers in Soviet industry', *Soviet Studies* (January 1960), pp. 229–36, on which our account relies.

2. *Inzh. Trud* (1934), no. 1, p. 20.
3. Rukeyser (1932), p. 154.
4. Scott (1942), p. 43.
5. Ibid., p. 117.
6. Ibid.
7. Kravchenko (1947), p. 174 (metallurgical plant at Nikopol in the Ukraine).
8. Serge (1937), p. 10 (Elektrozavod in Moscow).
9. Eastman (1940, citing *The New International* (February 1936) (a Donbass coalmine).
10. See for example, the discussion in *Za Ind.* (12 January, 9 February 1933).
11. *Pravda* (11 August 1934); *Za Ind.* (14 February 1935).
12. *Inzh. Trud*, (1931), nos. 19–20, p. 434.
13. A. Etchin (1928), p. 36.
14. See for example, a Central Committee decree of April 1930, 'On measures for attracting ITR to production'; a decree of the Sovnarkom RSFSR, 'On improving housing conditions for ITR' (October 1930); a similar injunction on housing from Narkomtrud RSFSR (November 1930). (*Inzh. Trud* (1930), no. 7, p. 190; S. Lifshits, *O spetsialistakh* (1930), pp. 99, 165).
15. Ibid., p. 166; a similar complaint was made at the VMBIT plenum of December 1930 (*Inzh. Trud* (1930), nos. 22–3, p. 705).
16. *Za Ind.* (19 September 1931).
17. *Za Ind.* (5 December 1931).
18. *Za Ind.* (23 June 1932); *Pravda* (10 August 1932).
19. *Za Ind.*, (20 July 1932.)
20. See *Za Ind.* (18 October 1931) for a decision of the Mossoviet to this effect. The introduction of special shops was 'particularly warmly welcomed by the ITR', according to an ITS official [*Za Ind.* (30 October 1931)].
21. See March 1932 Sovnarkom decree 'Towards the rapid improvement in housing conditions for scientists, engineers and technicians . . .' *Za Ind.* (26 March 1932).
22. *Inzh. Trud* (1935), no. 2, p. 58. In 1932, 48 million rubles were spent on ITR cooperative housing, in 1933 55 million (*Inzh Trud.* (1934), no. 1, p. 20). In 1934 about one-half of the 82 million earmarked for this purpose was spent (*Inzh. Trud* (1935), no. 2, p. 56).
23. On the abolition of restricted stores for specialists, see J. Scott (1942), p. 72; V. Serge (1937), p. 184. Serge states that the stores for top officials continued 'half-secretly'.
24. Kravchenko (1947), p. 175.
25. Scott (1942), pp. 128, 185.
26. See, for example *Inzh. Trud* (1929), no. 19, p. 573f.
27. See for example, *Za Ind.* (2 September 1932 and the following days); *Inzh. Trud* (1932), nos. 25–6, p. 586.
28. For articles stressing the importance of differentiated material reward in improving productivity, see for example, *Za Ind.* (6 September 1931, 24 November 1931, 1 January 1932, 22 May 1933); *Pravda* (13 July 1932,

10 August 1932, 14 November 1933); *Inzh. Trud* (1935), no. 2, p. 58.

29. Stalin, *Voprosy Leninizma*, p. 367.

30. Kravchenko (1947), p. 175.

31. According to Ciliga, who had a spell in a Leningrad prison in 1930, engineers not only fulfilled their professional functions but were also privileged in the matter of food and were treated with respect. ' "They are the engineers" "we are the engineers" were phrases of particular significance; even in prison, they exuded a feeling of superiority over the common run of Soviet citizens' (A. Ciliga, *The Russian Enigma*, pp. 152–3). F. Utley, who worked as an economist for the textile industry in the early 1930s, describes an engineer of her acquaintance who had been in and out of prison three times: 'He was by then quite philosophical about it. He was highly qualified and between imprisonments he received a good salary and lived well . . . Even during the periods he was an unwilling guest of the OGPU, he was comparatively well treated' (F. Utley, *The Lost Illusion*, p. 63).

32. Ciliga (1940), p. 268.

33. Stalin, *Voprosy Leninizma*, p. 374.

34. *Lenin i Stalin o Molodezhi* (1939), p. 309.

35. *Vestnik Kommunisticheskoi Akademii* (1931), no. 1, pp. 85–6.

36. N. Bukharin, *Culture in Two Worlds* (1934), p. 18.

37. This point is developed in Gramsci's essay, 'Americanism and Fordism', in *Prison Notebooks*, pp. 277–318.

38. 'It will no longer be practical to leave its [the industrial system's] control in the hands of businessmen working at cross-purposes for private gain, or to entrust its continued administration to less than suitably trained technological experts . . . the material welfare of the community is unreservedly bound up with the due working of this industrial system and therefore with its unreserved control by the engineers, who alone are competent to manage it' (T. Veblen, *Engineers and the Price System* (1921) p. 33).

39. Cited from O. Bauer's *Capitalism and Socialism after the War*, in *Za Ind.* (29 November 1931).

40. Stalin (1976), p. 767f.

Bibliography

I OFFICIAL DOCUMENTS

(a) PROTOCOLS OF CONGRESSES AND CONFERENCES

(i) *Party*
Devyaty S''ezd RKP (b) (Moscow, 1960)
Desyaty S''ezd RKP (b) (Moscow, 1960)
Odinatsaty S''ezd RKP (b) (Moscow, 1961)
Dvenadtsaty S''ezd RKP (b) (Moscow, 1961)
Pyatnadtsaty S''ezd VKP (b) 2 vols. (Moscow, 1961)
Shestnadtsataya Konferentsiya VKP (b) (Moscow, 1961)
Shestnadtsaty S''ezd VKP (b) (Moscow, 1931)
Semnadtsaty S''ezd VKP (b) (Moscow, 1934)

(ii) *ITR*
Zanyatiya Pervogo Moskovskogo Oblastnogo Delegatskogo S''ezda (Moscow, 1918)
Otchet o Zanyatiyakh 2-i Moskovskoi Oblastnoi Konferentsii Oktyabr 1918 (Moscow, 1918)
Stenograficheskii Otchet Rabot 1-go Vserossiiskogo S''ezda Inzhenerov (Moscow, 1923)
Vsesoyuzny S''ezd Inzhenerov i Tekhnikov, 2-i (Moscow, 1924)
Vsesoyuzny S''ezd Inzhenerov i Tekhnikov Chlenov Profsoyuzov, 4-i (Moscow, 1929)
1-aya Vsesoyuznaya Konferentsiya Rabotnikov Sotsialistcheskoi Promyshlennosti (Moscow, 1931)
Soveshchanie Khozyaistvennikov, Inzhenerov, Tekhnikov, Partiinykh i Profsoyuznykh Rabotnikov Tyazheloi Promyshlennosti (Moscow, 1934)

(b) COLLECTIONS OF DOCUMENTS

Direktivy KPSS i Sovetskogo Pravitelstva po

Khozyaistvennym Voprosam, vol. 1: 1917–28, vol. 2: 1929–45 (Moscow, 1957)

Industrializatsiya SSSR 1929–32 (Moscow, 1970)

KPSS v Rezolyutsiyakh i Resheniyakh, vols. 2–5 (Moscow, 1970–71)

Sobrangie Zakonov i Rasporyazhenii Raboche-krest'yanskogo Pravitelstva SSSR, Parts I and II, 1928–33

Spravochnik Partiinovo Rabotnika, Vyp. 8 (Moscow, 1934)

VKP v Rezolyutsiyakh i Resheniyakh, vol. 2 (Moscow, 1941)

(c) STATISTICAL PUBLICATIONS

Beilin, A., *Kadry Spetsialistov SSSR* (TsUNKhU, Moscow, 1935)

Inzhenerno-Tekhnicheskiye Kadry Promyshlennosti (VSNKh, Moscow, 1930)

Kadry Tyazheloi Promyshlennosti v Tsifrakh (Moscow, 1936)

Komsostav Promyshlennosti (uchraspredotdel TsK RKP (b), (Moscow, 1924)

Kogan, A. *Inzhenerno-Tekhnicheskiye Kadry Leningradskoi Promyshlennosti* (Leningrad, 1930)

Nash Promyshlenny Komsostav (uchraspredotdel TsK RKP (b)), (Moscow, 1923)

Novye Kadry Tyazheloi Promyshlennosti (1930–33)

Shmelev, V. A., *Voprosy Podgotovki Inzhenerno-Tekhnicheskikh Kadrov* (Moscow, 1931)

Sostav Rukovodyashchikh Rabotnikov i Spetsialistov (Moscow, 1936)

Sotsialisticheskoe Stroitelstvo SSSR (Moscow, 1935)

Trud v SSSR (Moscow, 1936)

II NEWSPAPERS AND JOURNALS

(a) NEWSPAPERS (the agencies publishing the newspapers are given in brackets)

Izvestiya (Central Executive Committee of the Congress of Soviets)

Krasny Shakhtyor (Shakhtino–Donetsk okrug party committee)

Pravda (Central committee of the party)
Sotsialisticheskii Donbass (Donetsk oblast party committee)
Sovetskii Sibir (West Siberian krai party committee)
Torgovo-Promyshlennaya Gazeta (VSNKh)
Trud (VTsSPS)
Za Industrializatsiyu (VSNKh/NKTP, 1930–35)
Some issues of the following enterprise newspapers were
    consulted:
*Barrikady; Dinamo; Elektrozavod; Martenovka; Rychag; Stalin-
    skii Udarnik.*

(b) JOURNALS (the agencies publishing the journals are given
    in brackets)

Byulleten Oppozitsii (Trotskyist opposition)
Front Nauki i Tekhniki (started publication in 1931, the
    result of a merger between the journals *Nauchny rabotnik*
    and *Varnitso*)
Inzhenerny Trud (VMBIT)
Inzhenerny Rabotnik (Ukrainian ITS)
Partiinoe Stroitelstvo (Central committee of the party)
Planovoe Khozyaistvo (Gosplan)
Predpriyatiye (Journal of the Moscow Club of Red Directors
    1923–27, then a VSNKh/NKTP journal)
Sotsialisticheskii Vestnik (Menshevik journal, published in
    Berlin during the period covered in the study)
Sovetskaya Iustitsiya (Commissariat of Justice)
Varnitso (Journal of the All-Union Association of Socialist
    Scientists and Technicians)
Vestnik Inzhenerov (All-Union Association of Engineers)
Za Sotsialisticheskuyu Zakonnost (RSFSR procuracy)

III BOOKS

Andrle V., *Managerial Power in the Soviet Union* (1976)
Azrael, J., *Managerial Power and Soviet Politics* (Cambridge,
    Mass., 1966)
Avrich, P., 'Workers Control in Russian industry', *Slavic
    Review*, vol. 22 (1963), pp. 46–63
Avtorkhanov, A., *Stalin and the Soviet Communist Party*
    (Munich, 1959)

Bardin, I., *Zhizn Inzhinera* (Moscow, 1938)

Bendix, R., *Work and Authority in Industry* (New York, 1956)

Berliner, J. S., *Factory and Manager in the USSR* (Cambridge, Mass., 1957)

Bienstock, G., Schwarz S. M., Yugow, A., *Management in Russian Industry and Agriculture* (Oxford, 1944)

Braverman, H., *Labour and Monopoly Capital* (New York, 1976)

Brinton, M., *The Bolsheviks and Workers' Control* (London, 1970)

Brodsky, L., 'Ideino-politicheskoe vospitanie tekhnicheskikh spetsialistov dorevolyutsionnoi shkoly v gody pervoi pyatiletki', *Trudy Leningradskovo Polytekhnicheskogo Instituta im. Kalinina* no. 261 (Leningrad, 1966)

Bukharin, N., *Ekonomika Perekhodnogo Perioda* (Moscow, 1920)

Bukharin, N., 'Burzhyuaznaya revolutsiya i revoliutsiya proletarskaya', *Pod Znamenem Markisizma*, no. 7–8 (1922)

Bukharin, N., *Culture in Two Worlds* (New York, 1934)

Byli Industrialnye (Moscow, 1973)

Carr, E. H., *The Bolshevik Revolution*, vol. 2 (1952)

Carr, E. H., *Socialism in One Country*, vol. 1 (1954)

Carr, E. H. and Davies, R. W., *Foundations of a Planned Economy*, vol. 1 (London, 1969)

Ciliga, A., *The Russian Enigma* (London, 1940)

Conquest, R., *The Great Terror* (London, 1968)

Direktor—I.A. Likhachev (Moscow, 1971)

Dobb, M., *Soviet Economic Development since 1917* (London, 1966)

Dzherzhinskii, F., *Izbrannye Proizvedeniya*, 2 vols. (Moscow, 1957)

Eastman, M., *Stalin's Russia and the Crisis of Socialism* (New York, 1940)

Emelianov, V., *O Vremeni, o Tovarishchakh, o Sebe* (Moscow, 1974)

Etchin, A., *Partiya i Spetsialisty* (Moscow, 1928)

Etchin, A., *O Edinonachaliya* (Moscow, 1930)

Fainsod, M., *Smolensk under Soviet rule* (London, 1958)

Fedyukin, S., *Sovetskaya Vlast' i Burzhyuaznye Spetsialisty* (Moscow, 1965)

Fedyukin, S., *Velikii Oktyabr i Intelligentsiya* (Moscow, 1972)

Fischer, L., *Machines and Men in Russia* (New York, 1932)

Friedrich, C. and Brzezinski, Z., *Totalitarian Dictatorship and Autocracy* (Cambridge, Mass., 1956)

Gramsci, A., *Prison Notebooks* (London, 1971)

Granick, D., *Management of the Industrial Firm in the USSR* (New York, 1954)
Hirsch, A., *Industrialized Russia* (New York, 1934)
Istoriya Kirovskogo Zavoda (Moscow, 1966)
Its s Dek. 1924 po mart. 1927 (Moscow, 1927)
Iz Istorii Sovetskoi Intelligentsii (Moscow, 1966)
Jasny, N., *Soviet Industrialization, 1928–1952* (Chicago, 1961)
Khavin, A. F., *U Ruliya Industrii* (Moscow, 1968)
Kravchenko, V., *I Chose Freedom* (London, 1947)
Kuibyshev, V., *Stati i Rechi*, vol. 5 (Moscow, 1935)
Larin, Yu., *Intelligentsiya i Sovety* (Moscow, 1925)
Lenin, V. I., *Polnoe Sobranie Sochinenii* (5th ed., Moscow 1958–65)
Lenin i Stalin o Molodezhi (Moscow, 1939)
Lewin, M., *Political Undercurrents in Soviet Economic Debates* (London, 1975)
Lewin, M., *Russian Peasants and Soviet Power* (London, 1968)
Lifshits, S., *O Spetsialistakh* (Moscow, 1930)
Littlepage, J. D. and Bess, D., *In Search of Soviet Gold* (New York, 1939)
Lunacharsky, A., *Intelligentsiya v ee Proshlom i Nastoyashchom* (Moscow, 1924)
Marx, K., *Capital*, vol. 1 (London, 1970)
Marx, K., *Theories of Surplus Value* (London, 1951)
Medvedev, R., *Let History Judge* (London, 1972)
Molotov, V., *O Podgotovke Novykh Spetsiakistov* (Moscow, 1928)
Nove, A., *An Economic History of the USSR* (London, 1972)
Ordzhonikidze, G. K., *Stati i Rechi*, 2 vols. (Moscow, 1956)
Osinsky, N., *O Stroitelstve Sotsializma* (Moscow, 1918)
Preobrazhensky, E., *The New Economics* (London, 1966)
Prokofiev, V., *Industrial and Technical Intelligentsia in the USSR* (Moscow, 1933)
Protsess Prompartii (Moscow, 1931)
Rabota Profsoyuzov Sredi Spetsialistov (Kharkov, 1929)
Rozmirovich, E., *NOT, RKI i Partiya* (Moscow, 1926)
Rukeyser, W. A. *Working for the Soviets* (London, 1932)
Schwarz, S. M., *Labour in the Soviet Union* (London, 1953)
Scott, J. *Behind the Urals* (New York, 1942)
Schneider, E. V., *Industrial Sociology* (New Jersey, 1969)
Serge, V., *Destiny of a Revolution* (London, 1937)
Stalin, J., *Problems of Leninism* (Peking, 1976)

Stalin, J., *Voprosy Leninizma* (Moscow, 1952)

Trotsky, L., *Sochineniya* (Moscow, 1925–7)

Trotsky, L., *Terrorism and Communism* (Ann Arbor, Mich., 1961)

Tucker, R. ed. *Stalinism* (New York, 1977)

Veblen, T., *Engineers and the Price System* (London, 1921)

Volskii, A., (Machajskii, W.) *Umstvenny Rabochii* (Berlin, 1968)

Voprosy Ratsionalizatsii (Moscow, 1925)

Weber, M., *Economy and Society* (New York, 1968)

The Workers' Opposition (The Opposition Platform) (Solidarity, pamphlet no. 2, n.d.)

Yanowitch, M., 'Trends in differentials between salaried personnel and wage workers in Soviet industry', *Soviet Studies* (January 1960), pp. 229–36

Name Index

Subject Index

Accidents, industrial, 91, 104, 118

Administration, autonomy of, 84–6, 130, 134, 153–4; collegial, 16, 20, 31, 35, 114; elective, 20; one-man, 113–16, 157: change to, 16, 31, 36, and party interference, 35, 87, 89–90, 107, 119–20, 156, philosophy behind, 19–20; and party organisations, 110–11, 119–23, 156; and trade unions, 32, 33–4, 109–11, 113–16, 133; *troika*, 109–16, 117, 131, 133, 157

Administrators, *see* Managers

Agriculture, collectivisation of, 3, 4, 42, 57, 153; state control of, 2, 57, 101–2, 149

All-Russian Association of Engineers (VAI), 25; conference, 1922, 26

All-Russian Union of Engineers (VSI), conference, 1918, 14–15; dissolution, 25

All-Union Central Council of Trades Unions (VTsSPS), 25; Engineers' and Technicians' Sections, *see* ITS

All-Union Conference of Engineers' and Technicians' Sections, 1924, 26–7

Appointment, rights of, 110–11, 112, 120, 133

Assessment and Conflict Commission (RKK), 33–4, 110, 113

Beloretsk party organisation, 90

Bolshevik Party, *see* Party

Bolshevik will power, 48–50, 150

brak, penalties for, 102, 121–2

Cadres, training of, 60–1, 72

Caste separateness, 27, 30, 50–1, 76–7, 128, 152

Central Committee, plenums: 1928, 50, 52, 60; 1929, 44–5; 1930, 45

Central Trade Union Council, 113, 118

Chemical industry, earnings, 136

Chief engineers, 66–7, 138

Class struggle, 3, 9, 42, 46, 101, 122, 149–50; and ITR recruitment, 60, 78

Clothing industry, earnings, 138–9

Coal industry, earnings, 138–9; party interference, 88–9

Coercion, state, 90–106, 107, 108, 150, 154

Collectivisation, agricultural, 3, 4, 42, 57, 153

Collegial boards, 16, 20, 31, 35, 114

Command planning, 9–10, 29–30, 80, 153

Commissariat of Heavy Industry (NKTP), 83

Commissars, *see* Directors

Communist Party, *see* Party

Competition, socialist, 51, 94

Conflict, ITR-worker, 123–9, 130, 134

Council of National Economy, 13

Counter-revolution, *see* Wrecking

Courts, and industrial control, 101, 102–5, 130–1

Criminal law, and state control, 91, 92–3, 94, 99–101, 102–3, 107

Culture, technical, 147–8

Democratic Centralists, and industrial organisation, 20

Directors, appointment, rights of, 110–11, 112; autonomy of, 84–6, 130; and ITR, 85–6, 98–9; red, 22; recruitment, 64–6; and specialists, 24, 29–31, 36, 85–6, 98–9; training, 65–6

Discipline, industrial, 130, 131–2

Donbass region, 39; coal industry, 88–